ARMED FRONTIER

DIÁLOGOS SERIES

KRIS LANE, Series Editor

Understanding Latin America demands dialogue, deep exploration, and frank discussion of key topics. Founded by Lyman L. Johnson in 1992 and edited since 2013 by Kris Lane, the Diálogos Series focuses on innovative scholarship in Latin American history and related fields. The series, the most successful of its type, includes specialist works accessible to a wide readership and a variety of thematic titles, all ideally suited for classroom adoption by university and college teachers.

Also available in the Diálogos Series:

Understanding Latin America's Economy in the Twenty-First Century by Jeff Dayton-Johnson

Driving Terror: Labor, Violence, and Justice in Cold War Argentina by Karen Robert

Frontier Justice: State, Law, and Society in Patagonia, 1880–1940 by Javier Cikota

Anti-Catholicism in the Mexican Revolution, 1913–1940 edited by Jürgen Buchenau and David S. Dalton

The Struggle for Natural Resources: Findings from Bolivian History edited by Carmen Soliz and Rossana Barragán

Viceroy Güemes's Mexico: Rituals, Religion, and Revenue by Christoph Rosenmüller

At the Heart of the Borderlands: Africans and Afro-Descendants on the Edges of Colonial Spanish America edited by Cameron D. Jones and Jay T. Harrison

The Age of Dissent: Revolution and the Power of Communication in Chile, 1780–1833 by Martín Bowen

From Sea-Bathing to Beach-Going: A Social History of the Beach in Rio de Janeiro, Brazil by B. J. Barickman

Gamboa's World: Justice, Silver Mining, and Imperial Reform in New Spain by Christopher Albi

For additional titles in the Diálogos Series, please visit unmpress.com.

ARMED FRONTIER

Warfare and Military Culture in the
Texas–Northeastern Mexico Borderlands
1686–1845

Luis Alberto García-García

Translated by VÉRONIQUE LESOINNE and
LUIS ALBERTO GARCÍA-GARCÍA

University of New Mexico Press
Albuquerque

Original Spanish edition © 2021 by Fondo de Cultura Económica
English translation © 2025 by the University of New Mexico Press
All rights reserved. Published 2025
Printed in the United States of America

Library of Congress Cataloging-in-Publication Data

Names: García, Luis Alberto, 1981– author translator | Lesoinne, Véronique, 1965– translator

Title: Armed frontier : warfare and military culture in the Texas–northeastern Mexico borderlands, 1686–1845 / Luis Alberto García-García ; translated by Véronique Lesoinne and Luis Alberto García-García.

Other titles: Frontera armada. English | Warfare and military culture in the Texas–northeastern Mexico borderlands, 1686–1845

Description: Albuquerque : University of New Mexico Press, 2025. | Series: Diálogos series | Original title: Frontera armada: prácticas militares en el noreste histórico, siglos XVII al XIX. | Includes bibliographical references and index. Identifiers: LCCN 2025006805 (print) | LCCN 2025006806 (ebook) | ISBN 9780826368751 cloth | ISBN 9780826368768 paperback | ISBN 9780826368775 epub

Subjects: LCSH: Mexico, North—History, Military—17th century | Mexico, North—History, Military—18th century | Mexico, North—History, Military—19th century | Texas—History, Military

Classification: LCC F1314 .G3713 2025 (print) | LCC F1314 (ebook) | DDC 355.009764/09032—dc23/eng/20250710

LC record available at https://lccn.loc.gov/2025006805

LC ebook record available at https://lccn.loc.gov/2025006806

Founded in 1889, the University of New Mexico sits on the traditional homelands of the Pueblo of Sandia. The original peoples of New Mexico—Pueblo, Navajo, and Apache—since time immemorial have deep connections to the land and have made significant contributions to the broader community statewide. We honor the land itself and those who remain stewards of this land throughout the generations and also acknowledge our committed relationship to Indigenous peoples. We gratefully recognize our history.

Cover illustration: detail of Segesser II. Courtesy of the Palace of the Governors Photo Archives
Designed by Isaac Morris

Composed in Adobe Jenson Pro

CONTENTS

List of Illustrations ▸▸ vii

Prologue ▸▸ viii
  LUIS ALBERTO GARCÍA-GARCÍA

Acknowledgments ▸▸ x

Introduction ▸▸ 1

Chapter 1
  The Development of the Spanish Medieval Military Ethos ▸▸ 6

Chapter 2
  The Northeast and Its Medieval Character ▸▸ 35

Chapter 3
  The Coming of the Enlightened Modernity ▸▸ 70

Chapter 4
  The Era of Nationalism ▸▸ 111

Chapter 5
  The Northeast in Flames ▸▸ 141

Conclusion
  Outcome and Final Considerations ▸▸ 167

Notes ▸▸ 178

Bibliography ▸▸ 223

Index ▸▸ 238

ILLUSTRATIONS

FIGURE 1. Lienzo de Tlaxcala Codex ▸▸ xiv

FIGURE 2. Segesser II (right side detail). 1720–1729 ▸▸ 2

FIGURE 3. Map of the settlements under study and the provinces to which they belonged ▸▸ 34

FIGURE 4. The New Kingdom of León ▸▸ 38

FIGURE 5. Province of Texas ▸▸ 39

FIGURE 6. Nuevo Santander ▸▸ 40

FIGURE 7. Comanche and Lipan attack routes during the 1840s ▸▸ 160

PROLOGUE

LUIS ALBERTO GARCÍA-GARCÍA

There is a historiographic narrative of how borderland communities in the American Southwest and northern Mexico developed historically as places where armed violence was commonplace from the sixteenth to the nineteenth centuries. Furthermore, these communities had a warrior and military culture that influenced the formation of a frontier society in response to a constant state of war against Indigenous groups. Several historians have studied this aspect: Héctor Aguilar Camín in *La Frontera nómada: Sonora y la Revolución Mexicana* (1977), Friedrich Katz in *The Secret War in Mexico: Europe, the United States, and the Mexican Revolution* (1981), Daniel Nugent in *Spent Cartridges of Revolution: An Anthropological History of Namiquipa, Chihuahua* (1993), Ana María Alonso in *Thread of Blood: Colonialism, Revolution, and Gender on Mexico's Northern Frontier* (1995), and more recently Lance R. Blyth in *Chiricahua and Janos Communities of Violence in the Southwestern Borderlands, 1680–1880* (2012) and Luis Medina Peña with *Los Bárbaros del Norte: National Guard and Politics in Nuevo León, 19th Century* (2014).

I have also studied this topic. In my book *Guerra y frontera: el Ejército del Norte entre 1855 y 1858* (2007), I discussed how, during the War of Reform (1857–1861), an army was formed in northeastern Mexico that fought in this civil war based on the local experience of the "Indian"[*] wars. This force played a prominent role in this conflict, and many of its members were protagonists of the political-military evolution of the second part of the Mexican and frontier nineteenth century. This was not so different from some River Plate armies of the same period or the Villista forces during the Mexican Revolution half a century later. While writing that work and analyzing the others, the existence and importance of the role played

---

[*] During the colonial period, the term "Indian," Indio in Spanish, was a sociolegal category of the stratified Ancien Régime.

by military organization and self-defense traditions in the northeastern frontier culture of nineteenth-century Mexico became evident. At the same time, I realized that if this process were analyzed only from the nineteenth-century temporality, many of the origins and particularities of these traditions would be left out. Thus, to achieve a better understanding of these historical phenomena, I decided that I had to research the subject that included the colonial period.

Later, as a graduate student, I took the "Spanish Borderlands" seminar under the direction of David J. Weber. During this course, the need to broaden the analysis of the peculiarities of frontier military culture became apparent. The overused argument that the northern frontier populations developed their traditions of organized violence as a reaction to Indigenous attacks seemed incomplete and reductionist. I had to look for the origins of these customs and practices beyond a war against Native Americans, which eventually led me to trace their roots to the Castilian frontier of the thirteenth century.

The next question was to delimit the geographical area since, having found this vein, I initially thought of including in the study other border areas of Latin America with similar problems, such as Argentina, Uruguay, or Chile. This was unfeasible given the limitations of time and resources, so I decided to focus in-depth on a single area: northeastern Mexico and Texas. I made this decision because this geographic area has been much less studied compared to northwestern Mexico and the regions of New Mexico, Arizona, and California. In addition, choosing populations from both sides of the Rio Grande would be a study with implications beyond the regional; this text is intended to contribute significantly to understanding the region within national and cross-border dynamics.

The book project is a testament to my dedication to this topic. After the manuscript was rewritten in Spanish, it was honored with the Atanasio G. Saravia Award for professional research in Mexico in 2018. The book was later published by Fondo de Cultura Económica in 2021. Kenneth Andrien, recognizing the historiographical value of the text, suggested an English version for a wider audience. This version is the result of my commitment to this research.

ACKNOWLEDGMENTS

I want to thank the History Division of the Centro de Investigación y Docencia Económicas, where I had the opportunity to stay during the August–December 2012 semester. I found a stimulating and conducive environment to outline and begin this project during my stay at this institution. I want to mention Luis Barrón and Clara García Ayluardo, who helped me navigate the CIDE in administrative and academic matters. I would especially like to thank Luis Medina Peña, who invited me to collaborate with him at that institution. This text results from that collaboration, which has continued without interruption during the past few years. Medina Peña read the original project and then the draft. His experience and knowledge of the subject were invaluable.

My time as a graduate student at Southern Methodist University (SMU) was instrumental in getting this project off the ground. I want to mention Kenneth Andrien, who helped me to delve into the Spanish American colonial world. I would also like to thank several professors at this institution (names accompanied by † indicate deceased individuals): David J. Weber (†), James K. Hopkins, Peter Bakewell, Edward F. Countryman, Ben Johnson, Jeremy Adams (†), Thomas J. Knock, Neil Foley, Alexis M. McCrossen, Daniel T. Orlovsky, Sherry L. Smith, Kathleen A. Wellman, and John Chavez. I owe them my understanding of North American borderlands and hemispheric history. Outside SMU, many scholars gave me advice and feedback. I want to thank Miguel González Quiroga, Brian DeLay, Andrew Torget, Andrés Reséndez, Sami Lakomäki, Paul Conrad, James Nichols, Sean F. McEnroe, and especially my mentor and friend Artemio Benavides Hinojosa (†), who was always interested in my professional development. Likewise, at the Universidad de Monterrey (UDEM), I found a generous space to complete this project. I have received tremendous support from my colleagues in the Social Sciences department of that institution: Patricia Fernández, Osvaldo Tello, Arturo Azuara, Claire Wright, Alejandra Galindo, Jesús Rubio, Philipe Stoessle, José Luis Berlanga, Javier Rolón, Eduardo Aguilar, Pamela Cacciavillani, and Melissa Ávila. I also received generous help from archivists and librarians during my research trips. I am particularly in debt to Jesús Ávila (†) from Archivo General

ACKNOWLEDGMENTS

del Estado de Nuevo León, Donna Guerra from Trinity University, and Joshua Lupkin, now at Harvard.

I am equally grateful to the cohort of friends and colleagues who helped me navigate life as a graduate student in North Texas: Jennifer Seman, George Diaz, David Rex, Matthew Babcock, Aaron Sanchez, Gabriel Martinez Serna, Ruben Arellano, Barbara and Bruce Mickey, Sarah Robertson, and particularly Ryan Booth. I am also very grateful to Mildred Pinkston and Sharron Pierson, who for six years helped in every administrative aspect of the PhD program. Andrea Boardman and Ruth Ann Elmore from the Clements Center were always attentive and friendly.

In addition, many colleagues were involved in one way or another. Rodrigo Moreno instructed me in the intricate militant world of the Mexican independence period. In Monterrey, I received a lot of help from colleagues and friends such as Alberto Barrera Enderle, Sergio Guajardo del Hoyo, and Victoria Andrea Martínez Cortés. Finally, I thank my parents, Gerardo García Ibarra and Lily García Silva, for their constant support.

ARMED FRONTIER

FIGURE 1. Lienzo de Tlaxcala Codex. Universidad Autónoma de Nuevo León, Colección Digital.

Introduction

THE PICTURE ABOVE IS A FRAGMENT OF THE *LIENZO DE TLAXCALA*, A MESOAMERICAN codex portraying the destruction of the Mexica Empire and other events of the sixteenth-century conquest of Mexico by the Spaniards and their Native allies. Surprisingly, the mounted conquistador is not wearing metal armor. Neither is he using the typical crested helmet, or *morrión*, which modern stereotypes so often associate with the conquistadores. Instead, he wears a simple hat. Most of the European men who followed Cortés were too poor to possess metal armor; undoubtedly, this conquistador belongs to that category. Instead of an expensive suit of armor, he uses the attire of the light cavalry forces of Castile and Andalusia, which just half a century earlier had been the militarized borderland between Christian and Islamic Iberia. The horseman's protection is a doublet, a type of leather jacket armor, and he is armed with a lance and a heart-shaped shield. This type of shield was originally of Arab design and known as *addárqa* before the Spaniards adopted and renamed it as *adarga*. These small but important details suggest that this Spanish conquistador is dressed and equipped in a manner practically unchanged since the eleventh century. This practical and affordable gear and clothing was ideally suited for the kind of low-intensity, raid-based warfare that characterized the borderlands of medieval Iberia. Note also that he is fighting alongside Tlaxcalan allies against Indigenous enemies. The system of alliances proved invaluable for the Spaniards as they penetrated inland throughout the Americas. Like his garb, this tradition of cultivating allies across ethnic lines also traces back to the context of medieval Spain.

Now let us jump forward two full centuries to consider a second image, a portion of the Segesser II codex painted around 1720 by Pueblos in New Mexico under Franciscan direction. The image portrays the destruction of a presidio's Spanish soldiers by a confederation of the Great Plains tribes allied with French soldiers. Note again the figure of the Spanish soldier. Comparing him with the conquistador from the previous image, we can see that the two soldiers' gear and clothing are nearly identical. Indeed, after two hundred years, the most noticeable change is the length of the hat's brim. In fact, other sources document the use of weaponry,

FIGURE 2. Segesser II (right side detail). 1720–1729. Courtesy Palace of the Governors Photo Archives (NMHM/DCA), 149804.

such as the adarga in northern Mexico as late as 1834.[1] Like his sixteenth-century predecessor, the Spanish horseman depicted in the Segesser II painting fights alongside Native allies, perhaps Puebloans. He is also facing a European enemy, not Moors nor Mexica, but rather French soldiers in typical eighteenth-century fashion, some of them wearing tricorn hats.

Taken together, these two pictures, as well as other testimonies, suggest a noticeable continuity in the military system that the Spaniards used in their North American borderlands from the time of Cortés until well into the nineteenth century. This continuity had its origins in medieval Spain. Although the military system of the Spanish borderlands was transformed and adapted to new circumstances, its core features remained mostly unchanged. This style of waging war faced challenges not only from Native American traditions but also from Enlightenment modernity as embodied by the Bourbon administration, and finally from the emergence of Mexico and the United States as new nation-states. This book argues that the local military organization in the northeastern borderlands of New Spain/Mexico retained an eminently medieval Iberian character from the earliest Spanish presence in the area during the seventeenth century until the second half of the nineteenth century.

This study examines four particular settlements, which provide a representative sample in the region: San Antonio and Laredo in modern-day Texas, and Lampazos and Bustamante in the northeastern Mexican state of Nuevo León. All four of these populations were integrated through military cooperation, trade, and family bonds, and they formed part of a line of communications connecting northern Mexico and Texas. Studying them side by side highlights the similarities in their basic principles of military organization and cultural patterns. At the same time, they offer a diverse sample of populations, illustrating the different ethnic groups and colonization models characteristic of the broader region. Bustamante began as a Tlaxcalan agricultural town, while Lampazos began as a mission and later developed into a military settlement. Laredo was a settlement for military settlers, and San Antonio included a mission, an agricultural settlement, and a presidio. In this way, we can track and analyze the historical patterns in the region extensively and in depth.

Several historians, including Brian DeLay, Sean F. McEnroe, and Luis Medina-Peña have produced groundbreaking recent studies of this region.[2] Other previous studies of the area, however, have tended to be overly descriptive and not analytical, often treating each military settlement as unique and unrelated to others in its historical development. This study, in contrast, explores the common characteristics of each while at the same time placing it within the broader imperial, national, and hemispheric contexts, using a comparative framework similar to those found in studies of the Atlantic world by scholars like Jorge Cañizares-Esguerra, Daniel K. Richter, and others.[3] Such a study can help to explain how a similar cultural background of the European settlers in North America—both Spanish and English—contributed to shaping the culture of the United States, understood in continental terms. For purposes of literary variety, I use the terms frontier and borderlands interchangeably, defining them both as areas of cultural exchange that produce a unique result across time and space.[4]

This book answers several interconnected questions: How did the Spanish military organization in the borderlands of medieval Iberia influence that of northeastern New Spain/Mexico and other borderland regions in Latin America? How different were the northeast's social structures and military organizations from Spain's communities under study? How significantly did the change in political order from community-royal rule to modern citizenship in the Mexican nation-state affect the communities under study? How did the geopolitical transformations during the nineteenth century affect the ways those communities organized themselves for war? In order to answer these questions, we must trace the evolution of the Spanish borderlands military systems from the Middle Ages through the nineteenth century.

The first chapter begins with the Spanish Reconquista (711–1492) and then examines the Spanish colonization of North America until the Chichimeca War (1545–1600). The chapter traces the common patterns of warfare in medieval Iberia, analyzing their evolution over time. It shows how Castile's character as a frontier society in a permanent state of war shaped its political institutions. Although the closure of Spain's borderlands in 1492 ushered in a more modern centralized state, the medieval model of warfare and colonization of the borderlands endured in other geographical areas as new generations exported these patterns throughout the western hemisphere. This chapter lastly explains why, in the borderlands of North America, the medieval military heritage was able to last and evolve, while it died out elsewhere.

The second chapter explains the process of colonization and settlements in the northeast borderlands during the seventeenth and eighteenth centuries. It shows the influence of medieval institutions on the area's colonial experience and how they became firmly rooted in the culture of its inhabitants through their protracted experience of warfare. This chapter illustrates how these frontier values endured in northeastern New Spain, while in Spain itself they had disappeared centuries before. It also explores the contrast and evolution of war and political participation in the northeastern borderlands, highlighting how they differed from contemporary Spain. Additionally, it describes how these ideas and practices affected the region's Native inhabitants as well as the ways Native people reacted, adopted, and integrated them. Although Spanish authorities continually tried to bring the area into conformity with the legal forms of metropolitan Spain and central New Spain, local traditions stubbornly persisted. Chapter 3 focuses on the emergence of the Bourbon dynasty and the imposition of its administrative policies, adopted from France in northeastern New Spain. It explores the consequences of the clash between the Bourbons' centralizing administrative reforms and the more traditional ideas of inhabitants of the region. The chapter also analyzes how broader geopolitical changes complicated that process, as the northeastern frontier became central to Spain's imperial security for Spain because of French, British, Native American, and later American expansionism into the area.

The fourth chapter studies the impact of Mexican independence in the region, focusing on the transition from a constitutional monarchy to a federalist republic with a proactive nationalistic agenda. During this period, Mexico drew upon the cultural inheritances of the French Revolution and the Cadiz Constitution to establish new political and military institutions such as the National Guard, National Militia, and Civic Militia. The chapter explores how these innovations impacted the local traditions of the northeastern borderlands without fully erasing the influence of their medieval origins. The final chapter explores the rupture of the region from the rest of the Mexican nation-state during the complicated period of 1835–1845. It examines how the local inhabitants were antagonized against governmental policies because of the refusal of the central government to recognize and use the regional structures of defense and political order. The chapter also studies the effects of the Anglo colonist's presence in the region and the increasing scale and frequency of Indigenous raids. Those factors made local structures based on gaining political voice through military participation stronger during the rest of the nineteenth century.

CHAPTER 1

The Development of the Spanish Medieval Military Ethos

SPAIN EXPERIENCED A TRANSFORMATION PROCESS THROUGH EIGHT CENTURIES of Islamic presence during the Middle Ages. This fact meant that Spain had a unique and different development from the one lived by the rest of Western Europe at the time. Even though this had repercussions in many areas, this book addresses the enduring consequences in the military sphere. In the Iberian Peninsula, the conflict between Muslims and Christians led to the formation of a borderland society in which military organization became an integral part of the culture. This chapter analyzes the common patterns of Spanish-Castilian society and its military organization during the Middle Ages and the early colonization of America during the sixteenth century. It also looks into the Andalusian-Muslim counterpart and its North African links to explain their influence on the emergence of a militarized society in Castile. Moreover, it explores the conflicts of the period known as Reconquista, not just the conflict with the Muslim presence but the wars among the different Christian Iberian kingdoms and their expansion overseas to Italy, North Africa, the Canary Islands, and the Americas. This section focuses on the strategies adopted during this period and how they developed. It also examines the role and motivations of individuals of both sides to participate in warfare, the way they were organized, the different categories of participation in military actions, the ways they were regulated, and the social categories that derived from war. Thus it shows why such a model of military colonization was successful in some situations while not in others. Finally, the chapter elucidates why this military culture fell into disuse in Spain while it experienced a new resurgence in America.

SPAIN (CASTILE) DURING THE MIDDLE AGES

In AD 711, a Muslim army from North Africa invaded the Iberian Peninsula. That force destroyed Visigothic rule and incorporated most of the invaded territory into the Damascus Caliphate. Some areas, however, were still under Christian rule, areas that the invaders were unable to or did not want to conquer. Different from the fertile lands in the south incorporated by then to the newcomers' order, the rugged and less productive areas of the north were not considered worthy of conquest. Those independent enclaves formed the nucleus of Christian resistance and acted as the spearhead for future invasions of Muslim territory.

Soon after the shock of the swift Moorish invasion, what remained of the Christian nobility organized the resistance. First, in the far north, mainly in Asturias, in the year 722, a nobleman, Pelayo, defeated a Muslim force in the mountains. In 801, Luis of Aquitania occupied Barcelona. In turn, Asturias became a kingdom that grew to extend over parts of the entire north, from Galicia to the Pyrenees. Later on, because of the fragility of the Christian nobility, the Asturias Kingdom was absorbed by another realm that initially had been an Asturian periphery: León. In this way, by the beginning of the tenth century, the kingdom of León was well established on the territorial basis of Asturias and would later form the nucleus of the kingdom of Castile.[1]

Originally, Castile was the borderland territory between the Kingdom of León and Muslim Spain. This area was in the corridor through which Moorish expeditions raided the northern Christian areas for pillaging. Therefore, it had a role in defending northern Spain simply due to its strategic geographical location, which would shape not only the character of its warriors but also the profile and actions of its rulers. Some historians suggest, not without evidence, that the name Castile refers to all the fortifications and castles existing in that territory due to the high level of war activity. Strategically, the Castilian enclave was critical for the security of the Christian north. For León, occupying, populating, and defending it was imperative. The problem was the scarcity of resources needed to carry out this endeavor. In a permanent state of war, such a frontier was not an attractive place in which to reside. So to attract colonists, the Leonese authorities had to grant privileges that, in the end, would be important for the institutional development of Castile. The Leonese crown decreed that those men who decided to colonize Castile would be free of any serfdom and would receive lands under the condition of settling and defending them. Contrary to the rest of feudal Europe, there were no juridical restrictions against peasants who owned lands. This tradition became so deeply rooted that even in the middle of the fourteenth century, there were *behetrías* in Castile, villages that had the right to elect their lord to be their political leader. They could also reject their lord if he affected the interests of the place's inhabitants, something unique in Europe then. As a result, the proliferation of small properties characterized the region.[2]

Castile was an open society in which, in some way, men were not perpetually confined to *castas*, or social classes. There was a social order where the high nobility was at the peak, a low nobility whose members would later refer to themselves as *hidalgos* were in the middle, and finally the commoners, who were called *villanos*, occupied the "lower" level. This class hierarchy was not rigid, though, and everyone could conceivably reach the upper level through military merits, and constant warfare against the Moors provided the opportunity for this social mobility.[3] Anyone could return from combat with the spoils of war; slaves, goods, horses, and other animals helped to improve their socioeconomic status. By the simple act of capturing a horse, a foot soldier could become a knight. A captive laborer, good armor, or livestock could all improve a man's fortune and social condition.[4] Although the king had some permanent troops at his disposal, the vast majority of Castilian armed forces were independent armies composed of individuals seeking social benefit through war. So Castile had a contractual and popular society that differed from the monarchical, aristocratic, and unitary way of doing things in León.[5]

This distinctive Castilian culture, which revolved around military aspects, developed during the period that historians call the Reconquista; the process involved the armed struggle between Spain's Christian and Muslim factions. This conflict began a few years after the Arab invasion, around AD 772 with the battle of Covadonga, and ended in 1492, when the Catholic kings captured Granada. The use of the term Reconquest implies two simple but fundamental ideas to determine that what the Kingdoms of Castile and Aragon were doing was a just war. First, the disputed territory was to be liberated from a foreign aggressor. Second, it was a religious crusade in which the Moorish opponents were considered infidels and had to be converted or expelled. There was also the question of legitimacy: someone would have to claim to belong to a royal line that predated the Muslim invasion. The Visigothic lineage, however, had been completely destroyed when King Rodrigo had died in the Battle of Guadalete in 711, so it was necessary to invent such a lineage. The way to do this was provided by the Mozarabic* monks who migrated to the north and claimed that the kings of Asturias were the heirs of the Visigothic tradition. As the Asturian kingdom gradually expanded toward Galicia, Alfonso III (866–910) took up the monks' proposal and put it into practice. One way of strengthening the discourse of legitimacy was for the monarch to promote the cult of the Apostle Saint James, essentially a Galician saint, who would eventually become the symbol of the Reconquest. According to the legend, the Apostle James appeared at the fictitious Battle of Clavijo in 844 and helped the Christian army of King Ramiro I of Asturias to victory. This legend was created and incorporated into traditional folklore to legitimize the Reconquest. At the beginning of the tenth century, Ordoño II (914–924) created the Kingdom of León, which would replace Asturias as the "legitimate" heir to the Visigothic monarchy. But the advance of Castile as the vanguard of the Kingdom of León made it grow in importance. Castile gradually reduced its ties with León until it became an independent kingdom and replaced León as the driving force behind the Reconquest.[6]

At the same time, Muslim political unity in the Iberian Peninsula was fragmenting. In 1031, the Caliphate of Cordoba collapsed amid internal conflicts between Arabs and Berbers. This allowed the Islamic governors of al-Andalus to govern themselves and become petty monarchs. The caliphate was thus divided into many independent kingdoms known as *taifas*. This state of affairs was exploited by the Christian kingdoms of the north since the Muslim dominions, divided and weakened, offered no resistance. Therefore, they were forced to pay tribute and occasionally received Christian military aid in their internal conflicts and vice versa. In 1085, when Castile took the important city of Toledo, the Muslim kingdoms realized that the Christian advance threatened their existence, so, in desperation, they asked for help from their North African allies, the Almoravids. The latter were ultraconservative Muslims and lacked the cultural sophistication of their Andalusian coreligionists, but they were good warriors. The Almoravids retook some territories and reunified Muslim Spain in 1103. Such an alliance put the Christian kingdoms of the north in serious trouble, and they were forced to be on the defensive during this period. The Almoravids' power in North Africa, however, began to wane under pressure from other Berber groups, who eventually displaced them. By 1172, after the expulsion of the Almoravids, the Almohads took

---

* Mozarabs were Christians who adopted the Arabic culture.

CHAPTER I

political control of the Islamic regions of Spain. The Almohads, another extremely radical Muslim group from North Africa, proved to be even more radical in their interpretation of Islam than their predecessors had been.[7]

On the other hand, the religious fervor of Christianity, expressed in the Crusades, would feed the Reconquest movement, primarily through French adventurers. During this period, religious orders of a military nature appeared: the Cistercians founded Calatrava in 1150 to defend the city of the same name. Alcántara was established in the same spirit in 1154, and the Order of Saint James began protecting pilgrims on their way to Santiago de Compostela in 1170.[8]

At the beginning of the thirteenth century, the Christian kingdoms formed a united front against the Almohads. The battle of Navas de Tolosa in 1212 was the turning point in the Reconquest. There the alliance of Castile, Aragon, and Navarre kings defeated the Islamic dynasty. This victory opened the way to the Guadalquivir valley in Andalusia. By 1248, Seville had fallen into Castilian hands. The only Islamic region left on the Iberian Peninsula was the kingdom of Granada, now ruled by the Nasrid dynasty, which had sprung from local Muslim lines. The Nasrid dynasty was weak, and to survive Christian pressure it became a vassal of the crown of Castile. At the same time, however, the Nasrid dynasty sought support from its Moroccan coreligionists, the Marinids. Ironically, the new Muslim partners were more interested in gaining control of Granada than ensuring the Nasrid defense against the Castilians. The Marinid presence further complicated the situation in Granada, as they were involved in alliances and betrayals, sometimes even allying themselves with other Christian kingdoms such as Aragon. Thus, with no other choices, the Nasrid sought help from their Christian rivals and changed the game of alliances. Finally, the Marinids' pretensions ended with their defeat at the hands of Castile in the Battle of the Salado in 1340. This action marked the beginning of a long pause in the Reconquest until the end of the fifteenth century.[9]

The figure of Rodrigo Díaz de Vivar, El Cid, helps us to understand the prototype of the warrior princes who emerged during this period on the borderland between the Muslim and Christian kingdoms. Diaz de Vivar was a member of the lower nobility who fell out of favor with the Castilian king, Alfonso VI, who banished him from Castile. He assembled a small military force in exile and dedicated it to the war against the Moors. This force accumulated large amounts of booty and gained great social prestige. Thanks to this, the army of El Cid began to receive money to protect towns, not only Christian but also Muslim cities, such as Zaragoza. The *Cantar del Mio Cid*—the Castilian equivalent of *La Chanson de Roland*—is a romance that portrays life on the Castilian frontier through the figure of El Cid. One of the main themes of El Cid's deed is how this type of warrior generated a livelihood through war and how this opened up opportunities for social mobility and access to power. The reading of the poem is compelling in that these military and political values defined Castilian society. The belief that war was a more prestigious and lucrative way of life than other activities, such as trade, would determine the character of Castilians for centuries to come, as would their quest for conquest in the New World.[10]

An equally important aspect of the military activities of that time was the organization of the self-defense of the villages, which led to the creation of municipal militias. The borderland towns played an important role in containing the Muslim military campaigns: they had the dual function of populating and defending the region.[11] Unlike the armies of the nobility, the militias of the towns were well-organized, with their own system of operations and command. The rules required them to hold regular *alardes*: military reviews and parades. And, as in the armies of the nobility, the figure of the *caballeros villanos* arose in the militias, a kind of knightly investiture earned by participation in the Reconquest. The militias supported the king, as happened in the battle of Navas de Tolosa. Avila, Salamanca, and Segovia were present in all the battles fought by the Castilian monarch. Their most important role, however, was to protect the vast frontier.[12]

For this reason, as we have seen, they received privileges such as tax exemption and the right to have their political organization, although always as vassals of the king. This policy starkly contrasted with the Carolingian laws that dominated the rest of Europe, which only allowed knights and nobles to enjoy these privileges.[13] The cities with militias were generally fortified and were important centers of institutional, fiscal, economic, political, and military connections and were located strategically for the defense and expansion of Christian territory. The frontier protection was based almost entirely on these types of towns.[14] The entire defensive system functioned by incorporating new populations that were not originally Castilian, giving them access to the social practices of military participation. Such was the case with the Mozarabic population of Toledo.

These militia towns used their position as borderland enclaves to negotiate and obtain as many concessions, privileges, and exemptions as possible. By law, these militias had an independent command and could be used according to the interests of the towns that sponsored them. But there would come a time when the Castilian monarchy would see the system of cities with militias as an obstacle to the centralization of power.¹⁵ On the other hand, using this militia system in border towns would not end with a pause in the Reconquest. Although a period of large-scale military activity against the Moors had ended, a low-intensity war continued on the Andalusian frontier between the advanced populations of Castile and the Muslims of Granada. For this reason, the municipal authorities of the Andalusian settlements continued to use this system of municipal militias.¹⁶

From 711 to 1340, there were many battles and not a few sieges, but such encounters were costly both financially and in human lives. Thus the most commonly used form of warfare was fast raids, designed not to take territory but to plunder, enslave enemies, and destroy their populations. It was a war of attrition, a cheap way to weaken rivals by pressuring them with constant and unexpected raids. This way of fighting was called *guerra guerreada*. Depending on the scale of the attack, the words *cabalgadas* and *algaras*, among other names, designated these quick, intense, and brief encounters. Sometimes they included foot soldiers, but most often only mounted forces were involved.¹⁷ During this time, Castilian frontiersmen adopted the Arab riding style, called *jineta*, with short stirrups for light cavalry.* Of the booty obtained, one-fifth belonged to the king as a tribute, known as the *quinto real*, and the rest was divided among the expedition participants. This tradition, which was also practiced by its Islamic counterpart as the *ganima*, split the profits of the armed expedition among its members. In other words, a whole system emerged to make the war profitable and sustainable while weakening the enemy's financial base. By the fourteenth century, Castile had a well-established military organization derived from the Reconquest. While it is true that some aspects of the organization were a common practice in other parts of Europe, in Castile and other kingdoms of the Iberian Peninsula this kind of organization established a broad base of participants among its inhabitants. Moreover, the Iberian population had incorporated such conflict economically and culturally as an integral part of their way of life. Therefore, the first great pause in the Reconquest did not cause this type of military organization to disappear in Castile; on the contrary, it evolved and was perfected, in part due to the growing power of the monarchy.¹⁸

---

* The other style of riding was known as *A la brida*. Of French influence, it consisted of a saddle with long stirrups, which allowed the rider to settle firmly. This helped to withstand greater impact so he could use the lance from a solid base. This was the preferred riding style of medieval knights to launch their powerful cavalry charges.

According to the religious cosmology of medieval Iberia, the social orders established by God were the *oratores*, represented by the clergy and the Catholic Church; the *laboratores*, such as laborers, farmers, or artisans, whose function was to produce goods; and finally, the *bellatores*, the warriors, whose social role was to defend and protect the previous two. Becoming a member of the Castilian nobility in the Middle Ages meant responding to calls to arms. The Siete Partidas, the first legal code written in Castilian, was clear in this regard, defining the armed duties of the subjects of Castile. This code established the figure of the caudillo—a military leader—as a legal category in the organization of war and on whom fell the responsibility of organizing the defense. So the king had established a private defense system based on individuals who were directly under the command of the royal authority.[19]

The figure of the caudillo as a military leader had existed in Castile since the beginning of the Reconquest. They were figures who made war and paid for it. In a sense, they could be considered businessmen. With the Siete Partidas, the Crown regulated the functions of caudillos, which constituted an implicit recognition of their quasi-independent functions and powers. In this way, the Crown established support for the military effort by privatizing war; it used this ingenuity extensively during the Reconquest and other Castilian military enterprises. Thus, specific individuals agreed to subordinate their military power to the king's authority in exchange for privileges such as access to the nobility and economic benefits derived from war and plunder. According to the Siete Partidas, "there is no other warlord than the lord major, who is understood to be the king or the one appointed by him."[20] These caudillos made their royal authority known through the ritualized use of flags, banners, or pennants, depending on the ruling monarch.[21]

Another example of crown-sponsored military leadership was the *adelantado*, a title given to the discoverer or peacemaker of a region previously outside royal jurisdiction. This category appeared in the eleventh century and was recognized by the king in the mid-thirteenth century. Those granted this status had civil and criminal jurisdiction over the territory under their control. The Siete Partidas defined the figure of the adelantado as "the man who is involved in an act indicated by the hand of the king."[22] He had three functions: "to punish wrongdoers, the other was to help people obtain their rights, and the third was to warn the king of the state of the country."[23] At first, it was just a title for an envoy of the king to deal with legal matters. But since most adelantados resided on the Crown's frontiers, it soon became a title for someone who ruled a remote territory. Initially, their title was Adelantado de la Frontera or Adelantado de Andalucía.[24] By the fifteenth century, in some cases, it became a patrimonial right.[25] This practice developed in the context of medieval Spain and the Reconquest. Undoubtedly, the role of individuals in defense, or rather the privatization of military enterprises, was a growing phenomenon in medieval Iberia, especially in Castile. Moreover, this system would soon find a promising horizon of continuity in overseas enterprises, first in the Canary Islands and on the coast of Africa, and then mainly on the American continent.

The pause in the Reconquest (1340–1482) did not mean peace; during this long period, Castile concentrated on securing its power and expanding its borders at the expense of its Christian neighbors. Most of the fourteenth and fifteenth centuries were periods of constant warfare between Castile, Aragon, and Portugal. The latter kingdoms, in turn, sought to make territorial gains at the expense of Castile, leading to a spiral of armed conflicts between the three crowns. Catastrophes were the order of the day because, in addition to the great epidemics of the bubonic plague, the nobility and the king of Castile had profound disagreements about the distribution of power, which led to several internecine wars. At one point, Castile was fighting in three different wars simultaneously and ended up getting involved in the Hundred Years' War by allying itself with France, forcing Portugal to do the same with England. There were, of course, years of peace and truce, but in general the period was marked by decades of continuous warfare: Castile was at war with Aragon and Portugal in one way or another from 1356 to 1431. The English Channel was an extension of the frontier war, in which both sides attacked the enemy's coasts to plunder and take booty. In a sense, they were naval cabalgadas. Although the peace with the Moorish kingdom of Granada ended in 1406, this kingdom was not much affected by the resumption of hostilities since the other wars Castile faced limited it to practicing a low-intensity war on the Muslim border. That is, the Christian and Muslim settlers on both sides limited themselves to raids to obtain booty for the war, but there were no ambitions for territorial expansion or to change the political order of the adversaries.[26]

In 1452, with Castile's internal affairs stabilized, King Henry IV undertook a crusade against the Moors to gain prestige and keep the nobility busy and distracted. This effort produced some trophies, such as the conquest of Gibraltar, but in reality it was a conflict of attrition rather than decisive battles. Again, in 1464, internal Castilian conflicts prevented the kingdom from continuing the war against Granada. The nobility rebelled against King Henry IV, and there were another twenty years of internal armed conflict, once again involving Portugal,

Aragon, and France. Finally, in 1484, Isabella, queen of Castile, and her husband, Ferdinand of Aragon, emerged victorious from the conflict. These monarchs formed an overwhelming force that unified most of the Iberian Peninsula under their authority. In short, although the Reconquest would have had a pause in the conflict against the Moors, in reality there was no period of lasting peace. Castilian society lived through a long period in which war played a central role, hardening and militarizing it. Throughout this period, the conflict in the Muslim marchland remained latent, punctuated by brief periods of violence and its peculiarities.[27]

THE LAST FRONTIER: GRANADA

During the hiatus in the Reconquest (1340–1482), the Moorish kingdom of Granada in Andalusia experienced a low-intensity war, as we have seen. While Castile did not launch a new campaign in the form of a Reconquest on the Andalusian frontier, there were continuous small-scale hostilities involving attacks and looting for livestock, crops, and captives. These events resulted in deaths, surprise attacks, and reprisals; harassment was common and therefore accepted as almost normal by the inhabitants of the area to the extent of not interrupting the dealings and diplomatic relations between Christians and Muslims.[28]

Armed conflict was always a private affair. The peace treaties agreed to with the Muslims by councils, the nobility, and feudal lords meant little or nothing to the entrepreneurs of the cabalgadas. On this frontier, anyone could wage war at will; nobles with a thirst for political power, social prestige, or economic benefits participated in it. Also, uprooted men, almost bandits, made a living from this peculiar warfare. The military actions were quick incursions destined to plunder the enemy's towns and farms, to take captives, and even to kill indiscriminately to weaken them for future incursions. These actions were not considered illegal, as they were well established in laws, decrees, and accepted practices of the time. They were part of the population's borderland culture, where violence became a way of life, mainly organized and carried out by knights and militiamen who refused to become peaceful settlers after the conquest of Andalusia.[29]

There were different categories of participants in this peculiar state of frontier warfare: *almogávares, almocadenes,* and *adalides*. Almogavar, from the Arabic *al-mugawir* (one who makes a military expedition) and *al-mujabir* (the bearer of military news), was the name given to those who lived by robbery, violence, and the taking of prisoners. Therefore, they lived by practicing guerra guerreada and raiding the frontier for immediate gain. These groups, formed on both sides of the borderlands, Moors and Christians, were small armed groups feared and hated by the local settlements. The almocadén, from the Arabic *al-muqadam* (local military chief), was the local Christian warlord or military chief who raided Granada and for whom violence was a way of life. The town council paid for his predatory expeditions, and he was considered a public official. Then there were the adalides, from the Arabic *al-dalid* (scout), who were knights and military leaders experienced in this type of warfare. Appointed by the king and his military delegates, they knew the terrain and were usually bilingual, fluent in Spanish and Arabic. They were experts at scouting, setting up ambushes, identifying smoke signals, distinguishing between dust created by cattle or by armed forces, and following a trail accurately. The chronicles of the time referred to their peculiar fighting style, saying that they fought like Moors.[30] Finally, there were the *homicianos*, a legal term for murderers who, if sentenced to death, were pardoned if they agreed to help colonize the Andalusian marchland. The king granted this privilege of pardon and colonization to consolidate strategic places such as population centers or fortresses. In this way, the figure of the homiciano became widespread in the borderland towns of the fourteenth and fifteenth centuries.[31] According to tradition, these homicianos were authorized by the king but acted individually on their initiative and motives; that is, it was another way of waging war under private concessions, a different type of war entrepreneurs.

Among the Moors we also find almogávares and almocadenes. Ambush and night raid were their preferred methods of operation; they moved undetected to take herds and prisoners. This military behavior of the guerra guerreada was practically the same as that of the Christians, but the Moors did not have the considerable human resources the Christian kingdoms had. For this reason, they always tried to attack by surprise at night to increase their effectiveness. A Christian chronicle of the time says that they completely dominated the aspect of guerra guerreada and that, thanks to their tactics, two hundred Moors could do more damage than six hundred Christians. They always attacked on horseback, with few provisions and no armor other than the protection of their shield. They were experts at luring the enemy into their ambushes, with no other goal than to appropriate or destroy the enemy's resources.[32] This way of fighting would remain deeply imprinted in the Castilian imaginary since a century later, it would be related, in almost identical form, to the attacks of the nomadic Natives of North America.

The capture of people was a fundamental motivation for the development of this peculiar system of frontier violence. Captives could be sold as slaves, exploited as labor, ransomed, or exchanged for other prisoners, depending on various factors such as social class. The Grenadian Muslims could make large profits from the ransom payments, but for the prisoners of low social class, such as shepherds, laborers, or merchants, their liberation was practically impossible and they were condemned to perpetual slavery. And some captives, particularly women and children, became renegades, adopting the religion of their captors. Such individuals seemed the most dangerous to their former side because of their knowledge of both cultures, their uprooted condition, and their religious opportunism.[33] This type of person became a common feature of the last Iberian frontier, as their biculturalism was a valuable natural product of a borderland interaction.

PERIOD OF TRANSFORMATIONS AND CONTINUITIES

When the last truce ended in 1482, the Catholic kings had already consolidated their power; they then turned their attention to Granada. This moment would be the last time the traditional military organization of the medieval period was used in the Iberian Peninsula. The war against the Muslims of Granada was to last ten years; it involved riding, sieges, and battles, but now the Castilians had overwhelming military superiority. This was possible mainly due to the resources that only a unified monarchy could command, which translated into the creation of an armed force of unprecedented size and to the use of firearms on a large scale. Added to this was the participation of the Aragonese naval power, which made it possible to blockade the coast of Granada, isolating it from the outside. On the other hand, the Moors were divided, and the Catholic kings took advantage of this to attack. This last war of Reconquest involved soldiers operating under the direct command of the royal authorities, armies formed by the nobility, municipal militias, and mercenaries. In 1487, after a long siege, the fifteen thousand Muslim inhabitants of Málaga were enslaved by the Catholic monarchs, who repeated, now on a large scale, the traditional behavior of the victors in the region. In January 1492, Granada fell into the hands of the Catholic kings, thus completing the Reconquest.[34]

CHAPTER I

From then on, there was no longer any need to continue promoting internal expansion through economic and political concessions. Spain took the path to becoming a centralized state; its monarchs were no longer willing to share their authority as they had done during the Reconquest. In addition, during the reign of Ferdinand and Isabella, Spanish influence increased in other areas: they initiated expansion in North Africa, obtained Naples, fought France for hegemony in Italy, and began the conquest of the Americas. These actions caused friction with the Castilian nobility, who saw their former privileges diminished. In addition, the Crown's policies aimed at consolidating Spain as a continental power to counter the power of France, so it formed dynastic alliances with other powers, such as the Holy Roman Empire. In 1497, Philip the Beautiful, son of Emperor Maximilian of Austria, married Juana, daughter of Ferdinand and Isabella, from whom the future monarch, Charles, was born. Alliance with another power, England, was achieved when in 1501, the daughter of the Catholic kings, Catherine, married Arthur, the heir to the English throne. Such alliances brought an increased flow of foreign advisors and bureaucrats to the Castilian court, and the old nobility was furious, jealous of losing their influence and privileged status. The situation exploded when Ferdinand placed his grandson Charles, who had been raised in Burgundy, on the Spanish throne. The new monarch, who at the time could barely speak Spanish and whose court was mostly made up of foreigners, was to be not only king but also Holy Roman Emperor. Thus, after Charles was crowned king in Brussels in March 1516, a revolt broke out in Castile, whose inhabitants saw in this act a coup d'état. In this conflict, some nobles did not respect the royal authority and tried to take justice into their own hands carrying out vendettas against their rivals to expand their dominion and influence. In some regions, the vassals rebelled against their lords; the cities convened their general assemblies, known as courts, to supplant the royal power. In short, the central authority of the state was far from being enforceable, at least initially.[35]

At first, the uprising was nothing more than a minor revolt. Still, when Charles was crowned emperor in 1519, things went from bad to worse: Castile saw this act as a threat because its traditional power as a kingdom that had been the leader of the Reconquest and protagonist of the discovery of America would be diminished, and it would now be only a minor part of a great empire in the making. In Toledo, a revolt known as the *"comuneros"* broke out. Initially, the city authorities set three goals for their movement: (1) to not pay new taxes, (2) to reject the Empire because it meant sacrificing Castile to dynastic entities, and (3) to defend their interests in case the king ignored their demands. The conflict would grow, and by 1520 there was unrest throughout Castilian territory. The rebellion had gotten out of control and had become a kind of revolution.[36] Essentially, it was a clash between an old order that would not disappear and a new one that had not yet been born.

In addition to its political implications, the comuneros revolt is interesting for its military peculiarities. The municipal militias played an essential role in the uprisings, using the military knowledge they had inherited from the Reconquest, such as their ability to mobilize quickly and their effectiveness in combat.[37] Soon after, the situation changed: the high and middle nobility realized that the rebellion threatened their privileges, perhaps even their lives, much more than the Empire did, so they decided to renounce it and support the emperor. By February 1522, Charles had crushed the rebellion; the destruction of the city of Medina del Campo, home of the conquistador Bernal Díaz del Castillo, made clear what would happen to those who opposed the nascent Carolingian Empire.[38] The purpose of the rebellion was to preserve the old egalitarian order, but the conditions that had produced it disappeared with the consummation of the Reconquest, the discovery of America, and the new dynastic arrangements in Europe. The high nobility was well established and had no intention or motivation to continue to support the old meritocratic structures of a military nature. All of this would lead to the complete transformation of Castile into a hegemonic kingdom, leaving behind its medieval traditions and becoming the focal point of a state that sought to centralize Spain. The old warrior and egalitarian society had no place in the new configuration. With no more wars to fight in its immediate surroundings, the era of independent military characters on the Iberian Peninsula was over. The old structures, though, would find a fertile space for their survival when transplanted to new territories.

CHAPTER I

THE TRANSPLANTATION OF THE MEDIEVAL MILITARY TRADITION TO THE FRONTIER STRUGGLE OF OVERSEAS TERRITORIES

The first overseas adventure of the Castilian Crown took place in the Canary Islands, discovered in 1336 by the French, who first attempted to exploit them. Castile began exploratory and predatory expeditions in 1393, and in 1402 it incorporated the establishments previously founded by France. Borderland experiences in Spain influenced military efforts that fell to private investors. Following the tradition of hiring private entrepreneurs to reconquer and expand frontiers, the king entered into *capitulaciones* that fixed the rights and obligations of each party.[39] Another institution of the same type was that of the adelantados, such as Alfonso de Lugo, who received the hereditary title of Adelantado de Canarias in 1503. Lugo was a representative figure of his time, imbued with the medieval values of the Iberian marchlands and favoring the acquisition of privileges through military conquest. He participated in numerous encounters with the Natives of the Canary Islands, whom he finally defeated after several campaigns.[40] Another characteristic of this type of medieval private military colonization was the use of the *"requerimiento,"* a process by which the Natives were requested to accept being subjects of the king and to become Catholic Christians. If the islanders rejected the requirement, which was generally the response to such a demand, they were treated as enemies and enslaved. This formula had already been used against the Moors, such as in the capture of Malaga in 1487. There were frequent raids to enslave the Natives.[41]

Here we can identify another characteristic of Reconquest: the use of Native allies. This meant that Natives conquered in one place could become conquerors in another. This strategy of incorporating allies allowed them to be integrated into the new political order, along with its consequent social mobility, according to the laws of Castilian military participation. The Crown sought to create permanent settlements in the Canary Islands, so the rights of colonization and *vecindad*, a form of citizenship, consisted of acquiring land through occupation; this system was known as *repartimiento*. Such a structure worked well as long as the Canary Islands remained an outpost far from royal authority. In 1526, however, the king established the Real Audiencia in the islands, a court appointed by the crown to rule on civil and criminal matters. This was a decisive step in the formal establishment of royal authority, as had been done years earlier in the conquered lands of Spain.

The creation of a royal institution such as the Audiencia had several effects, one of which was that the territory in which it was established ceased to be a frontier.[42]

During the sixteenth century, some areas of the Mediterranean became frontiers of the Spanish monarchy. Among them was North Africa, a strategic point for the security of the Andalusian coast due to the danger of predatory expeditions of Moorish origin that ended in plunder and enslaved inhabitants. In those times, the Reconquest was part of a recent past; it was so present in the consciences that some claimed it had not ended but was continuing on the African continent. By 1509, the Spanish had captured the cities of Melilla, Mazalquivir, and Oran on the North African coast. There they reproduced the same borderland institutions established in the Middle Ages, such as the practice of sharing the spoils of victory and military meritocracy as a method of social advancement, by which the nobility secured the administration of the place. Hernán Cortés himself tried to regain fame and royal favor by participating in the failed expedition to Algeria in 1541. Self-financed soldiers served the dual function of military and colonizing force. The system of presidios, military forts to protect the population from attack, was established in the North African possessions. Homicianos were even used as a military force. Some Berber tribes were used as allies, while others remained enemies. From the enclaves taken, the Spaniards launched cabalgadas to seize booty and slaves, as had been practiced decades earlier in Castile. These military garrisons were only strategic points on the African coast; they never became colonies defended by soldier-settlers. Even if the Church had appealed to the crusading spirit, religious zeal would not have compensated for the lack of economic gain; undoubtedly, the Muslim Mediterranean was losing importance in Spain's imperial vision, which turned its focus to the Atlantic and northern Europe.[43]

Another critical frontier for Spain that emerged in the Mediterranean after the Reconquest was Italy, where the Crown had dynastic and strategic interests. As early as 1497, Spanish forces captured the city of Ostia in the Apennine Peninsula. Their interests in Naples, which clashed with France's, sparked a war in 1501. The Spanish landed a veteran force from the recent war in Granada, which put into practice the tactics learned in the Reconquest: surprise attacks, ambushes, and highly mobile light cavalry. Wherever possible, the troops plundered and pillaged, as they did at Monte Cassino. Castilian surnames, such as Pizarro, appeared on the lists of soldiers in this war. Along with the changes in objectives and a new geopolitical reality for Spain, an era of military transformations began. Gonzalo Fernández de Córdoba exemplified these changes. He was a veteran nobleman who participated in the conflicts with the Moors and the civil wars and later commanded the Spanish forces in Italy. In this endeavor, he was not using his own resources but was paid directly by the monarchy, which consequently dictated orders to him, marking the beginning of the modern age in the military forces.[44] At the same time, the armed forces underwent a transformation: the army formations changed into infantry units armed with pikes and firearms. These famous *tercios* would become a highly effective military force for the next 150 years. The tercios radically differed from the medieval armies that fought for social status and wealth; they were the beginning of modern armies paid for by a nation-state. In any case, some of the terminology of the Reconquest continued in use. The Spanish garrisons in Italy, for example, were called presidios and formed the bases of the tercios that fought in Europe on behalf of their king in the sixteenth and seventeenth centuries.[45] These new presidios did not function like the original institution of serving as a support base for soldier-colonizers in the marchlands. When the conflict with France ended in 1504, the situation of the soldiers who had acquired their military training during the Reconquest became uncertain. Some of them joined the campaigns in Africa, and others became mercenaries. Castile, Spain, and Europe were changing.

OLD CONTINUITIES IN A NEW WORLD

The year 1492 was an important one for Spain. It marked the end of seven centuries of conflict and the discovery of America. In a way, both events symbolized the end of the medieval order and gave way to the beginning of the modern era. But not only that, this transition brought with it the start of a political process not seen since the dissolution of the Roman Empire: the centralization of power in the head of the Spanish monarchy. Thus the effects of the events of 1492—the end of the Reconquest of the Iberian Peninsula and the discovery of America—were transcendent and far-reaching in the course of history, profoundly altering the geopolitical situation of Spain and Europe. In the Iberian Peninsula, not only did a kingdom with an unstoppable hegemonic tendency emerge, but upon achieving this hegemony, it necessarily became involved in European affairs and due to its transoceanic expansion would contribute, with few virtues and many defects, to the design of the rest of the world. The beginning of a new era, however, did not mean that the previous medieval heritage suddenly disappeared for Spain; the medieval imaginary survived in many areas of life and politics. Some historians have pointed to the continuity of attitudes between El Cid's quest for booty after he and his men took Valencia in the eleventh century and the enormous quantities of gold and silver that Francisco Pizarro took from the Inca capital of Cuzco.[46] Other historians refute the idea of an "Autumn of the Middle Ages" in Spain.[47] Instead they claim that the Spanish established a medieval world in the Americas.[48] Most historians agree that the Spaniards, especially the conquistadors who arrived in the Americas in the fifteenth and sixteenth centuries, had a vision and a table of values, beliefs, and traditions forged in the Iberian Middle Ages that they naturally sought to reproduce in the New World.[49]

When Columbus arrived in 1492 in lands unknown to Europeans, a world of opportunity opened up in the small Caribbean islands and later in Cuba. At first, the only productive activity was alluvial gold mining. A quick solution to obtaining labor was to use the Natives under the formula of repartimiento service. The *encomienda*, whose origin traces back to the conflict-ridden medieval Castilian frontier, was applied, and in the Caribbean it became a form of control only over people, not over land, which necessarily led to the enslavement of Indigenous populations who refused to serve in this system.[50] Thus slave hunting became a profitable occupation in the region. The Spaniards called these expeditions cabalgadas, which were similar to the procedures used in Granada thirty years earlier. These expeditions took place in what is now the Caribbean, Panama, Colombia, and Venezuela.[51] In 1513, a document called the *Gobernación Espiritual y Temporal de las Indias* (Spiritual and Temporal Government of the Indies) ordered the collection of the fifth royal tax on the proceeds of these expeditions.[52] The Crown soon realized that it would be difficult, if not impossible, to impose a centralized and bureaucratic authority in this early stage of colonization since the new territories were far from the metropolis and were still frontiers. In the early stages of colonization, the Castilian monarchy, instead of wasting resources trying to establish a royal bureaucracy that would be too costly to operate in such a scenario, decided to delegate administrative and political powers to individuals who would invest in colonizing ventures.[53] This measure saved money, but at the same time it meant the revival of the old Castilian frontier traditions that were disappearing in the Iberian Peninsula.

As overexploitation depleted the human and mineral resources available in the Antilles, the need to search for new lands to find these elements became apparent. Between 1517 and 1518, several expeditions explored the coast of Yucatan. In 1519, the Spanish organized an expedition in Cuba to penetrate the continent, led by a Castilian hidalgo named Hernán Cortés, who led a small force of about

CHAPTER I

six hundred men.[54] Most of his men brought their own supplies and military equipment, as was customary at the time. This mini-army gave Cortés the title of Adelantado.[55] The first act of the conquistador from Extremadura to legitimize his actions was to create a cabildo in what would become the city of Veracruz. By doing so in the name of the king, he legitimized the expedition, showing that it was a private enterprise independent of the governor of Cuba and that it used its own resources, albeit under royal authority. It did not take him long to define his goal: the Aztec Empire, which covered an area of 160,000 square kilometers, with its capital in Tenochtitlan, located in the middle of Lake Texcoco in central Mexico, and which would finally surrender in 1521 following a naval siege at more than two thousand meters above sea level. None of the writers of the time, or their immediate successors, could have imagined the circumstances that reality offered Cortés and that fed his legendary stature despite the maneuvers of the Spanish monarchy to minimize his epic. Many factors contributed to this victorious outcome. One was military technology, especially firearms and steel. Another was the spread of pathogens: Europeans unwittingly introduced diseases such as smallpox, which devastated Native populations. The most important factor, however, was the division between different Indigenous factions. The Spanish took advantage of this weakness and allied themselves with various Indigenous groups, including the Tlaxcalan. It is likely that although the Iberians had a technological advantage, the fall of the Aztec Empire would have been impossible without the support of Tlaxcala and its thousands of warriors.

 The profile of the conquistadors who came to Mexico and to the Americas in general is well illustrated by the careers of two men. The first is Hernán Cortés, a hidalgo originally from Extremadura, one of the poorest regions of Castile. Although he received some education in law, he was, like most young men of his time, more interested in a military career. He had the option of joining the army and fighting in Italy but decided it would be better to try his luck in America.[56] The other example is Alvar Núñez Cabeza de Vaca, the grandson of Pedro de Vera, one of the conquerors of the Canary Islands. His mother was Teresa Cabeza de Vaca, a noblewoman from Jerez de la Frontera, an Andalusian town with a long tradition of fighting against the Moors. Eventually, Alvar Núñez would become an adelantado in Paraguay.[57] Both men belonged to the lower nobility and tried to make their way into the new frontiers with their resources to gain wealth and improve their social status by military means.[58] This seems to have been the general pattern of leadership in the Americas: second-class nobles from the poorest areas of Spain, mainly Castile, with enough formal education to manage a military enterprise and then establish colonization based on an incipient civil administration, exercised from the beginning in the name of the king and no one else.

As for the rest, various evaluations have already been made of those who accompanied Cortés on the Mexican adventure and made diverse contributions to the common enterprise. In terms of their origin, the most representative places from which the conquistadors came were Andalusia (30 percent), Extremadura (19 percent), and Castile (24 percent).[59] All these regions under Castilian authority had lived in a constant state of war during the Middle Ages. These conquistadors/colonizers formed the core group of *encomenderos* in New Spain who sought to emulate their medieval predecessors' forms of control over land and labor. The conquistadors recreated the search for economic opportunity and social advancement through violence.

As already mentioned, despite their audacity and courage, the conquistadors depended on the help of their Indigenous allies, mainly Tlaxcalans, to achieve victory. Tlaxcalans occupied an independent territory surrounded by the Mexica Empire and lived in a constant state of war with their powerful neighbors. This circumstance, in a way, represented a parallelism with the frontier situation on the Iberian Peninsula a few years earlier. At first, the Spaniards and Tlaxcalans fought each other, but after three inconclusive encounters, both groups formed a strong alliance. Thus Tlaxcalans participated in every armed encounter against the Aztecs: the first entry into Tenochtitlan, the Noche Triste, Otumba, and the final siege of the Aztec capital. Later they accompanied the Spaniards on other expeditions, such as the Panuco expedition in 1522, the conquest of Guatemala in 1524, and the Nuño de Guzman expedition in 1530.[60] As a result of the alliance and these conquests, Tlaxcalans received notable privileges, such as being placed under the direct administration of the Crown and having the right to receive encomiendas.[61] Their leaders were allowed to use firearms and ride horses, privileges denied to the rest of the Indigenous population. Cortés even invested some Tlaxcalan nobles as knights.[62]

There was an apparent and paradoxical contradiction between what was happening in Spain and what was taking place in the new territories annexed to the Crown. While in Europe, some institutions, such as the town council (cabildo) and the manors (*señoríos*), were suppressed in favor of royal power; they lived a revival in the Americas.[63] In Spain, Charles V had recently consolidated the imperial authority after a conflictual process that included armed uprisings such as the comuneros. For this reason, the Spanish Crown, which had centralized power in the Iberian Peninsula, was unwilling to disperse it in the Americas by creating a new aristocracy. From the beginning of the American conquests, the clergy countered the strength of the old conquistadors. For this reason, and also because it was interested in exploiting the Indigenous labor force, the clergy soon opposed the encomienda, arguing that it was a form of slavery. Although the Crown did not suddenly abolish the encomienda to the conquistadors, it refused to make it hereditary. As the newly incorporated territories grew in importance, the Crown began to administer them more rigorously. The arrival of a professional bureaucracy would further reduce the power of the conquistadors in the political and administrative affairs of the colony.[64] In turn, the Indigenous allies would begin to lose their privileges during the second half of the sixteenth century. Among them, the most important, exemption from tribute, was revoked in some places. The authorities treated them as conquered rather than as allies. The administration of the center of New Spain, from which the conquest and colonization expeditions originated, was absorbed into the growing governmental machinery of the empire. Thus the old order, already extinguished in Spain and which the conquistadors had attempted to maintain in the new territories, began to lose momentum and vitality in the great urban centers of the Americas by the mid-sixteenth century. The northern frontier, however, would present an entirely different panorama from that of the center of the developing colony since it would offer essential and decisive opportunities to keep the old system functioning.

THE CHICHIMECA WAR AS A PATTERN OF MILITARY DEVELOPMENT ON THE NORTHERN BORDERLANDS

After the conquest of the Mexica, the eagerness to gain riches encouraged the Spanish to explore different areas of North America. In 1545, large deposits of silver were discovered in Zacatecas, about six hundred kilometers northwest of Mexico City, and colonization efforts in New Spain shifted northward. The Spaniards would find a very different situation in these territories from what they had previously encountered in Mesoamerica. The Indigenous groups of the region, the Zacatecos and Huachichiles, commonly known as the Chichimecas,* were nomadic hunter-gatherers who lacked a central government, and the Mexica and other Nahua groups had been unable to incorporate them into their empire. Instead of open warfare, the Chichimecas practiced raiding and surprise attacks for plunder. Thus the Spanish entered an extremely complicated conflict that lasted half a century (1550–1600) and became known as the Chichimeca War. A Spanish witness described the Indigenous attacks as fighting and skirmishing, just like the Moors of Granada.[65] This witness described a style of warfare similar to that practiced by the Moors in Andalusia half a century earlier. The northern conquistadors, perhaps a new generation, had a memory, probably by hearsay, of the frontier wars in the peninsula, which is why the comparisons are frequent and repeated in the same sense. The new conquest scenario was thus similar to previous military experiences in Europe and Africa: a permanent conflict in a frontier region where irregular actions were the norm. The communication routes between the northern mining centers, such as Zacatecas and San Luis Potosí, were the battleground of the Chichimeca War. The Spanish trade that supplied the mines and extracted the product from them attracted the Natives, who dedicated themselves to attacking and plundering the caravans and populations of the region. The Spaniards, in turn, needed labor for the mines, which led them to seek slaves among the local Indigenous population. These two factors provoked a large-scale conflict that would significantly affect Spanish penetration in the north for the next three centuries.

---

* The Nahua people initially used the term Chichimeca to designate those native populations living north and west of the Valley of Mexico. The Spaniards, however, reinterpreted this term and gave it a connotation of barbarism and lack of civilization, a product of medieval conceptions of savage peoples. During the sixteenth century, the Iberians used it to generically designate the Indigenous groups of the north, such as Tepehuanes, Cazcanes, Huachichiles, and Zacatecos, among many others. They were associated with nomadic practices, warrior character, and a lack of political structure. In reality, this demonstrated a lack of understanding of the variety and complexity of the native cultures of the north, as many were agricultural and had complex political organizations. This term continued to be used well into the eighteenth century. Charlotte M. Gradie, "Discovering the Chichimecas," *The Americas* 51, no. 1 (July 1994), 67–88.

CHAPTER I

Among the Chichimeca groups, warfare was essential to their sociopolitical organization.[66] They practiced a type of warfare, as already mentioned, based on raids by groups of about twenty warriors, who after the raid were divided into small parties to make pursuit more difficult.[67] In 1560, the targets of the attacks were only ranches, travelers, or trains of mules carrying goods. A decade later, the intensity of the raids increased, and they came to loot and destroy villages. By 1580, the raids had reached places near Mexico City and Guadalajara.[68] The Chichimecas had no urban centers to destroy, and they lacked almost all material possessions, unlike the inhabitants of the Mexica and Inca empires.[69] In addition to raiding and looting, the Chichimeca added other practices, such as taking captives, mainly women and children, to sell or exchange with other Indigenous groups, since almost all of them practiced ethnic incorporation. Contact with their Spanish adversaries led them to modify their war practices. Some of these groups adopted the same tactics as the Spaniards, such as posting sentries to guard their camps; ambushes were usually carried out at dawn, something they learned from their Iberian enemies and their incursions at first light. They adopted the use of European swords and metal knives. In some cases, they enthusiastically embraced the use of horses, which made them highly mobile and dangerous. Their nomadism was tempered to some extent by the trade they began to practice among the tribes as they began to accumulate stolen animals in corrals for exchange with other Natives. Finally, the Chichimecas changed their political organization to confront their enemies more effectively: they organized themselves into tribal confederations to launch much larger attacks against the Spanish settlements.[70]

As with most Spanish colonization efforts in the Americas, the expansion to the north was private. Thus private individuals were responsible for defending the territory they occupied and had to organize against Chichimeca incursions. The encomienda played a fundamental role in the defense of the new settlements; the crown granted the encomenderos only the labor and tribute of the Natives in exchange for Christianizing them under their tutelage and defending the territory. It was a medieval institution used during the Reconquest, although it included only Indigenous labor and taxes, not land ownership in the Americas. The Spaniards also adopted the medieval tradition of founding cities to serve as defensive zones, as they had done in Andalusia. The founding of the towns of Jerez de la Frontera in 1569 and Zacatecas and San Miguel* in Guanajuato

---

* Refers to present-day San Miguel de Allende, not the town of the same name in Nuevo León.

were examples of this defensive policy. San Miguel, located on the route between Zacatecas and Mexico City, was founded in 1555. Settlers in these settlements were required to have weapons and horses for defense as a condition for being granted land. In some of these foundations, the practice was to bring Indigenous groups from the central areas, already Christianized and willing to cooperate with the Spanish, to confront the Chichimeca adversaries. In San Miguel, there were Otomies who acted as diplomatic agents and militia settlers, making the place a Spanish-Indigenous defensive post, using alliances with Natives as Cortés had done years before.[71]

Military commanders were high government officials or wealthy men expected to use their resources in this war against the Indigenous inhabitants.[72] Villages were required to build forts to defend travelers and their neighbors.[73] The Spanish based their war tactics on punitive raids, called *entradas*, which consisted of groups of nine to fifty horsemen who entered Indigenous territory to destroy their camps. These forces used Indigenous allies, with whom they formed numerous parties; there are testimonies that they sometimes consisted of as many as four hundred men.[74] There were also armed horsemen on the roads who tried to guard and help against Chichimeca attacks. These efforts were not based on an overall strategy but on individual initiatives that sometimes succeeded and sometimes failed. Ultimately, these measures alone did little or nothing to pacify the region.

The practice of incurring personal expenses to organize the defense created problems. The main one was that the conquering colonists wanted the opportunity to obtain material gain to compensate for their costs. The most common way to achieve this was to enslave the Chichimecas to pay for the expenditures of war and raids. Many Spaniards refused to participate in military actions unless they were allowed to enslave captured Indigenous people, which led to abuses, the most notable of which was the capture of peaceful Natives.[75] By the 1570s, the increasing scale of the raids forced the viceroy to adopt a policy of "blood and fire," which achieved little except a few successful raids. What it did accomplish was to escalate the level of violence precisely because the Chichimecas were gaining more and more followers to fight against the Spanish population, creating an endless spiral of war.[76]

In the years after 1570, Spanish penetration and expansion to the north became extremely difficult. One solution was to organize all Spanish forces under direct royal command. During this decade, Viceroy Martín Enríquez de Almanza took the first administrative steps to achieve general coordination of the war effort by appointing military supervisors.[77] Another step was to increase the viceroyalty's military budget to one-third of the total war expenditures, with the remaining two-thirds collected from the encomenderos, miners, and merchants.[78] Consequently, the defense remained mainly private, albeit with considerable Crown participation. As one moved down the military ladder, other problems arose. While there were permanent soldiers with assigned salaries, these were so low that the military sought to increase their income by other means. For this reason, and to try to reduce Indigenous slavery, the viceregal authorities sought to have soldiers paid an official salary. These soldiers, though, had to provide their own equipment, weapons, and horses.[79] In an effort to save money, some measures overrode others. The administration tried to give military command to people with experience fighting the Chichimecas, usually landowners and miners.[80] The concession of commands to the rich and powerful of the region would become, with time, a symbol of social status that, together with the sale of these positions, would later reinforce a landowning aristocracy that would last until the country's independence. Diplomacy and bribery also became part of the royal agenda: Gifts of clothing and trinkets were given to the Chichimecas with the promise that the flow of gifts would continue on a regular basis and that past hostilities would be forgiven. This policy of friendship continued as long as the means for its purchase were available.[81]

Among the measures the colonial authorities took was creating a centralized military system based on presidios. These were forts and garrisons near the roads to protect against Chichimeca attacks. Presidios were not a new defensive tactic; as noted above, they were used in Spain during the wars against the Moors and in other peripheral zones of the Spanish empire, such as North Africa, Italy, and later in the Philippines. Even the Portuguese, who shared a military past similar to the Castilians', had presidios on the coasts of Africa and Asia. In Spanish North America, the use of presidios began in 1570 during the Chichimeca War. At first, they were small forts made of adobe, with garrisons of twelve soldiers; with time, they increased in size and number of troops. On some occasions, the term presidio defined a place to which a garrison was assigned without necessarily having a fort. Such an arrangement provided some security to the area, but the number of soldiers was never sufficient, and the quality of the troops and their officers was not always the best. Some officers and suppliers engaged in illegal business with the money allocated to their garrisons, basically stealing it. Others committed excesses against the Native population, and some were known slave hunters. Even so, with all its flaws, the institution of the presidio became an integral part of the military strategy to secure the Spanish frontier in North America until the nineteenth century. In 1581, the Council of War authorized the payment of 450 pesos per year to each presidio soldier, a salary that some officers and commanders considered insufficient.[82] This salary would remain unchanged for two centuries.

The use of paid troops was costly and there were never enough soldiers to guard the entire territory with the necessary efficiency. Therefore, an alternative and complementary measure was the creation of Spanish towns that served explicitly as a defensive barrier. These defensive towns were located along the different routes to the north. Generally, their first settlers had some war experience and owned their weapons, horses, and military gear. In theory, the purpose of these settlements was to provide protection along the roads. Some of these outposts would also serve as places to gather the pacified Chichimecas and later integrate them into a sedentary life. Some examples of towns with this strategic structure were Celaya, founded in 1570, San Miguel in 1555, León and Aguascalientes in 1575, and Jerez in 1569; but, as with the institution of the presidio, these towns were insufficient to defend the region.[83]

Tlaxcalans played the most crucial role among the groups of Indigenous allies. In 1590, Viceroy Luis de Velasco y Castilla began negotiations with Tlaxcalan leaders to send four hundred families north and found eight towns. The authorities believed, correctly, that it would be much easier to integrate the Chichimecas into settled life in towns inhabited only by Tlaxcalans rather than by Spaniards.[84] In 1591, capitulaciones were signed with Tlaxcalans, guaranteeing them and their descendants the title of hidalgo in perpetuity, exemption from taxes and tributes, the right to an autonomous political organization separate from neighboring Spanish settlements, land, the use of firearms, and the right to ride horses. On the northern frontier, which was then beginning to take shape, there were six original settlements, one of which was in Saltillo, in the province of Coahuila. These population centers were generally prosperous and successful; their descendants encouraged the creation of other Tlaxcalan settlements on the northern frontier. The viceroy repeated the experience with other Indigenous groups, making similar concessions to the Cholultecas, Mexicas, Huejotzingos, and Otomies. Still, none of these groups would be as numerous as the original Tlaxcalan project.[85]

At the end of the sixteenth century, war expenses were so high that the viceroy decided to use diplomacy to resolve conflicts on the frontier. Concerning the Chichimeca issue, the Spanish authorities reduced spending on soldiers and tried to take control of the military force. The authorities also made peace treaties with some groups, offering them provisions such as food and clothing, in contemporary terms a sort of social subsidy.[86] Diplomacy had already been used similarly and extensively in the Iberian Peninsula during the medieval period, especially when Castile had to negotiate with the various Muslim kingdoms to fight against Christian neighbors. At that time, diplomacy represented a complete reversal of the previous practices of "blood and fire." Another fundamental change in the colonial north was the introduction of missionary work throughout the frontier. The number of friars began to increase significantly in the 1580s, as it turned out that missionaries tended to be more effective in establishing a dialogue with Chichimeca groups than did soldiers. By 1590, the Chichimecas were more accustomed to this process of psychological penetration, which involved evangelization on the part of the regular clergy, and a slow process of assimilation began. As a result, the war was over by 1600.[87]

The Chichimeca War, which proved to be a field of experimentation and testing, illustrates the strategies and tactics of colonization and conquest that the authorities and colonizers would use in the northeast. The missionary advance would grow in magnitude and importance during the seventeenth century, as the viceregal administration favored it. On the other hand, the presidios and permanent garrisons were also part of the advance and defense of the frontier in the northeast. The Crown attempted to administer them directly, but this control was far from efficacious given the distances involved. The problems that arose in the administration of presidios and garrisons during the Chichimeca War, such as corruption and the domination of local interests, would plague the management of these defensive sites until independence. Private investment to advance colonization and solve military issues, an essentially medieval practice, would continue, which is why the encomenderos would endure until the eighteenth century. Soldier settlers who obtained land and status through their military participation continued to be of great importance, as did the search for economic rewards in the form of land, booty, or slaves. All these practices would face resistance from the Crown's policies. Undoubtedly, these appropriation strategies practiced on the northern frontier had their roots in medieval Spain, and although modified and adapted to the North American context, they would retain their essence, as it was the only way to acquire new territories at a low cost since the Crown wanted an inexpensive empire. At the same time, they would continue to be an obstacle to the Crown's attempts to consolidate its control over the processes of colonization and conquest.

THE DEVELOPMENT OF THE SPANISH MEDIEVAL MILITARY ETHOS

The cultural heritage of eight centuries of conflict between Moors and Christians left a deep imprint on Spanish society, particularly concerning its military organization and attitudes toward warfare. Castilian-Spanish society developed a system of colonization and conquest for frontier zones on the peninsula that was used and perfected during the centuries of the Reconquest. In essence, to use contemporary terms, this system was based on individuals rather than the state, and the possibility of profit played an important role. At that time, that was the driving force for warfare; no one helped his lord (or lady) to make territorial conquests if they were not associated with profits for the captain, his soldiers, and the accompanying host. Participation in the war was a form of social mobility par excellence, and at the same time it served no less to obtain political rights. It was also used to incorporate and assimilate other populations, sometimes of different ethnicities, into the scheme of alliances in war; likewise, it ensured sources of income via taxes and levies imposed by force and the right of conquest. When the Reconquest ended in 1492, the unification process in Spain began through an increasingly centralized state. This entailed a change in the political administration, which was to grow and become more bureaucratic, and consequently, the organization for warfare also changed. It is almost a rule: If an incipient state grows with the acquisition of new territories, centralizing efforts increase, not only in its civil bureaucracy but also in its military bureaucracy. It is an inevitable process, and it is well known that Philip II, not too distant in time from Isabella of Castile, tried to direct his vast empire with letters from his desk in El Escorial. Despite the intentions of the monarchy, values and attitudes did not change from one day to the next, as they were firmly rooted, especially in places as distant as the northern frontier of America. Medieval attitudes toward war were part of the mentality of the time and played an important role in Spain's transoceanic expansion, and even though its days were numbered in Spain due to the end of the conflict on the Christian-Moorish frontier, that way of life found fertile ground in the Americas. The conquests of the Mexica and Inca empires were achieved by relying upon this learning. Although the administrative incorporation of these new frontier zones soon followed the path of metropolitan Spain, the medieval heritage of military values, attitudes, and organization moved on to play a key role in the peripheral areas of the American continent. The northeastern frontier of New Spain in North America became a space where Spanish military colonization was based entirely on the medieval ethos and would endure for centuries.

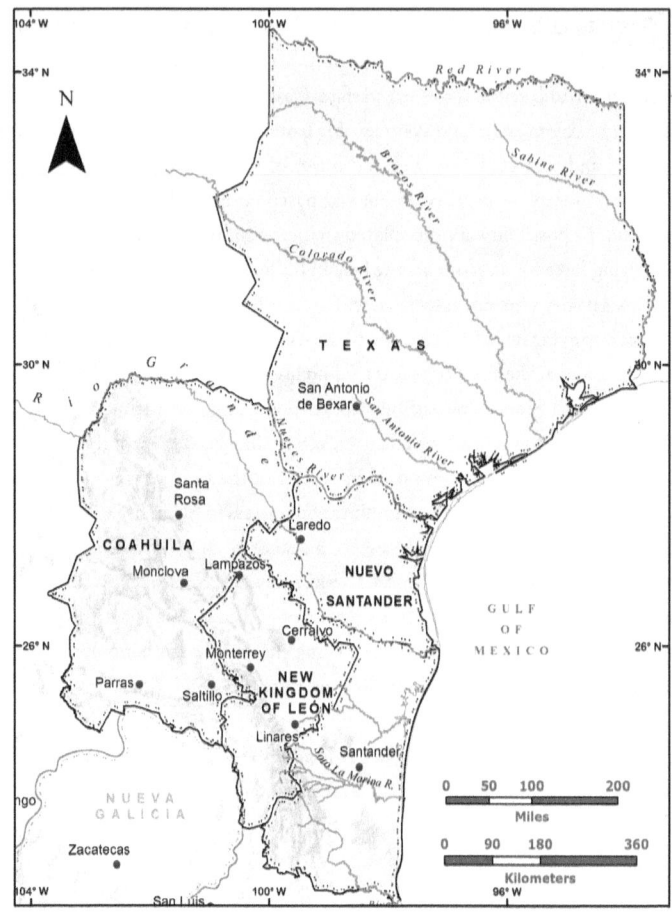

FIGURE 3. Map of the settlements under study and the provinces to which they belonged. Gabriela Arreola Meneses.

CHAPTER 2

The Northeast and Its Medieval Character

AFTER THE FALL OF THE AZTEC CAPITAL, THE SPANIARDS COLONIZED OTHER areas around Mexico City-Tenochtitlan. By the mid-sixteenth century, they started to advance northwards, laying the foundations for an entire expansion over North America. The ways and means they used for this expansion were those that had already been used previously in the Iberian Peninsula since the time of the Reconquista and, later, in the Canary Islands and the Caribbean. This chapter analyzes in detail the expansion strategy and the traditions inherited through it to characterize the colonization type of the northeastern borderlands of New Spain. It begins by explaining the colonization process in the region through the creation of the provinces of the New Kingdom of León, Texas, and Nuevo Santander between the late sixteenth century and the eighteenth century. The section shows the various origins and processes of the settlements under consideration in this work: San Miguel de Aguayo, Lampazos, Laredo, and San Antonio. At this point, it is necessary to emphasize that the region's colonization was to be accomplished within the framework of the private initiative, which, as previously mentioned, was a clear inheritance from the borderland enterprises—military and colonizing—carried out during the Reconquista of the Iberian Peninsula. This approach to the subject will explain the colonization process at various levels, such as that of the political and the military leadership, the governing through governors and mayors, the way these used their military power to gain political credibility, and how the various family clans controlled the political structure of the settlements. Such a pattern was also practiced by individuals who, when colonizing the area, would bring with them not only traditions of action and military financing typical of the Spanish Middle Ages but also traditions that could be called civic, such as the concepts of citizenship and political representation, in which both ethnic origin and group cohesion were important.

CHAPTER 2

THE COLONIZATION OF THE NORTHEAST

The colonization of the northeastern region began in the late sixteenth century. In 1579, right during the Chichimeca War, the settling of the New Kingdom of León took off with the capitulaciones granted by Philip II to Luis Carvajal y de la Cueva* in Toledo, making this advance party into a private enterprise. Originally, the New Kingdom of León started at the Tamesi River, stretching northwest of the Mazapil mines and north of Saltillo and its dependencies. Noticeably, the authorization conceded for colonizing extended over a vast and, in places, undetermined territory, which led to conflicts with other jurisdictions. The colonization project had its ups and downs. The first one was when Carvajal lost support in the Court of New Spain and ended up dying in prison, accused of Judaizing, in 1591. The colonization resurged in 1596, and after multiple problems regarding its limits with the neighboring provinces, its area was reduced to about thirty-seven thousand square miles. The original Native population comprised Indigenous semi-nomads whom the Spaniards generically categorized as Chichimecas. Like in Zacatecas, the Spanish population profited economically through the encomienda or directly by hunting slaves. During most of the seventeenth century, the latter proved to be one of the most profitable activities in the region. At the same time, the proslavery attitude made the territory an area of permanent conflict, since the Indigenous people reacted with attacks and rebellions.[1]

The hamlet of San Miguel de Aguayo played an important role during the early colonization process of the New Kingdom of León. This settlement was founded in 1689 by the Tlaxcalan colonists coming from Saltillo, descendants of those who had participated in the original enterprise of 1591. The strategic location north of the New Kingdom of León made San Miguel a critical defensive position against attacks by Natives, such as the Tobosos. This settlement would also include a community of Chichimecas known as the Alazapas. At first, they settled in a hamlet nearby called San Antonio, and as time went by, the Alazapas ended up integrating in San Miguel. The Tlaxcalans of San Miguel kept the same privileges as their ancestors had earned since the sixteenth century, such as holding the title of hidalgo, the exemption from tributes, and the authorization to

---

* The figure of Luis Carvajal y de la Cueva will be analyzed at a later point.

bear firearms and ride horses.² Such entitlements were an important part of the military strategy adopted during the Chichimeca War and would be used during the whole colonial period until 1821.

The settlement of Lampazos started in 1690 as a mission north of San Miguel de Aguayo, under the care of the Franciscan missionaries who controlled the spiritual instruction of the region's Indigenous peoples, known as Tlaxaguichi. In 1745, the Natives rose up because a lay brother had shot and killed one of theirs. That same year, the viceregal authorities allowed the refoundation of Lampazos, now as a villa inspired by the colonization model established in San Miguel de Aguayo. But Lampazos would not be peopled by Tlaxcalans but by Spanish *vecinos*; the new settlers were to form militias both to protect the territory from Apaches and to "restrain them [the local Natives] from a new uprising."³ The villa was established with thirty Spanish vecinos (not counting their relatives) from nearby settlements and provinces and about 140 Native Americans.⁴ Once more, the strategies the Spaniards had used during the sixteenth century were in vogue during the eighteenth century.

The colonization of the northeast formally began with the establishment of the New Kingdom of León, but it did not end there. Other provinces, such as Texas, followed a similar colonization pattern. This province would occupy the coastal plain north of the Nueces River, spreading about a hundred miles inland from the Gulf of Mexico. It was originally inhabited by groups of hunters-gatherers and others who practiced agriculture, Natives without political unity, such as the Karankawas and the Hasinais. The French were first trying to establish a colony in this area in 1685, but the attacks by the Natives destroyed the settlement two years later. The French presence raised the Spanish authorities' interest in the region, so they made nine exploration expeditions between 1687 and 1690. In 1693, the establishment of a missionary and military post called San Francisco de los Tejas in the eastern part of the northern province failed. During the early eighteenth century, the French established a post in Natchitoches, from where they would trade with the Coahuila province of New Spain. The viceregal administration, vigilant of its territories, replied with the refoundation of missions in eastern Texas and establishing the San Antonio de Béxar Presidio in 1717. Initially, the province was governed from Coahuila, and the new settlers were Native to the neighboring provinces. Starting in 1722, it was ruled by a military governor named by the viceroy; after 1739 the governor would usually be named by the authorities in Spain.⁵

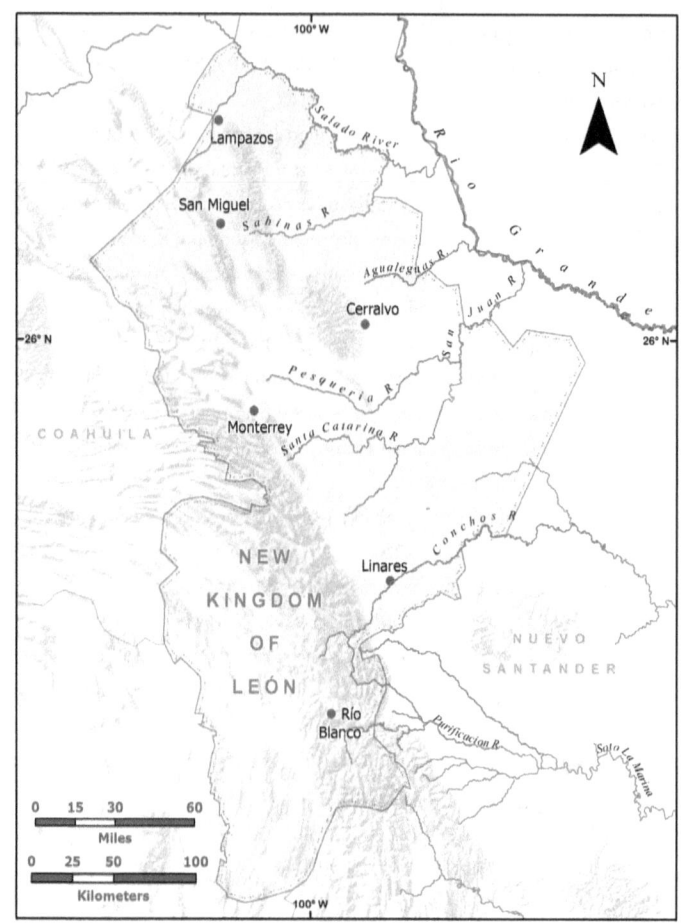

FIGURE 4. The New Kingdom of León. Gabriela Arreola Meneses.

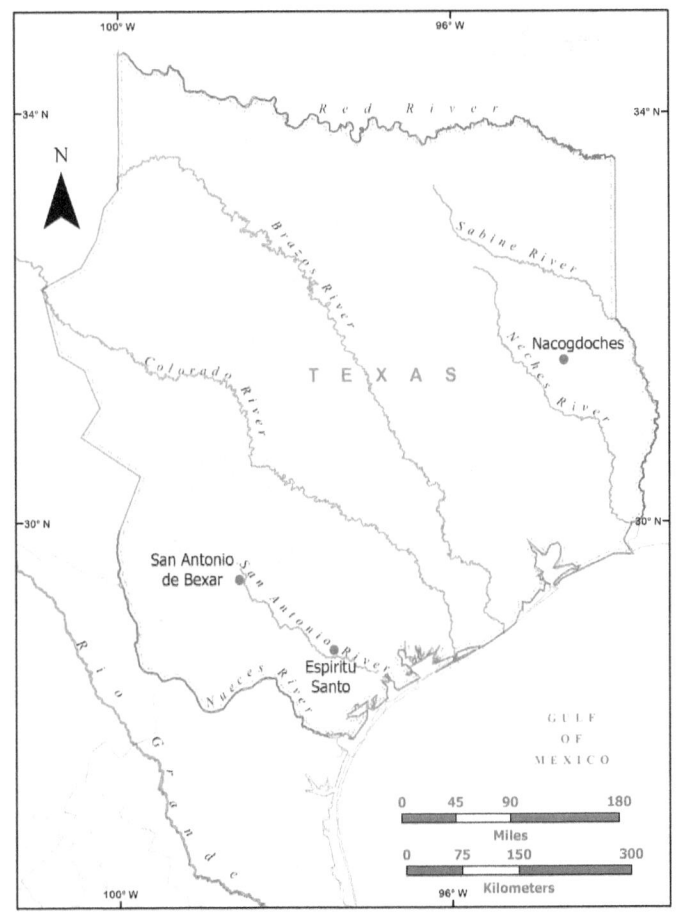

FIGURE 5. Province of Texas. Gabriela Arreola Meneses.

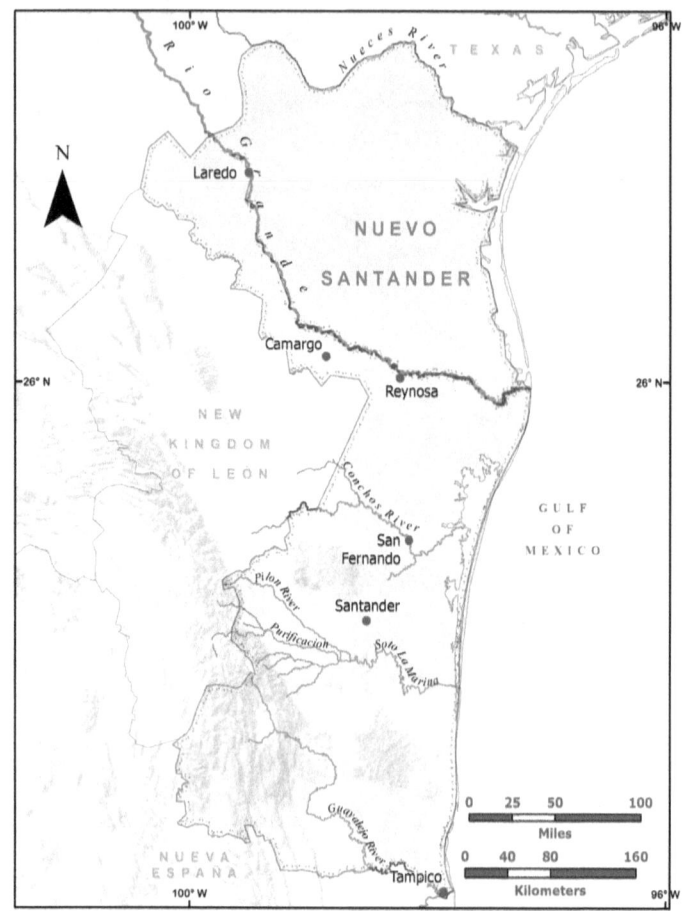

FIGURE 6. Nuevo Santander. Gabriela Arreola Meneses.

THE NORTHEAST AND ITS MEDIEVAL CHARACTER

From its very foundation, San Antonio was a military post, a presidio with a garrison, whose soldiers were, for the most part, Native to the northerly provinces of New Spain. Afterward, some Franciscan missions started appearing around San Antonio. In 1731, new immigrants arrived from the Canary Islands and founded the San Fernando community on the outskirts of the presidio, integrating a single community that revolved around the military administration of the presidio. This community was under the authority of the fort's commander since the territory was considered to be military territory. Thus, made up of a presidio, missions, and immigrants, the community of San Antonio, in and of itself, condensed all the colonization strategies implemented in the area since the Chichimeca War.

After the foundation of the New Kingdom of León and Texas during the sixteenth and seventeenth centuries, the colonization of the northeast was to conclude with the creation of Nuevo Santander. That province's jurisdiction encompassed the territory delimited to the west by the New Kingdom of León and Coahuila, to the north by Texas, to the South by San Luis and Veracruz, and to the east by the Gulf of Mexico, or "Seno Mexicano." As in the other provinces, its original population was made up of groups of hunters-gatherers and farmers. This area remained outside the Spanish sphere of influence until 1748, when José de Escandón was charged with initiating the colonization of that territory, for which he greatly made use of settlers coming from the New Kingdom of León. Nuevo Santander started with a military government under the viceroy, and the governor was usually an army officer.[6] Laredo was founded in 1755 as part of the pacification project of Nuevo Santander and was located about 150 miles to the south of San Antonio in Texas. The objective was to establish an outpost between the Rio Grande and the Nueces River to help improve communications with Texas, as well as to protect the area from Apaches. This settlement was founded by Tomas Sánchez on the Rio Grande's northern riverbank, with about eighty people coming from the New Kingdom of León. Laredo constituted an essential part of the military colonization enterprise for the Nuevo Santander Province under the authority of José Escandón, and it was subordinated to the military authority.[7]

The four settlements—Lampazos, San Miguel, San Antonio, and Laredo—were part of the line of communications toward the north and cooperated in various ways (see fig. 3). In 1777, for example, a caravan of muleteers from San Antonio de Béxar transporting French tobacco (quite probably the product of smuggling) through Louisiana was attacked by Natives while crossing the province of the New Kingdom of León. Don Juan Bautista Prunecha, who identified himself as vecino of San Antonio, sent his servant for help as the caravan tried to resist the attack. The servant asked for help in the nearby town of San Miguel, which answered by sending an armed corps of twenty-eight men.[8] This incident demonstrates how the area was connected not just by commercial exchange but also by a more relevant fact: the assistance of armed parties for defensive purposes. Given that it was military territory, cooperation was taken for granted in case of an attack or of hostilities, and the communities understood it to be so and assumed it within a well-established framework. This legal framework was directly correlated to the one used during the sixteenth century, which in turn was derived from the one current in medieval Spain.

In summary, the colonization of the northeastern borderlands of New Spain began in the late sixteenth century and continued well into the eighteenth century. The strategies for the colonization and appropriation of the territory were essentially the same as those the Spaniards had used in the medieval borderlands during the Reconquista: they consisted of private enterprises of a military nature. This pattern was utilized as an administrative tool in frontier areas, maintaining the marked military character in the northeast, which, unlike the central area of New Spain, subsisted in an intermittent state of war.

THE MACRO LEVEL OF THE EXPANSION: GOVERNORS, EXPLORERS, AND MILITARY LEADERS

In 1579, Luis Carvajal y de la Cueva was first in obtaining the king's *capitulaciones*, so as to conquer, colonize, people, and pacify the New Kingdom of León, which, at least in that document, included parts of Coahuila, Nuevo León, Tamaulipas, and Texas. Carvajal was Portuguese, a Native of Mogadouro, and had made his wealth as a slave hunter in Africa; he arrived in New Spain around 1568. Being sharp, he managed to grow in influence and soon became the mayor of Tampico in the Pánuco Province (present-day southern Tamaulipas). Carvajal brought with him thirty-nine families (about 196 people) from Spain and Portugal for the project of the New Kingdom of León. This supposed colonization was actually an enterprise meant for hunting Indigenous people to sell them as slaves in the mining regions of Zacatecas and San Luis Potosí. Because Carvajal was not part of the original wave of colonists from central New Spain, such activity, right in the midst of the Chichimeca War, preoccupied the Spanish authorities. Both circumstances caused him serious problems with the viceregal administration, to the point where he was accused of Judaizing. For this he was sent to prison, where he later died.[9] The case of Carvajal illustrates how the early colonization of the northeast was based on risky private ventures, just like the conquest of Tenochtitlan in the early sixteenth century and the expansion of the Spanish power in the Caribbean and the Canary Islands during the fifteenth century.

The colonization project of the New Kingdom of León resumed in 1596 with Diego de Montemayor, an experienced colonizer of the north who had participated in the foundation of Saltillo under the command of Alberto del Canto. Montemayor used soldier-colonists with experience in borderland colonization projects. His treatment of the Natives was not much different from Carvajal's; indeed, during his government, Indigenous slavery persisted in the region, which increased the violence. Montemayor died in 1611 without having officially appointed his successor to the governorship. During the next twelve years, some officials were designated or put in charge, but no official governor was named,[10] since no one had the sufficient financial means nor the influence that the position required. Despite this making for a period of uncertainty, more soldier-colonists would arrive, and marriage alliances would build family networks. In this way a political-military structure formed that was to remain in place for various centuries.

Martin de Zavala took on the governorship of the New Kingdom of León from 1626 to 1664, the year he died. He was the son of a rich family from Zacatecas whose wealth came from mining. His father, Agustin de Zavala, had participated in the foundation of San Luis, together with Miguel de Caldera. Agustin lobbied strongly for his son Martin to be granted the governorship of the New Kingdom of León. Not only did Martin de Zavala have an aristocratic education, but also military experience in Flanders. Thanks to these impeccable credentials, he obtained capitulaciones to pacify and settle the kingdom; they conceded him the power to grant encomiendas and to pass the title of governor on to his son or some other successor. Zavala turned out to be an enterprising governor and a good administrator: he introduced cattle farming as commercial activity in the area, which would define the region's rural vocation practically until the present time. During his governorship, he was responsible for forcing the Natives to work as laborers on an institutional scale, with violence if necessary. Zavala maintained the tradition of conquest in borderland areas when in 1656 he requested the title of adelantado. Hence, we can say that he followed the same path as Carvajal, that of combining the leadership of the political administration and the military leadership, a pattern that lasted until the nineteenth century.[11]

Zavala had an important collaborator, Alonso de León, born in the city of Mexico. De León participated in punitive incursions against the Natives, founded some settlements, occupied administrative and military positions, and was also an encomendero. He became Zavala's right-hand man, and in 1655 he went to Spain to present Zavala's report on the New Kingdom of León to Philip IV. His son, Alonso de León "El Mozo" ("the Younger"), would also reach important political and military leadership levels. Born in Cadereyta, in the jurisdiction of the New Kingdom of León, at the age of sixteen he traveled to Spain with his father in 1639. There he joined in a naval expedition against the English. In 1660, he returned to the northeast, leading various incursions inland against Indigenous peoples. In 1682, he complained before the viceroy of the excesses of the then governor, Juan de Echeverría. In 1683, with the support of the royal authorities, he was named governor of the New Kingdom of León, a position he occupied until 1684. Due to rumors of a French settlement in the north, de León led four expeditions between 1686 and 1689 and reached the Rio Grande and Baffin Bay on the Texas coast. In 1689, he found that the Natives had completely destroyed the French settlement. Two years earlier, de León had become the governor of Coahuila, the neighboring province. In 1690, he founded the mission of San Francisco de los Tejas in eastern Texas and finally died a year later.[12]

The last colonization project in the northeast took place in the eighteenth century, under the leadership of José de Escandón. Born in Santander, Spain, in 1700, he moved to Yucatan, in New Spain, at the age of fifteen, an important event since it was Escandón's first experience in a borderland military organization. Yucatan was considered frontier territory because the Spanish authorities had been unable to incorporate and control the Maya population, especially in the area of Peten (now in Guatemala), where there was an independent Indigenous base until 1687, when it was destroyed by a Spanish force from Yucatan. Nevertheless, there never was effective control of the region by the Spaniards, which is why they created presidios with garrisons, which the Natives repeatedly destroyed, massacring their soldiers.[13]

In 1729, the Spanish authorities even came to the extreme of bringing immigrants from the Canary Islands to people some areas of Yucatan.[14] The Yucatecan panorama was similar to that of northern New Spain. Martin de Ursúa y Arizmendi, the governor of Yucatan from 1690 to 1715, who in the end managed to subdue the Peten region, had a mentality and an action pattern similar to that of Escandón in the Sierra Gorda and Nuevo Santander later on. When he arrived in New Spain, Ursúa had begun his military career as sergeant major in the viceroy's militia. Thanks to political connections and great ambition, he managed to become governor of Yucatan in 1690. A descendant of the conquistadors, Ursúa behaved like one and even expected the recently incorporated inhabitants of Peten to pay him tribute in the same way the first conquistadors expected it in their encomiendas.[15] In 1708, he even demanded to be given the title of adelantado, which the Crown ended up granting him.[16]

All this occurred shortly before Escandón arrived in Yucatan, which demonstrates that these military structures and traditions were deeply rooted. The ambitious adolescent would learn from them; they were his military training school. Escandón saw his first war experiences when he joined Merida's encomenderos company, where he reached the grade of lieutenant. Then, in 1727 in Querétaro, he would reach the grade of sergeant major* thanks to the crushing of an Indigenous revolt in Celaya, and he put into practice his knowledge as a military colonizer in the Sierra Gorda. Located between the present-day states of Querétaro, Hidalgo, and Guanajuato, this mountainous region is difficult to pass through and is almost inaccessible.[17] This area had remained something of an independent island, unconquered and, in administrative terms, not incorporated to the viceroyalty of New Spain. It was a de facto interior borderland.

In 1738, Escandón began to incorporate that territory through three military campaigns.[18] This is how the young Escandón grew in relevance and acquired fundamental experience for future campaigns on the northern border. In the Sierra Gorda, Escandón tried to bring the Indigenous and Spanish populations together, but the ecclesiastical authorities who had established missions in the area opposed his plan. In the end, Escandón was able to establish vecino-soldier populations to surveil the region.[19] He believed that the military vecinos (colonists) were the

---

* The grade of sergeant major in the seventeenth-century Spanish military was almost the equivalent of that of a general.

ones best suited to that task because "having to lead their families and possessions and to plant their crops on their own land so stimulates them to the defense of the country, that in no event do they abandon it; this is what the experience in the eight settlements I have founded in the Sierra Gorda has proven to me."[20] According to Escandón, he was the one responsible for financing this enterprise that did not cost the royal treasury anything.[21]

The colonization project of the Seno Mexicano (present territory of Tamaulipas and southern Texas) started in the late 1730s. A number of personalities tried to lead the project, mainly from the New Kingdom of León. One of them was José Fernández de Jáuregui, governor of such province; another one was Antonio Ladrón de Guevara, vecino of the New Kingdom, and finally, Narciso de Montecuesta, mayor of Valles, province of San Luis.[22] To many people's surprise, José de Escandón was chosen to head this project, due to a large extent to his experience in the Sierra Gorda and to his political connections. In his plan, he proposed to establish twelve settlements between 1749 and 1755, starting with the foundation of Laredo. Public order would be headed by Escandón, followed by his subordinate captains.[23]

As seen above, in the late seventeenth century, the settlement pattern preferred by the Crown was the use of garrisons—presidios—and missions. But by the eighteenth century, the Crown was trying to replicate what the English were doing in their settlements in North America. The Crown stressed, however, that the establishment of the new settlements would be a pacification and colonization project, not one of conquest.[24] In reality, this was simply a repetition of the Ordinances of New Discoveries and Populations of Philip II in 1573, inspired by the New Laws of 1542, which had been promulgated to avoid the conquistadors' abuses toward the Native population.[25] The fact that in the mid-eighteenth century the Crown had to refer to laws promulgated during the sixteenth century made it evident that the same problems were still rampant. Escandón could not escape from tradition, however, and in the draft of his original project he referred to the enterprise in Nuevo Santander as a conquest.[26] In reality, the territorial expansion took place under the old schemes of land appropriation. In all practical terms, Escandón was acting as a de facto adelantado since by undertaking an expedition with his own resources,[27] he was repeating the same colonization pattern as the one used by Luis de Carvajal and Martín de Zavala, but on a much larger scale. All this is relevant because even though, at the time, the Nuevo Santander project looked like a new territorial expansion model, it ended up being a repetition of the old strategies that persisted in the borderland areas of the Spanish empire.

POLITICAL AND MILITARY LEADERSHIP AT THE LOCAL LEVEL

In the borderland settlements of the colonial era, the political and military leadership was concentrated in the hands of a single authority figure.[28] This was a reproduction at the local level of the same system used in the borderlands to administer provinces through governors who also held those functions. In the northern settlements, those who headed the local administration also held the post of *alcalde mayor* (head magistrate) or *justicia mayor* (head justice) at the same time as they flaunted the title of *capitan a guerra* (war captain). In San Antonio, for example, the commander of the presidio was also justicia mayor. Just like the governors, these local functionaries were persons with their own important resources and means who could help organize and rule over the general population. In this way, the settlements studied here used this structure to profile the local leaders to such a degree that the authority figures would all come from the same families for generations, thus creating a local elite that rested its power in the concentration of the political-military leadership. In the long run, this elite—known in the historiography of the Mexican nineteenth century as the local or regional dignitaries—would be extremely important for the adoption of federalism from 1824 onward.

Such fusion of the political and military power can be noted in Laredo in 1755, when the settlement was founded by Tomás Sánchez. A Native of the outskirts of Monterrey, in the New Kingdom of León, Sánchez worked as a rancher in Coahuila and was knowledgeable in the characteristics of the northern borderlands. The viceroy authorized him to found the township of San Agustin de Laredo as part of Escandon's project. Sánchez referred to this project as "advancing its townships and dominions [of the Crown]"[29] and committed himself to establishing the township at his own expense. The deed of the foundation of Laredo indicates that Tomás Sánchez was "one of the soldiers who served to the satisfaction of his lordship during the conquest, pacification, and settling" of the region of Nuevo Santander.[30] He was authorized to lead thirteen families to the new settlement. The royal authorization linked to the document where such measures were set forth even calls it the "capitulación" of Sánchez.[31] In exchange for such services, the viceroy conceded him the titles of captain and justicia mayor.[32] In this way, Tomás Sánchez and the other political-military leaders of the borderland settlements basically reproduced the manner in which the former adelantados would operate locally.

Hence, the politico-military system of the borderland settlements allowed for the emergence of an autochthonous elite, which took in hand the local positions of leadership that it would obtain in various ways and inherit for several generations. An example of how this system would work is the lineage of Capt. Diego Ramón (1641–1724). There is not much information about his father, Joseph Ramón, who probably was born in Spain, but it is known that he was a figure of a certain standing, since he had obtained the grade of sergeant major. By 1703, Diego Ramón had completed more than thirty-seven years of military service in the northeast of New Spain and had resided in Boca de Leones, a settlement in the vicinity of San Miguel de Aguayo, and in Lampazos, both in the New Kingdom of León.[33] In 1674, he participated as a soldier in an expedition to the region of Coahuila and Texas and later accompanied Alonso de León in his expeditions to Texas in the late seventeenth century. In 1691, Ramón acted as temporary governor in Coahuila, and in 1699 he participated once more in an expedition to Texas. Thanks to these various raids, in 1703 he was named commander of the presidio of San Juan Bautista in Coahuila. Four years later, he took part in a punitive incursion against the Natives on the Nueces River in Texas.[34]

The son of Diego Ramón, Capt. Domingo Ramón (?–1723) also became an important leader in the politics and military activities in the northeast. During the years 1716–1717, he headed expeditions that founded six missions in Texas.[35] His brother, the alferez Joseph Ramón, served in the garrison of Boca de Leones.[36] Domingo Ramón died from wounds he had received in an encounter with the Karankawas in Texas when he was commander in the presidio of La Bahia. His son, Diego Ramón, succeeded him at the command but was later removed from the position. Afterward, he became lieutenant at the presidio of San Antonio de Béxar and briefly commanded the presidio of San Xavier de Horcasitas in Texas. Finally, he concluded his military career as alferez at the Texan presidio of San Sabá in 1757.[37]

Diego's brother and Domingo's son, Antonio Ramón, reached the grade of alferez at the presidio of San Antonio de Béxar. Later, his son, Juan Ignacio Ramón, also undertook a military career as a soldier at the presidio of La Bahia in Coahuila, starting in 1774. By 1783, he had reached the grade of alferez, and five years later he would be lieutenant of the company of Lampazos, a township in which he became one of the most prominent inhabitants. Between 1777 and 1781, he accompanied royal visitor Teodoro de Croix on his journeys to northern New Spain. In 1791, he acted as lieutenant governor of Lampazos, thereby taking charge of the political administration. Between 1805 and 1807, he served in the company of Lampazos in San Antonio and Nacogdoches; three years later, he joined in the armed uprising of Miguel Hidalgo and ended up being executed in 1811.[38] This relation of the Ramón clan shows how for two centuries one family was involved in the local political and military administration in the region. It also highlights how military participation grew in relevance over several generations. Even if the Ramón family had never become powerful landowners—as occurred in other parts of central and western New Spain—they undoubtedly were symbolic of a lifestyle characteristic of the elite in the northeast. Even though they were neither rich nor powerful in land and cattle—actually almost no one was at the time—they nevertheless determined the political rhythm where they resided and held, to express it in Weberian terms, the monopoly of legitimate violence, which would turn out to be indispensable in order to define the post-independence state.

Another example of how the elite flourished and acted is the Urrutia family in San Antonio during the seventeenth and eighteenth centuries. This clan was born with José de Urrutia (1648–1741), a Basque who migrated to the American continent before 1691 and served in the garrison of the Neches River in Texas. There he stayed amidst the Natives and headed various campaigns against Apaches during his life. In 1697, he married his first wife, Antonia Ramón, daughter of Diego Ramón and sister of Domingo Ramón. This event illustrates how a family could strengthen its social status through a marriage alliance, in this case with the prominent Ramón clan. A local elite would thus grow, basing its power on politico-military control. In 1733, Urrutia was designated captain of the San Antonio presidio, a commanding post that would remain under the control of the Urrutia family for various generations. His son, Toribio de Urrutia (1710–1763), succeeded his father in the same post as presidio captain in 1740. In 1743, Toribio received the title of justicia mayor of San Antonio, and, like his father, he led multiple expeditions against Apaches. A man of certain means, he indicated in his service record that he had defended the territory "at his own expense."[39]

Toribio did not have descendants and was substituted by his nephew, Luis Antonio Menchaca (1713–1793). Luis Antonio was the son of Antonia Urrutia Ramón and of a soldier of the first garrison to be established in San Antonio in

1718; therefore, he was related to both influential families. As the grandson of José de Urrutia and the nephew of Domingo Ramón, Luis Antonio Menchaca maintained the military tradition. Given such a lineage, it should not be a surprise that in 1763 he became the captain and justicia mayor of the San Antonio presidio. At that time, the merits were not only personal but familial and were formally and officially valid. In his petition to the viceregal authorities to be granted the grade of captain, he not only mentioned his own service but also that of his ancestors in the defense of the northern provinces.[40] By 1779, he was one of the richest inhabitants of the region. His son, José Menchaca (1746–1820), also pursued a military career. He was alferez of the San Antonio presidio in 1771 and temporary commander of the same for nine months in 1780. Afterwards, he would be transferred as commander to the presidio of Agua Verde in Coahuila until his retirement in 1801, the year in which he returned to San Antonio. During the War of Independence (1801–1821), he involved himself with both sides, insurgents and royalists, changing sides depending on what best suited him. He was jailed by the royalists and died in prison in 1820.

The analysis of the influential families clarifies how their heads became the local politico-military leaders in the northern borderlands. None of this was original or foreign to what had happened in other latitudes of the Spanish empire overseas; at least, on the American continent, since the sixteenth century, there subsisted a tradition rich in medieval values initially developed in the borderlands of Spain during the Reconquista. The prominent families of the local communities of northeastern New Spain used the very same political-formal structures in the same way as the adelantados and caudillos of medieval Spain: the political power came from their capacity to provide the means to defend the territory under their authority. In some cases, these family networks lasted until some historical event would undo the status quo and a new elite would emerge. In other cases, the ties would last well into the nineteenth century, such as those of Tomás Sánchez and his descendant Santos Benavides, who became a prominent politician and military leader in Laredo after 1850.[41] This tradition of political representation through military participation was successfully used by the local individuals of the northeastern borderlands' communities to further their own interests.

THE NORTHEAST AND ITS MEDIEVAL CHARACTER

VECINDAD, POLITICAL REPRESENTATION, AND WAR

In the northern borderlands, political rights, social status, and defense cooperation were tightly interconnected. The concept of vecindad was directly related to some type of military service. Officially, since 1596, the first settlers of the New Kingdom of León received encomiendas.[42] Given that the consolidation of the colonization depended on the encomienda for protection in the face of the constant attacks by the Natives, by the mid-seventeenth century, the majority of the inhabitants were vecinos and encomenderos; hence, the two standings became interchangeable.[43] The legal documents of the time used these terms—vecino and encomendero—in this way until the eighteenth century.[44] Those who held such standing were required to own two sets of arms, horses, chainmail (or leather armor), a shield, and an arquebus. They also had to perform alardes—military parades—three times a year.[45] There is evidence that this tradition took place frequently.[46] Such parades were the way in which the vecinos demonstrated their resources and abilities to contribute to the common defense. What is more, that they had to own two sets of arms and other equipment meant that they had to be able to arm more people, at least one more person, for the defense.[47] This is how the status of vecindad was so important to sustain the politico-military structure of the borderlands.

The concept of vecindad originated in the eleventh and twelfth centuries, in medieval Castile, and defined a form of citizenship; it was indicative of the rights of the inhabitants of a recognized community. In the beginning, it referred to the privileges and duties of such individuals as were willing to settle down in lands that had been snatched from the Muslims through war. Among the privileges they enjoyed were the use of communal property, voting, and being elected to posts of local leadership. Their duties consisted of residing in the community, paying taxes and public expenses, and serving in the local militia. Vecindad was used not only to show the ties between the members of a community but also to establish and ground a social status among them. As was to be expected, over time the concept of vecindad changed, losing its relation to immigration, and it was used to define residents during the seventeenth and eighteenth centuries. Both the benefits and obligations of the vecinos largely varied depending on the location.[48]

CHAPTER 2

In Castile, at the beginning of the modern era, there were certain rules to follow to obtain the status of vecino. First of all, it had to be understood as a natural right that could be freely exercised. It was only available to the head of the family. In principle, only adult men could hold this status, but women could also assume vecindad if they took up the role of head of the family. Minors below the age of twenty-five could be granted vecindad in special cases, but in general neither women nor minors were eligible. Foreigners, too, could be vecinos as long as they were Catholic. Vecindad was based on individual intentions more than on a formal declaration, and the inhabitants of the communities could lose it if they failed in the performance of their responsibilities. In short, vecindad was socially acquired and negotiated. The second rule was that the heads of families had to be integrated into the community, which was determined by a number of factors, such as residency, marriage, and property ownership. By the eighteenth century, in Castile, the status of vecindad was well defined by all these characteristics.[49] On the other hand, even though vecindad still was a socially constructed and defined status, it had lost its medieval component of military service. The need to defend one's communities in an area over which they contended against the Moors lay well behind, which rendered the military requirements anachronistic.

On the American continent, the characteristics of vecindad evolved in a similar fashion. At the beginning, at the time of the conquistadors, the concept of vecindad was a mere replica of the medieval Castilian model. For example, local citizenship could be obtained simply by the fact of being one of the founding members of a community. Until the seventeenth century, there were still formal requests for vecindad, but the practice disappeared over time. The classification based on social reputation remained alive; the implicit vecindad prevailed, unlike in Europe, and new, previously nonexistent forms of exclusion emerged. People of mestizo, Indigenous, or African descent remained excluded from vecindad. This was totally contrary to the Castilian precedents, where the personal origins and genealogy were irrelevant. Indeed, what was wanted were settlers willing to militarily defend an area; their ethnic origin was not at play. On the other hand, in practice, such restrictions were loose, and there were cases where the inhabitants of a community, even if they were not recognized as vecinos, had the same rights and obligations. In the borderlands of the Spanish empire on the American continent, military service remained an essential requirement in order to be considered a vecino. An example of this peculiarity was Buenos Aires, where the threat of Portuguese and Indigenous people made military service a necessity.[50]

The New Kingdom of León was a borderland zone and maintained military participation through the encomienda as a requisite to retain the status of vecino. This condition was inclusive and not static. The inhabitants who were able to fulfill the military participation requirements obtained vecindad in the same manner they had in medieval Castile. Such flexibility is noticeable, for example, in that there were women who were included in the category of vecinos-encomenderos, as in the case of Mónica Rodríguez, whose name appears on the lists of the military parades.[51] She was a well-to-do woman, the granddaughter of Diego de Montemayor, the founder of Monterrey. She had married and procreated a son with Alberto del Canto, founder of Saltillo, one of the earliest colonizers of the New Kingdom.[52] It is unlikely that she would have participated in any military action; rather, it is possible that some relative or servant had taken the place that corresponded to hers on the battlefield. There is no record of how she obtained that status; it was likely by heritage or widowhood. Her legal status demonstrates to what extent it was important to appear in the military reviews and show off the resources one had for self-defense. Furthermore, it brings to light just how much the politico-military status was interconnected with kinship. As a descendant of the first conquistadors in the region and thanks to her marriage with another, Mónica Rodríguez was able to acquire and retain vecindad, provided she was in a position to support military actions.

Over the years, the Spanish Crown forbade the figure of the encomendero, since it did not want medieval lordlings in its empire who could contend with it for political power and because it served as a form of Indigenous enslavement system in disguise. But the relationship between vecindad and military participation remained, revealing a continuity that responded to manifest political needs: on the one hand, the austerity in spending on the part of the colonial administration, and on the other, the clear necessity for defense and conservation of the borderlands. During the military reviews as late as 1768, the vecinos kept on registering their arms and horses, as well as how many children and servants they could contribute to the military service.[53] It was the same manner of demonstrating one's capability of fulfilling one's military obligations as at least a century before. Women kept appearing on the lists, too, such as Doña Margarita de Benavides, a widow who brought arms, three sons, and three horses. Another case was that of Doña Margarita de los Santos Olivares, a widow with two sons and four horses. Another woman, Manuela Vela, a widow, brought one son and seven mounts.[54] Undoubtedly, the three women had inherited vecindad when they became widowed. Also, the social differences are noticeable given that two of them wore the title of Doña, a sign of eminent position. This is further confirmed by the fact that the former brought horses while the latter brought only mounts, which could be mules or donkeys, animals of lower value but still not to be turned down for military actions. In any case, these examples illustrate how, despite some differences in circumstances and assets, the armed service was useful to obtain vecindad, a title in no way despicable in the social and political order of the borderlands' societies at the time. In fact, they were categorized as vecinos of the borderlands, which exempted them from taxes, provided that they were ready for any war emergency, mainly attacks and uprisings by Natives.[55]

The right to political participation through the organization of the defense was a social tool that was politically useful for the colonists-vecinos, since by acquiring a certain level of authority, they could make good their interests. This was the case of the vecinos of Lampazos in 1765, when they removed from his position the mayor and war captain, Domingo de Abasolo. Among the many reasons for such an action were frequent episodes of public drunkenness, ignoring how many inhabitants lived in that place, abuse of his authority, inability to make the Chichimecas attend the religious services, and, most importantly, that on one occasion those Natives gave him a beating. This made him appear unable to act like a leader, and so the local Spanish settlers requested his dismissal.[56] To reinforce the legitimacy of their complaint, the vecinos appealed to their standing as "conquistadors and descendants of those who had won [the territory] at the cost of the blood they had shed and the goods they had lost" in the colonization process.[57] In this way, the vecinos were appealing to their military participation, to the services of their ancestors, the first settlers, and to their condition as continuators of a tradition of conquest in the borderlands. All this falls into the standing of vecindad obtained through social reputation and military capability. The governor decided in favor of the vecinos and referred to himself as "governor of the New Kingdom of León, of its Conquests and Frontiers." Thus he too was appealing to the military territory and borderlands character of his jurisdiction in order to legitimate his politico-military authority before the inhabitants of Lampazos. In the end, the local vecinos chose the former mayor, Pedro Joseph Flores de Abrego, as substitute for Domingo de Abasolo, given that Abrego was "one of the conquistadors of these places and in him concur the necessary circumstances for the political and military governance," in addition to his being capable of maintaining "the peace in this *vecindario*."[58]

The military parades, or alardes, were a way of assessing the political support in the region. In 1751, these lists registered thirty Spanish vecinos and forty-seven Chichimecas in Lampazos.[59] Two years later, after the mayor was removed from office, the numbers had fallen to twenty-two Spanish vecinos and fourteen Chichimecas.[60] The year in which Pedro Flores took charge, the numbers rose to almost double: thirty-seven Spanish vecinos and thirty-eight Chichimecas.[61] This evidences how the population had the opportunity to support or reject the public servants through military participation, which was quite relevant in a conflictive borderland. Any person wanting to be in command had to be able to demonstrate and maintain his military leadership. In turn, the locals would give their support through their war resources. It was a type of borderland social agreement similar to what had existed centuries earlier in the Iberian Peninsula.

This traditional way of exercising one's citizenship through military service, which was common in the borderlands, was not strictly limited to a certain gender or race. Traditionally, this scheme was applied in Castile during the Middle Ages when Mozarab and Mudejar populations were integrated into the Castilian system of vecindad and military participation. The same system integrated the Natives of northeastern New Spain: the Tlaxcalan settlement of San Miguel de Aguayo used that strategy to integrate the community of Chichimeca-Alazapas residents into the neighboring settlement of Santa María. In the beginning, this integration was partial, and on various occasions Alazapas fled to the mountains, while at other times they would secretly meet with hostile tribes such as Tobosos. The Tlaxcalans were suspicious of the Alazapas, but nevertheless, on various occasions, they joined forces against other tribes. In the 1730s, Alazapas participated in such encounters on foot, armed with bows and arrows. Fifty years later, some members of this group would ride on horses and bear firearms.[62]

Undoubtedly, this Tlaxcalan integration practice influenced other northern settlements, like Lampazos, with some variations.[63] In that town, instead of integrating various Native American groups, they would form units of Spaniards and Indigenous people. This community had started as a mission but never managed to incorporate the Native population into Spanish social practices. In 1745, a revolt took place that led the Indigenous inhabitants to abandon the mission and take refuge in a nearby mountain, just like the Alazapas had done in San Miguel. Some of them were armed with muskets even when the Spanish laws forbade it, which shows the inability of the locals to enforce such important dispositions.[64]

CHAPTER 2

Years later, Lampazos had become a settlement of about thirty Spanish vecinos and about one hundred Natives.[65]

Around the mid-eighteenth century, there were many military parades in the Lampazos community, where they made a point of showing the division in forces between the Spanish vecinos and the Indigenous settlers. Usually, the Spaniards used the traditional equipment, which included a leather armor, a leather shield, a sword, a spear, muskets, powder, ammunition, and the horses they could contribute. Obviously, not all had the same equipment, which revealed the social and economic differences among them. As for the Natives, most were armed only with bows and arrows; a few of them had firearms, swords, and horses. Also, there were those who used the titles of don, captain, and governor.[66] On one occasion, during one such alarde, they formed a line before Domingo de Abasolo, the mayor who had tried to force them to attend the religious services, and they ended up giving him the thrashing that led to his removal from his post.[67] In short, these displays of military force were a ritualized form of obtaining politico-social recognition and showing to their enemies that the community had the means to respond. Thus, the "Indians" became part of the community through their incorporation into the military system.

By 1790, the attacks and thefts by the Lipan Apaches* had become a constant threat to the population of Lampazos, and the military services thus turned out to be more necessary than ever. Hence the mayor issued an edict that ordered "all the vecinos in my charge" to have their weapons in good state and a horse ready "as has always been the custom in this vecindad," and those who, for lack of means, "could not have a musket, should have a spike or a spear" or "a bow and twenty-five arrows or a slingshot." This edict applied to "all persons ten years or older." For such persons who refuse to comply with these orders, the edict added, there would be a fine of fifteen reales that would be used for public works, and those "with spikes and arrows" should make bricks of adobe.[68] The edict did not distinguish between Spaniards and "Indians"; it referred to all the inhabitants as vecinos. We can infer that the people with firearms were people of certain means, mainly Spaniards; those who had bows and arrows were Natives; and those with slingshots most likely were from the lowest social class, possibly mestizo ranch laborers. Even the fines varied according to the economic capacity of the people,

---

* We will discuss this Indigenous group in the next chapter.

one in cash and the other in labor. Noticeably, in twenty-two years of interaction, the two groups modified their racial barriers through military service. Society had been stratified based on wealth and not race, which can be seen in how people could offer resources for the defense of the settlement. The Apache incursions helped reinforce this borderland community's process of greater social integration.

The ways of understanding the concept of vecindad varied a lot, depending on how they were applied in their place of origin, Spain, and in the northern borderlands. An occasion where this contrast becomes quite clear is what occurred with the arrival of new immigrants to San Antonio during the eighteenth century. At that time, the Spanish Crown was trying to strengthen its military presence in the periphery of the empire, like Texas, so it subsidized immigration to that area for people from the Canary Islands. The new colonists consisted of a group of fifteen families who had the full support of the authorities in Madrid; the latter were interested in dealing with subjects accustomed to handling themselves in accordance with the notions of vecindad effective in metropolitan Spain. In this way, there would not be any risk of dealing with almost independent communities that had organized themselves for war and that represented a potential risk of rebellions, like those that took place in sixteenth-century Spain.** From the get-go, the new settlers had problems with the vecinos already established in San Antonio, mainly because of issues of land distribution and access to water. In accordance with the Laws of the Indies, the king had granted the Canarian migrants and their descendants the title of hidalgo, which was in itself a noble title. Even if this was a minor title, the matter did not sit well with the original inhabitants of San Antonio, who had earned their social status and military stripes fighting in the borderland wars against Indigenous enemies, all that "at their own expense." In addition, the Canarians were granted the faculty to organize their own council (cabildo) and elect their own authorities.[69]

In reality, these concessions constituted a formal declaration of vecindad through an official document, a common practice then in Spain but not in its American colonies, especially not in the borderlands. Naturally, the new vecinos tried to take advantage of this legal chink to obtain the most fertile lands. Even more, the Canarians understood the military service and inherent obligations in

---

** We will discuss the subject of the absolutist Spain of the eighteenth century in the next chapter.

a very different manner from that customary to the descendants of the region's conquistadors and founders. Their political authorities would sometimes refuse to participate in war actions, arguing that they did not want to leave their own homes unprotected.[70] This type of attitude was contrary to the traditions well-established since the sixteenth century in a region where war actions were frequent and cooperation necessary, not to say indispensable, to survival. Inevitably, this situation led to a confrontation between the two groups of settlers.

Documents in hand, the newly arrived Canarians used the method of formal requests to the authorities and put the original inhabitants of San Antonio at a disadvantage, since the latter believed that their rights over property were protected by custom and the fact of fulfilling their military obligations without having to make a formal request for the deeds. This is how the islanders legally stripped the older vecinos of San Antonio of the land ownership and water rights they had acquired by custom and tradition. In a report, a friar of the nearby missions pointed out how unjust the situation was, saying that the newcomers had certain rights but did not belong to the initial group of founders of the place, where the original *vecinos criollos* had shed their blood to pacify and defend the area until then.[71]

Documents of that time show how the original vecinos argued the case.[72] They appealed to the social reputation they had acquired through the military service. In their defense, they referred to themselves as "residents in this presidio [San Antonio] who at our own expense have assisted in all the war functions that have arisen." They insisted they had done so "with our persons, arms and mounts and horses, in all the invasions that arose against Apaches among others who harass this presidio with extreme intensity."[73] They also requested the faculty to elect a mayor at their convenience to avoid any problems. In this contention, we notice how the tradition of acquiring the status of vecindad through social reputation was still current. Quite smartly, however, they avoided resorting to the argument that on their own merits, the political concessions granted to islanders be revoked, but rather demanded equal circumstances and that they be granted "the present privileges and exceptions that islander families enjoy by virtue of being settlers."[74] This meant that they were requesting the endorsement of their vecindad through a formal request, so as to argue legally in equality of conditions against the islanders. On the other hand, in spite of their unwillingness to participate in war matters, the new vecinos would eventually fulfill their duties in this respect. In the end, the tradition of vecindad and military participation remained as a well-established rule in San Antonio, mainly because the amount of hostility and danger around the location made it necessary. Even the captain of the presidio kept charge of the political administration.

WAR AS A LUCRATIVE ACTIVITY

Hunting slaves was an activity the Spaniards brought to the American continent, first in the Antilles, then in the Caribbean and South America. That activity was well-documented in the Spanish expansion to the north of New Spain. The growth of the mining industry in places like Zacatecas and San Luis during the sixteenth century required a considerable amount of labor, which made capturing Natives to be sold to the miners a highly profitable activity. This led the Natives to retaliate with violent raids on the Spanish settlements. During the Chichimeca War (1550–1600), the manhunts for slaves became a serious problem given that they angered the Native population and made the conflict grow bigger. To stop the violence, the viceregal authorities forbade the capture and sale of Natives. Nevertheless, the issue persisted simply because it was difficult to enforce these policies in remote areas like the northeast, where from the very start of the colonization, the custom of enslaving Natives was one of the main economic activities.[75]

The hunts for slaves, or *saca* [removal/extraction] *de indios*, were introduced in the northeast by Luis Carvajal during the foundation of the New Kingdom of León. Earlier, he had been involved in slave trafficking with the Portuguese from Cabo Verde in Africa. In the New Kingdom, he maintained that practice, selling captured Indigenous people to large mining centers.[76] Another colonizer of the northeast in the sixteenth century who was also involved in this activity was Alberto del Canto. He had participated in the colonization of the northern province of Nueva Vizcaya and was accused on multiple occasions of being a slave hunter. Around 1570, del Canto founded the town of Saltillo in Coahuila, from where he kept enslaving Natives. This business became so important that it was one of the reasons the Spanish emigrated to the northeast. This activity caused these regions to be more attractive when compared with the regions where there was only mining,[77] and even though the viceroys constantly tried to eradicate this practice they were unable to do so until well into the eighteenth century.

During the seventeenth century, the saca de indios grew in spite of the official prohibition. What is more, local authorities would turn a blind eye or would collaborate; indeed, occasionally, there were public slave auctions with permission from the current governors.[78] Other bondage systems were adopted to disguise that activity under legal mechanisms. The encomienda, for example, was adopted to accommodate slavery. Originally, in the Middle Ages, the encomienda system consisted of land and inhabitants of a conquered area that the Crown granted a soldier for his military service. On the American continent, the encomienda facilitated the exploitation of Indigenous labor, but it did not include the concession of lands. The main obligation of the encomendero was to provide and supervise the Christian instruction of the Natives in his custody.

In the northeastern borderlands, the encomienda had its own peculiarities. When a Spanish vecino located an Indigenous communal settlement (rancheria), he would request that he be granted an encomienda as a reward for his services to the king. At that moment, he would lead troops to the communal settlement and attack it by surprise. The Natives captured during such an attack would be shackled and led to some place where they would have to work under the surveillance of armed men. Once the labor period was over, the Indigenous men would be freed, so that the encomendero would not have to feed them, but the women and children would be kept as hostages to ensure that the men would come back. Each time there was the need for labor, the encomendero would repeat the process. Over time, and as a consequence of such practices, it was more and more difficult to find Indigenous settlements, and the expeditions would stretch ever further in the hope of finding slaves, even so far as to the north of the Rio Grande.[79] This behavior and the Indigenous retaliations it spurred in the form of uprisings, attacks, and cattle theft from the Spanish settlements are characteristic of the period.[80]

In 1672, the royal authority abolished the encomiendas once and for all; the *congregas* would take their place. This new institution consisted of a Spanish vecino being in charge of a congregated Indigenous population and controlling their work, but not being their owner.[81] Actually, it was a variant of slavery, and in all practical terms it was not different at all from the way of practicing the encomienda in the northeast. The Natives who ran away from the congregas could be declared rebels and sold as slaves. In this way, the new system was fomenting Indigenous enslavement under a new name.[82] The encomienda would persist in spite of its legal abolition. Local documents show that it was practiced almost until the eighteenth century. In 1715, there were 4,500 "Indians" in congregas in two Spanish settlements only, which shows that the overall number must have been much higher since there were more Spanish settlements with their respective congregas in the region.[83] Enslaving Indigenous people also became an act of manliness, according to testimony from that era: "he was not considered a man the one who did not go to the communal settlements of friends or enemies and take away the children from their mothers to sell them."[84] Another chronicle of the time describes the activity in the following manner: "There is absolutely no difference between catching those people and riding wild beasts; even in this they are alike."[85] There were also Natives who profited from slave trafficking, particularly those who had lived among the Spaniards and learned that habit. There even were armed conflicts between these Native groups and the Spaniards over the control of this activity.[86]

In the early eighteenth century, the dynamics of slavery had led to spiraling violence. Just in the New Kingdom of León, more than a thousand people died because of the Indigenous attacks between 1709 and 1715.[87] The situation came to the point where in 1713, the viceroy Fernando Alencastre Noroña had to intervene, calling the War Council to study the problem and find a solution. The viceroy reiterated in a decree that enslaving "Indians" was forbidden because it incited them to retaliate. Obviously, the Spanish population of the northeast completely ignored this resolution, just as it had always done with the previous ones. The viceroy then named an inspector (*visitador*), the lawyer Francisco Barbadillo y Victoria, who had plenipotentiary powers to take the measures he deemed necessary to end the Native slavery in the northeast.[88]

Barbadillo arrived in the region in January 1715 and immediately got down to work, implementing drastic measures to end the slavery, among which was the creation of a mobile company of seventy soldiers to patrol the area. His purpose was not simply to defend the region from Indigenous attacks but also to impede the manhunts for slaves on the part of the Spanish population. Barbadillo abolished the congregas and expropriated lands to give them over to the freed Natives, with the obvious intention of establishing Indigenous villages. In 1716, Barbadillo went back to the city of Mexico, the situation being apparently under control. But there was plenty of opposition by the Spanish vecinos, who harassed the missions and Indigenous villages looking for slaves, which once again led to war. In 1718, the governor of the New Kingdom of León, Juan Ignacio Flores, requested once more permission to distribute captives among the vecinos.[89]

The Spanish population's reluctance to change forced Viceroy Valero to send Barbadillo back in 1719, but this time as governor. During the four years of his administration (1719–1723), Barbadillo re-established the mobile company and the organization of Indigenous villages as well as establishing missions.[90] Barbadillo's measures were exactly those that the viceregal authorities had tried to implement more than a century earlier, during the Chichimeca War. All this back and forth between the viceroy and the local Spanish population over the enslavement of Natives barely illustrates, by the way, how difficult it was for the Crown to change the habits and traditions of some Spanish groups, especially in the borderlands. The medieval custom prevailed against the centralizing and rationalizing efforts of the Crown's representatives in the New World, and slavery would not disappear through decrees, but only when it became evident that it was no longer economically viable.

Using war as a means of obtaining slaves would continue in the northeast during the whole eighteenth century. There are reports that shortly after Barbadillo left in 1724, the governor of the New Kingdom attacked Indigenous villages, enslaving and killing many.[91] In 1726, the new governor, Pedro Sarabia Cortés, formally argued in favor of re-establishing the congregas. Later on, in the multiple colonization enterprises of New Santander, there were characters like the prominent vecino Antonio Ladrón de Guevara, who wished to keep enslaving Natives. In 1738, Ladrón de Guevara proposed colonizing Nuevo Santander with vecinos from the New Kingdom of León, who should receive "privileges of conquistadors and settlers [and] that the lands with the 'Indians'—just like the old congregas—should be given to the Spaniards."[92]

Even though it is true that the viceregal authorities did not support projects that enslaved Natives, which is why they rejected Ladrón de Guevara's proposal to colonize Nuevo Santander, this was not always the case, since the very same viceregal authorities contradicted one another. The character who finally had the privilege of colonizing that territory, José de Escandón, was not much different from Ladrón de Guevara. During the period in which he "pacified" the Sierra Gorda, he had established congregas and practiced slavery, and he even would be designated to re-establish the congregas in the northeast. When he was governor, he deported Natives captured in the Sierra Gorda to work on his ranches in Nuevo Santander.[93] Quite possibly, he had done the same with the Native tribes in the northeastern region; Ladrón de Guevara was his partner during the colonization of Nuevo Santander, so Escandón had allied himself with the elite that supported and fomented capturing Natives. In 1772, well into the eighteenth century, there was still a good number of cases of Indigenous slavery in Nuevo Santander.[94]

The irruption of Apaches in Texas during the first part of the eighteenth century changed the existing balance of power. In 1729, an attack by Lipan Apaches almost annihilated a whole troop of twenty-five soldiers from the San Antonio presidio. The Spanish forces tried to retaliate, but the presidio commander had to admit that even if they united forces with several presidios, it would be insufficient to ensure success. In order to have a minimum of efficacy, they required the support of the militias of vecinos from the neighboring provinces of Coahuila and New

Kingdom of León. But such participation had its cost. Since the militias of vecinos would be integrated at the expense of their members, the local military authorities had to explain to the viceregal government that the only reason the vecinos had participated in similar campaigns in the past was that they were given the opportunity to keep the Natives they captured. Forbidding enslaving those taken as spoils of war would mean that few vecinos would be willing to participate in fighting enemies.[95]

In the end, in 1732 they were able to launch a raid, which turned into a battle on December 9. The force comprised 102 men, 80 of them vecinos, as well as allied Natives. The governor of Texas, Juan Antonio Bustilla y Zevallos, had to finance the mounts and armament.[96] The vecinos accepted participating only because they were allowed to keep the booty of the expedition: they took 29 prisoners and more than 700 horses and mules.[97] So many animals, shared among the 80 vecinos, represented significant gain. The 29 Natives captured were women and children, the most prized prisoners for enslavement. The only information available about their (mis)fortune is that they were kept as prisoners, although it is quite probable that they ended up as slaves. This punitive expedition only confirmed the importance of war as a way of obtaining economic benefits; even if slavery was officially forbidden, the militias of vecinos accepted participating only in exchange for some material gain, in this case horses and mules.

The Crown always tried to avoid slavery, but the problem was that members of the military were involved in that activity. The royal ordinances were very clear: "no officer who would take as spoils of war some pieces (*piezas*) of 'Indians' of both sexes and ages in any war expedition in which they would manage to undo some communal settlements, may take them for himself nor distribute them under any reason or pretext whatsoever."[98] In 1750 still, there was evidence that the military officers in Texas took captive Natives as slaves. The friar Benito Fernández de Santa Anna, at the head of one of the missions of Béjar, accused the governor of having taken "two pieces of the prisoners" as a product of a war incursion.[99] The friar mentioned that the passion of the Spanish vecinos for taking captives was well-known by the Natives and had created an "implacable hate" in the "Indians."[100] Fernández also explained that many campaigns against Apaches had had as their sole purpose the capturing of slaves, which made it impossible to reach peace agreements with this ethnic group.[101]

Among the many traditions with medieval roots to obtain material benefits from war, like the encomienda/congrega, the requerimiento stands out. The latter functioned as a ritualized legal method that the Spaniards employed to declare war and enslave Natives. The ritual consisted of reading, before the Natives, a declaration that demanded them to submit to the royal authority and to adopt the Catholic faith. The refusal to comply with such requerimiento led to an immediate and automatic authorization for the Spaniards to kill, plunder, and enslave the Natives. The requerimiento's origins lay in the Arabic conquest tradition, in which the conquered people had to pay taxes to be able to maintain their religious practices; hence, it functioned as a source of income and labor. Later, the Spanish Christians adopted the method, eliminating the part about religious freedom. The first time they applied it was in the Canary Islands in the fifteenth century. Then, in the sixteenth century, Cortés and Pizarro used that tool in their conquest of the Native empires of the American continent.[102]

As a legal instrument for punitive war actions, the requerimiento had a long history in the northeast of New Spain. In 1631, the vecinos sent to the governor of the New Kingdom of León a request to read out a requerimiento. They argued it was necessary due to the continuous Indigenous attacks over more than thirty years, which had recently worsened. They said it would be useless to keep the "Indians" captive because they would most certainly escape and continue with their series of thefts and murders. Therefore it was essential to bring death and destruction upon them. Among the suggestions that the colonists made, the most remarkable one was the request to kill all adult males, or at least to cut their right hands off and to hamstring them so as to render them permanently useless. The women and children should be deported outside the kingdom to hispanize them and to make them lose "the natural evil of their fathers."[103] More generally, such a request questioned the Natives' real assimilation or acceptance of the Catholic faith, since they had never kept the peace for more than six months. All in all, it was an excuse to make the Indigenous women and children captive and be able to sell them as slaves in other provinces.

Through the use of the requerimiento as a legal tool, the vecinos of the New Kingdom of León tried to justify the use of violence. The colonists acknowledged that the kings of Castile had been authorized by the pope to conquer the Indies in a smooth and lenient manner. But, they argued, the conquests of Mexico and New Mexico had been carried out violently because "God favors and helps them [the conquistadors] in the conquests, even though they have been so cruel and bloody."[104] They asserted that the colonization of the New Kingdom of León should be undertaken "with all the means necessary to achieving the end of the conquest."[105] The petitioners found it necessary to refer to Saint Augustin and his ideas about the just war: That the ruler has authority, that the cause of the war is recognized, that the ruler acts with justice in mind and restores peace, and that the war be carried out without affecting innocent people. Through their machinations, these four conditions were present. They concluded that a just war "brings peace."[106]

A committee of theologians analyzed the petition and concluded that it fulfilled the requirements for being a just war. On the other hand, they mentioned their preoccupation with the possible secondary collateral damages to women and children in such an extermination war. The colonists answered that any excess would be accidental and not premeditated; they also emphasized that they were acting correctly, pursuant to the law, in accordance with the official rules of going to war in the case where the requerimiento was rejected by the Native inhabitants.[107] This legal formalism evolved. It was no longer the original request of submission to the king's authority by a recently discovered Indigenous population; rather, it was a punitive action against Indigenous people for their uprising. What did not change was the original principle of undertaking military action against those who refused to submit themselves to the royal power.

During the first half of the eighteenth century, the requerimiento would still be used as a legal tool for retaliation and punishment. At the same time as the authorities were trying to eradicate the encomienda and the congrega, the requerimiento remained an authorized protocol. In 1714, the governor of the New Kingdom of León, Francisco de Mier y Torres, sent his emissaries to negotiate with a group of rebelling Natives and hand them a requerimiento of peace pursuant to the law and war title.[108] This happened again in 1734, when the governor, Joseph Antonio Fernández de Jáuregui y Urrutia, requested resources from the royal treasury to launch three punitive expeditions against the Natives. His justification was that "the requerimientos of peace set forth by the law" did not suffice; therefore, it was necessary to use force. He suggested that those "Indians" had to be relocated outside of the province.[109] Thus, the requerimiento, a tool for diplomacy and war put to use since the Middle Ages, remained current in the northeastern borderlands of New Spain until the eighteenth century.

CHAPTER 2

RITUALS, SYMBOLS, AND PRACTICES

Religion played an important role in the organization and development of the defense in New Spain's northeast. In some cases, the military organization would revolve around an explicitly religious symbolism and calendar. The first documented records about military reviews in the region date to the seventeenth century; they established the specific date on which they had to occur year after year. Originally, they took place on three dates: the day of Saint Catherine, November 25, the day of the Lord's Incarnation, March 25, and finally, the day of Saint James (Santiago), July 25.[110] Adopting a known religious anniversary like that of Saint James bore a powerful symbolic value in the martial organization.

The figure of the Apostle Saint James had had a deeply rooted cult in Spain ever since the Middle Ages. During the Reconquista, he became a symbol of resistance and the patron saint of Spain's military effort, so much so that the name of Saint James was used as a battle cry.[111] At the beginning of the conquest of the American continent, Pizarro's and Cortés's soldiers would invoke Saint James during their battles against the Incas and Aztecs.[112] In the Spanish borderlands of North America, this cult made a big impact. In the eighteenth century, soldiers of the presidios and the militias still used Saint James's name as a rallying cry when engaging in battle against the Natives.[113] The tradition of holding military parades on his anniversary persisted well into the eighteenth century. In 1776, the governor of the New Kingdom of León, Melchor Vidal de Lorca, ordered the annual review of the province's militia to be held on July 25. He was quite clear when saying that since "immemorial times, it has been the custom in this province that the day of Saint James, the twenty-fifth of the coming month of July, every year, the companies of militias are inspected."[114]

Vidal de Lorca stressed that such reviews were not a "mere ceremonial formality, but with the greatest attention and care, as corresponds to being in a position to stop the barbaric 'Indians' in their constant raids."[115] This was a ritualized practice in which the neighbors participated under the coordination of the mayor and war captain. Unlike in the other central regions of New Spain, this custom maintained its military function in that area during the postcolonial era. The tradition was deeply rooted in the region; the communities of Lampazos and San Migel del Arroyo kept detailed lists of those eighteenth-century military reviews. The Jacobean tradition had another function too: the incorporation and integration of the Indigenous communities into the Spanish military traditions, given that it demanded the presence of all able men capable of doing some type of military service.[116] The military documents of the time show the Spaniards, Tlaxcalan, and Chichimeca doing this activity together in the same manner as it was practiced in the Spanish Middle Ages.

The military parades on the day of Saint James were not the only integrated religious rituals practiced in these Spanish borderlands. The religious practices during Lent and Holy Week were another method to bring cohesion to the communities for self-defense. In San Miguel de Aguayo, the rituals were performed as community bonds between Tlaxcalans and Alazapas. One of the customs was for the settlement's vecinos to wear their military equipment during the Holy Week festivities for the "guardianship of the Holy Host as for the processions that emanate from the divine services."[117] The official in charge pointed out that "it is the usage and custom in all the borderlands that the inhabitants should wear their arms," particularly during the services of the Holy Week.[118] Due to the tendency of the Natives to attack during the religious processions, the vecinos had to have their arms at hand, especially during Lent Fridays due to the processions along the Stations of the Way of the Cross.[119] In this way, the inhabitants participated in a ceremony that carried as much a symbolic function as a practical one.

The term they used to refer to the Natives who might attack during those processions is noteworthy: "enemies of both crowns."[120] This expression illustrates the fusion of various traditions that suggest the relevance of communal defense in the minds of the settlement's inhabitants, as well as how it is intertwined with religious ideas. The Tlaxcalan vecinos from San Miguel, originally Nahuas from Mesoamerica, were incorporating Chichimeca Natives of the Alazapas faction into a Spanish defense system through a religious-military practice. The expression "enemies of both crowns" refers on the one hand to the Spanish monarchy and on the other, implicitly, to Christ as the king of Christianity. From that standpoint, the enemies were not only defying the Spanish administration but also the divine authority, which transformed the defense into a religious duty similar to a crusade. The expression points to the sacred duty of defending the Spanish borderlands against the enemies of the faith, an understanding not much different from what had happened in earlier centuries, during the Reconquista, but incorporated with Tlaxcalans and Alazapas Natives right in the eighteenth century in the northeast of New Spain.

CHAPTER 2

Like the religious calendar, the heraldic symbols also had a powerful significance for the vecinos and the various Indigenous factions. One of them was the Cross of Burgundy, which had been used as the flag of the Spanish armed forces since 1506. Its design consisted of a red diagonal cross, like an X, which was a derivation from Saint Andrew's cross and resembled two red branches on a white field. This came from the story according to which Saint Andrew had died crucified on a similarly shaped cross. Its use was imported to Spain from Burgundy by Philip the Handsome when he married Joanna of Castile, daughter of the Catholic kings. Charles V adopted it, and it became the standard of the Spanish regiments on the European battlefields during the sixteenth and seventeenth centuries. This Burgundy emblem became a symbol of the Spanish military power and would be used in North America.

The ensign had great value since it could be used as a tool for diplomacy between the various Indigenous groups in the region.[121] In 1772, a group of five Tancahuayas visited the San Antonio presidio. According to a Spanish officer, these Natives were carrying a flag with the Cross of Burgundy as a peace symbol.[122] This demonstrated that Tancahuayas had learned to use a European Renaissance symbol as a tool of diplomatic relationships; it was an acknowledgment of the Spanish military power, a way of honoring the military standard. Shortly after, that Indigenous group was attacked by Apaches, who took the emblem as loot. Apparently, the flag had acquired special value for the Natives of the region. Comanches were another group that made use of this symbol. In January 1772, they stole animals from the inhabitants of San Antonio, and a group of soldiers captured four of them. The governor of Texas decided to free two of the Comanche prisoners and to send them to their camp to try to arrange a peace agreement. Forty days later, the freed Comanches returned in greater numbers to negotiate. According to documents of that time, the Comanches carried a peace symbol, a flag made of shifts on which they had painted a cross.[123] Although it is not mentioned whether it was a Cross of Burgundy, undoubtedly the Comanches had tried to reproduce it since they had incorporated a diplomatic symbol through the ritual act of honoring the military ensign.

Rather than an example of the territorial possession of a modern state, the last colonization enterprise in the northeast of New Spain in the mid-eighteenth century—the colonization of Nuevo Santander—was based on strategies whose origins were clearly medieval. Indeed, the whole expansion into the northeast of New Spain was based on this type of medieval structure. From the start, the expansion and colonization projects were private enterprises that revolved around powerful individuals who assumed military and political power. What is more, the military participation of the vecinos-colonists continued as a form of local citizenship, given that it carried with it the possibility of having a say in political matters. This civic culture can be traced back to the Spain of the Reconquista. Another characteristic that shares the same origin is the practice of war as an economic activity, which made territorial appropriation a sustainable business; it was the same way the war against the Moors had been sustained centuries earlier. One more proof of the medieval character of the colonizing enterprise in the northeast, until the case of Nuevo Santander, was the use of symbols with origins in the Middle Ages, such as the cult of Saint James or the ritual of the requerimiento. The military character of these religious festivities, traditions, and symbols remained alive in the northeast. In Spain, as well as in the large and rich urban areas of the empire, these traditions had lost their social function and military value; they lived on only as ornamental vestiges of another era. Metropolitan Spain, as the empire grew in size and strength, was moving away from the warring years of the Reconquista, while in the northeastern borderlands of New Spain, the Spanish colonization efforts continued using the social and military model of the Middle Ages due to the permanent state of war with the Indigenous populations. In other words, the peculiar context of the borderland region allowed for the conservation of the tradition. Not only did the borderlands represent a geographic space, but they also represented a particular way of life that had emerged from the medieval traditions that lasted for many generations in these territories. By the mid-eighteenth century, this culture, now naturalized in the special regional conditions, was profoundly ingrained in northern New Spain. At the same time, Europe was undergoing a consolidation process of the modern era, which, together with the Enlightenment, transformed its society. This gap, this cleavage—to use a trending term in political science—between the borderland society and the metropole, together with the arrival of the Bourbons on the Spanish throne, was going to have profound consequences in the empire. It would bring with it important and profound attempts to change the way of managing the borderland settlements of New Spain due to its strategic relevance in the imperial battles. Unavoidably, the north would enter a transformation process where the medieval character of the borderlands would set itself up against the new administration and its enlightened character.

CHAPTER 3

The Coming of the Enlightened Modernity

DURING THE EIGHTEENTH CENTURY, THE BOURBON DYNASTY IMPLEMENTED a series of administrative reforms for the whole Spanish empire. This was particularly noticeable in the changes within the Spanish armed forces. Based on the rationalism of the Enlightenment, those changes had their origins in France and Prussia and ultimately affected the European military order. The Bourbon reforms purported to reorganize the military structure of the northeastern borderlands of New Spain. There, a series of reforms of the same nature as those applied in Europe started taking place, such as the centralization of the military authority. These changes came as a consequence of the threats by the Anglo-Americans, the French, the Comanches, and the Apaches, who defied the Spanish position in North America. Due to the wars of independence, the Spanish colonial authorities planned changes in the military structures, but the inhabitants of the borderland communities adapted to, reinterpreted, or simply resisted the reformist measures. The local traditions of political participation in the military field persisted, and so did the defense in the hands of individuals. In this way, the ancestral customs in this matter lived on.

THE ARRIVAL OF THE BOURBONS AND THE POLITICAL CHANGES

In the last decades of the seventeenth century, the Habsburg dynasty that governed Spain suffered defeats in Europe in wars whose costs spiraled upwards and led to an inevitable economic crisis. The Habsburgs were incapable of building the centralized state they fiercely wanted because of the strong regional autonomies in the Iberian Peninsula and the aristocracy's political power.[1] The early eighteenth century brought relevant transformations for Spain and its empire. This started with the transition of the dynasty from the Habsburgs to the Bourbons, of French origin, after the War of the Spanish Succession (1700–1713), which involved France, England, Portugal, and the Netherlands. The new Bourbon king, Philip V, established the principles of a modern absolutist monarchy, such as the centralization of power, efficient spending, professionalization of the bureaucracy, compulsory military service, and fiscal reforms that included areas that had never been administratively incorporated, like Aragon and Catalonia.

After the dynastic conflict, Spain was in a steep decline. To reconstruct its economy, it needed to renovate the commerce with its American possessions. During the war, Spain was unable to supply its colonies, and French, British, and Dutch smugglers filled the void. When the Spaniards tried to limit the incursion of foreign merchants in their markets, the French and British navies inflicted a series of naval defeats upon them during the War of the Quadruple Alliance (1718–1720), and Spain had no remedy but to accept the foreign participation in the oceanic commerce. At the same time, the Bourbons initiated a series of internal changes in the administration of the Spanish empire, such as moving the Casa de Contratación (House of Commerce) from Seville to Cadiz, the establishment of the new viceroyalty of New Granada, and the imposition of a state monopoly on the tobacco trade in Cuba. These moves were part of a plan to generate income through taxes, eliminating monopolies and putting an end to a number of privileges that the criollo elite enjoyed. Such measures, however, were taken without analyzing the context and its political consequences, and so after fierce opposition and even some armed rebellions, the innovations would be abolished.[2] The new minister, José Patiño (1726–1736), learned from these errors and focused on the main problems affecting the empire's economic stability, such

CHAPTER 3

as smuggling, corruption, and foreign intromission. One of the priorities was to reconstruct the naval forces, so the number of shipyards grew. It was mostly a deterrent since they did not want to confront the British and their navy directly. Patiño maintained the monopoly on tobacco in Cuba but sweetened it with more acceptable terms for the producers and set the foundations to establish the viceroyalty of New Granada in 1739. Thanks to his leadership and bureaucratic knowledge, Patiño was able to achieve true changes, but most importantly he set the basis for future reforms.[3]

After Patiño, the second reformist wave was propelled by new politicians and public administrators like José de Campillo y Cossio. These reforms were, in turn, driven by the War of Jenkins' Ear (1739–1748) against Great Britain. Unlike in previous conflicts, on this occasion Spain was able to fight successfully, even managing to humiliate the British Navy by severely defeating it in Cartagena de Indias. There, after a long siege where tropical diseases decimated their forces, the British were forced to retreat. Another successful change was allowing ships to navigate individually instead of using the traditional system of fleets and galleons. At the same time, the Spanish Crown created new monopolistic companies to exploit the agricultural resources of the imperial periphery. Most of the new administrators established hard but reachable objectives: the liberalization of the economic structure, the expansion of maritime commerce, and the modernization and reduction of the fiscal burden. These reforms, however, led to the opposition of powerful groups, even rebellions in some cases, which they were able to suppress. The Bourbon administration's objectives varied and sometimes were contradictory, yet the success of the new policies in mainland Spain promoted their use overseas.[4]

During the second half of the eighteenth century, the transformations that the Bourbons had initiated went on. In 1759, Charles III stepped on the Spanish throne; he had prior experience in public affairs as king of Naples (1734–1759), a position in which he had launched a series of reforms to centralize the administration. Once in Madrid, he was set on following the same line for Spain and its territories overseas. In 1762, Spain found itself dragged into the Seven Years' War (1756–1763) in an alliance with France against Great Britain. But now the British fleet was bigger and more powerful, while the Spanish forces and garrisons were too few and too small to resist. In June 1762, the British brought a force of two hundred ships and 14,000 men in a risky operation to take Havana. The Spanish forces consisted of eighteen ships and a garrison of 2,300 soldiers. The Spanish Crown's subjects on the American continent were unable to send help to Havana, while the British were bringing reinforcements from Jamaica and their North American colonies. The loss of Havana was a humiliating defeat. To recover the city, the Spaniards had to cede Florida, and the British retained the whole of Canada. This catastrophe would accelerate the reformist and enlightened vision of Charles III, who considered the peace treaty with Great Britain to be only a temporary armistice until the next conflict would inevitably flare up. From then on, the Bourbon king's priority was the military reform rather than the economic and commercial deregulation reforms.

THE MILITARY REORGANIZATION OF THE SPANISH ARMED FORCES

In Bourbon Spain, the military transformations followed the same path as the commercial and administrative changes and were actually part of a larger process initiated in France during the second half of the seventeenth century. During that time, the French Bourbons transformed the way in which the armies would be administered in Europe during the eighteenth century; the standardization of the armed forces had begun. Now there was supervision of the providers, as well as an enrollment system and structured payment of the soldiers' salaries. The state would take responsibility for the equipment, supplies, and transportation of the armies. The Crown designated the officers who commanded the troops. All this implied the birth of a civil bureaucracy to manage the armed forces, integrated by intendants who supervised the army and navy and directly informed the War Ministry. Even if it didn't entirely put an end to the existing corruption, this organizational model meant progress in the matter and was copied throughout Europe.[5] Undoubtedly, one of the great defects with which this system was born was the official sale of officers' commissions to finance military expenses, while at the same time it became an important vehicle of social mobility for the bourgeoisie.[6]

Spain followed the French model during the time of the Bourbon reforms of the eighteenth century, and a whole new organization incorporated the army into the bureaucratic-administrative structure. As in France, the sales of army commissions became an important source of income for the armed forces,[7] but unlike in France, in Spain the monopoly over the corps of officers by the higher nobility limited the possibility of access and therefore the possibility of upward mobility for the lower nobility and the bourgeoisie. This is how the Spanish army became the bastion of the aristocracy, which later on would lead to numerous problems between the military hierarchy and the civil bureaucracy. In 1704, the Bourbon regime imposed selective conscription. To promote it there were incentives, such as exemption from other public duties or concessions of military jurisdiction, which gave soldiers immunity before the civil laws. Following the French precedent, the Crown granted promotions, and the central administration was responsible for supervising the military budget. Spain would discover, however, that maintaining such a military control structure proved to be very costly.[8]

Another problem that worsened the spending was that most of the time the contingent of conscripts would be incomplete. What is more, regions like Catalonia, traditionally resistant to any form of administrative centralization from Madrid, made it so that their quota of conscripts would not be met. Hence the modernization of the Spanish armed forces was not the product of a homogeneous process; the efficiency levels in the organization varied widely, and the command structure remained inefficient. The General Staff was nonexistent, which complicated the campaigns with large numbers of troops, and there were constant disputes among the commanders of the various regiments. In contrast with the state of affairs in France, the creation of a vast bureaucracy led to antagonisms because the authority was spread out among different administrative branches, which led to hostility and paralysis. In addition, those changes promoted corruption, like the financing of ghost units, and the sale of commissions favored poor, inefficient leadership.[9]

After the humiliating defeat by Great Britain in 1762, Charles III took it upon himself to reform the armed forces from the ground up. The Bourbon king decided to follow a different military model: that of the Prussian army, which was successful throughout the eighteenth century and was characterized by a process of state centralization and militarization of society, a process originally set up by Frederick II (Frederick the Great). Prussia had established military academies for the training of officers, the most famous one being the Berlin War Academy, founded in 1722.[10] The Prussian advances in military organization reflected the zeitgeist prevalent in Europe at the time: absolutism and Enlightenment, especially centered on providing a scientific order to the way things worked. Frederick II wanted his armies to function with the mathematical precision of a clock mechanism, which was only possible through the establishment of a fierce discipline. In his mind, this was to be "the foundation of glory and the conservation of the state," and he believed "that the slightest loss of discipline led to barbarism."[11]

In such a system, there was no place for personal initiative; the soldiers had no choice but to follow their officers' orders. The whole discipline mechanism revolved around obedience to the king, while the officers fought to maintain their privileges and the soldiers to avoid punishment for any breach of discipline. This structure was rooted in precision, itself arising from meticulous training, where movements, deployments, marches, and formations were precise. The objective had to have a tactical advantage in battle thanks to a precise execution by the troops.[12] This kind of discipline and mathematical precision in military maneuvers would have been unheard of in earlier centuries. After the Prussian successes on the battlefield, their model became the ideal to be imitated by the European armies of the time. The Bourbon dynasty in Spain adopted it during the reign of Charles III in 1768 and tried to export it to its American colonies.[13]

Charles III applied the Prussian military system to the Spanish forces during the second half of the eighteenth century. At that time, military academies, like those in Avila and Segovia, started appearing in Spain. The army adopted Prussian formations and tactics based on a strict discipline imposed by stern officers. Rearming constituted an important part of the reform, and the armaments factories ramped up the production of top-quality weapons. But even though the Spanish army markedly improved in its training and tactics, it lacked a logistical system and appropriate supply chain, which was a serious shortcoming in case of a major armed conflict. Like in the past, recruiting troops undoubtedly represented the worst headache for the implementation of military reform. To be able to avoid problems and riots, the army looked for volunteers, but there never were enough of them. Applying a quota of conscripts particularly affected the lower classes that could not request exemptions, and the regional opposition to this measure shifted the bulk of the recruitment to Castile and Andalusia. As a consequence of these imbalances, criminals and foreigners were enrolled. In theory, the Spanish army should have counted between seventy and eighty thousand men, but in reality it could barely gather half of that.[14]

The incorporation of foreign officers led to resentment from domestic officers and undermined the leadership capability of Spanish officers. On the other hand, the body of officers remained socially stratified by the domination of the higher nobility, which occupied the highest posts, while the lower nobility was assigned as noncommissioned officers and the recruits from the lower classes would fill the rows of soldiers. For the latter, not only was the path to promotion closed, but more often than not they were constantly affected by reductions in their salaries, sometimes living below the subsistence level without any hope of moving up in the ranks.[15] To be able to finance the army, Charles III maintained the practice of selling commissions, which, in some cases, managed to bring together half of the units' officers.[16] The number of staff officers was unnecessarily high, while there was a deficit of professional subordinates in spite of the creation of military academies. Given such structural problems, the Bourbon forces in the Old World suffered military disasters such as the failed expedition to Algeria in 1775, where the lack of military intelligence, war plan, logistics, and capable commanders cost Spain five thousand men.[17]

THE MILITARY REFORMS IN AMERICA

When the British forces attacked Havana, they surprised the Spanish forces on the American continent. In New Spain, the strategic port of Veracruz suddenly became vulnerable to an invasion. The viceroy Marquess of Cruillas saw the danger and tried to gather a militia force to repel a hypothetical attack. This was the usual defense procedure on the American continent: defending the coastal cities with a small force of the regular army with the support of local militias. This time, the problem was that never before had they seen a hostile force as numerous and as close as the one that had overtaken the Cuban city. From the start, Cruillas faced many problems in gathering and properly organizing a defensive force that, truth be told, looked more like a horde than like a military unit. The higher classes refused to provide workers to construct fortifications or to serve as militiamen. There were no weapons, and even worse, the few militiamen who made it to Veracruz were decimated by yellow fever, which immediately made the number of deserters rise. Finally, the recruitment and the forced contributions made the inhabitants of Veracruz resist.[18]

This chaos led the Spanish authorities to remake the defensive strategy of the American colonies always with local bases, given that the war in Europe made it financially impossible for the mother country to send troops to the American continent. In 1763, Charles III ordered the military system to be reformed, starting with Cuba. The main change was to arm and train American subjects following the guidelines developed in Europe; there would be regular army units but, at the same time, numerous duly trained militias. There was fear of arming the inhabitants of the colonies due to the implications of granting them military power. But in the face of the latent danger of the British troops attacking, there was no other option. In order to transform the militias into disciplined units, the authorities launched a process of recruitment and periodic training with arms and uniforms they provided. The officer had to come from the local elite, following the same pattern as in Europe.[19]

The military reforms were fairly easy to implement in Cuba, thanks to the reduced territory and size of its population, but they proved much more difficult to implement in much larger and richer areas, such as the center of New Spain. In 1764, Juan de Villalba y Angulo initiated the process of military reformation, but he soon had to face conflicts with the civil authorities for resources and the granting of military immunity. Two years later, Villalba gave up on the project and left it unfinished.[20] The transformation meant annoyances and sacrifices for the civilians in the viceroyalty's central areas, given that there was no inclination toward military service.[21] The military renovation provoked distrust in the colonial bureaucracy, as well as in the local elites, and increased the risk of a popular insurrection.[22] The authorities tried to make military service more attractive by introducing military immunity, which was already practiced in Europe. The immunity exempted the members of the armed forces from the civil jurisdiction and put New Spain's military far away from the reach of the common courts with regard to civil and penal matters. Moreover, these privileges could be extended to the wives, children, and servants of the soldiers.[23] Soon such immunity turned out to be a problem when a number of soldiers violated the law at pleasure. In some cases, rich storekeepers would enroll in the militia to be able to falsify weights and measures, sell forbidden alcoholic beverages, gamble, and organize fixed cockfights.[24]

A no less relevant obstacle was the integration of the officers' corps. In the beginning, they wanted most of their officers to be European, but given the conflicts in Europe, this proved impossible. The European officers' corps was growing older and becoming inefficient, and the officers were falling victim to personal vices such as gambling, alcoholism, and laziness, which required them to be replaced. Inevitably, the officers' posts were being more and more occupied by criollos.[25] To the vicissitudes of time, we have to add the social conflicts in the localities where the new replacements were serving since a good number of them were the dregs of the Spanish army.[26]

As in the mother country, in New Spain one of the most important sources of income for the administration was the sale of officers' commissions. The social status, the local command, and the elegant uniforms that such posts offered made them attractive to the eyes of the rich criollos. The families of the nobility never lost a chance to buy commissions for the male children who had no future in the family business. Thus the seeds of an army of castas were being sown since the officers belonged to the upper class, the only ones able to buy those positions. Such a tradition of the ranks of army and navy officers belonging to the great families can still be seen nowadays in many countries of Southern Cone, and its origins lie in those Bourbon times of the sale of commissions. In the early nineteenth century, the Prussian naturalist Alexander von Humboldt described the situation as follows:

> It is not the nation's military spirit but the vanity of a small number of families whose heads aspire to the title of colonel or brigadier, that has promoted the militias in the Spanish colonies.... It is amazing to see, even in the smallest provincial towns, all the store owners transformed into Colonels, Captains, and Sergeant Majors.... Since the rank of Colonel gives right to the treatment and title of lordship, which is ceaselessly repeated in the common conversation, it is now conceived of as the one that most contribute to the happiness of the domestic life, and it is the one for which the criollos make the most extraordinary economic sacrifices.[27]

Humboldt, a Prussian son of an officer who had served under the orders of Frederick II, found the Spanish colonies' military system quite ridiculous.[28] Charles III's original project of implanting the Prussian model in the American continent had largely turned into a pantomime. Among the new militia officers, there were those who wanted to show off their recently acquired social status through substantial expenditures. Some of the common eccentricities were making their units parade frequently, employing honor guards, and deploying large escorts in official labors in order to stand out in front of their jurisdiction's civil servants. Rude declarations and arrogant attitudes in civil matters on the officers' part inevitably led to conflicts with other authorities.[29] The impunity with which the commanders and officers with immunity behaved made those martial ranks a socially prominent activity, but one that did not deserve much military attention.[30] In some cases, the monied commanders and officers hired substitutes known as *alquilones* to perform their daily tasks. Obviously, these substitutes did a poor job in their commanding roles. As an example, there is the much-publicized case of one of such substitute officers who was supposed to be on patrol but actually was at a brothel.[31]

The military service of the militia type, however, led to a conflict between availability of troops and the labor necessary for the economy in cases of armed emergencies. The mother country's system of regular troops, in addition to being costly, produced conflicts with the productive society since it subtracted labor, particularly from agricultural work. Had it functioned optimally, the militia system the Bourbons implanted in their overseas territories would have produced good results. They did not, however, anticipate the potential recruits' reluctance to do their military service. To determine who was recruitable, there was a general census that showed the number of men eligible for military service, then there was a pause to see who would sign up voluntarily. When this failed or did not yield the expected numbers, those who had to serve to fill the quotas were designated. There were exemptions that could be purchased, of course, but for the most part these were out of reach for the lower classes. The viceregal administration tried to fill the quotas in other ways, such as by recruiting homeless men and criminals.[32] But because the category of homeless was not well defined in the law, they would grab common people to recruit them. Most of the time, it was a matter of a simple extortion where the officers would try to get a bribe to help the person evade the recruitment. The legal frameworks regarding military discipline, inherited from the mother country, did not help make military service popular since severe physical punishment was used to impose discipline, and a good number of soldiers died because of beatings they received from officers and sergeants.[33]

In theory, the recruits had to receive pay, but it became general practice for the payment not to be made, and when it was made, the amount proved insufficient to cover the basic needs of a family. Pensions were practically nonexistent and insufficient in the cases when they were granted. Those who became disabled in action would not receive any kind of compensation.[34] All this resulted in the lower classes having much to lose and almost nothing to gain by remaining in the army. It is almost a sociological rule that an ill-provisioned and ill-maintained army without resources will tend to live off its environment. The terrible economic

CHAPTER 3

conditions of the colonial militia led the troops to harass and threaten civilians, sometimes steal from them, and other times extort them, frequently with the complicity of their officers.[35] As was to be expected, the military reformation of the Bourbons affected the borderlands of the Spanish empire on the American continent, given that, together with the ports, these were the areas most in need of defense and military protection.

THE BOURBON REFORMS IN THE SPANISH BORDERLANDS IN NORTH AMERICA

The Bourbon administration imposed a series of changes in the imperial borderlands in which Enlightenment rationalism would be an integral part of the framework. By 1740, the concept of territoriality had changed, which would affect the empires' frontiers. The new mentality included a new, rational geographic conception that would justify any and all reformist measure that led to the physical occupation and direct control of the land. Within the framework of the construction of an absolute monarchy during the eighteenth century, there was an attempt to implant the royal authority in the borderlands through means based on a military-scientific approach. The logic behind this new approach was rooted in setting down geographic limits within which the Spanish authority's presence would be reinforced by a military deployment that would ensure the control of the properties. Hence, rationalism and military force became tools for the reorganization of the Spanish borderlands.[36]

During the first half of the eighteenth century, the Bourbons tried to reform the military system through administrative measures. In 1724, the viceroy appointed the Marquis Pedro de Rivera, governor of Tlaxcala, with military experience in combat against pirates in Yucatan, as general inspector of the northern province of New Spain. He was assigned the task of collecting data about the state of the presidios and elaborating a proposition to reform them. The purpose was to increase the defense capacity of those provinces in the face of possible external threats, as well as to optimize the use of scarce resources by homogenizing the forces and cutting expenses,[37] admittedly two contradictory goals in principle.

Rivera's inspection lasted forty-three months, during which he visited twenty-three presidios. He crossed the provinces of Nueva Vizcaya, Sonora, Arizona, Nayarit, New Mexico, the New Kingdom of León, and Coahuila, covering around ten thousand miles. In his travels, Rivera compiled a vast amount of data, such as topographical descriptions and the longitude and latitude of the locations of the described places.[38] In this effort, he demonstrated a high sense of geographic consciousness through mathematical measurements, but his main objective was the reorganization to optimize resources. With regards to the region that occupies us, we must point out that Rivera visited the presidio of San Antonio in Texas and those of Cerralvo and Cadereyta in the New Kingdom of León. There the general inspector interviewed officers and soldiers in addition to revising the accounting books.[39] Thereafter he made recommendations, such as reducing the number of soldiers in the San Antonio presidio, since at that time the hostile Natives did not represent an immediate threat and from his viewpoint a small garrison could defend the fort. As to Cadereyta, he determined that its population had grown large enough not to need a presidio and recommended that the garrison be moved to the north, to the hamlet of Boca de Leones, close to San Miguel de Aguayo and Lampazos. To act in a regulated manner, Rivera reorganized the functions and payments of the presidios in accordance with the *Reglamento para la Guarnición de la Habana, Castillos y Fuertes de su Jurisdicción, año 1719* (Rules of the Garrison of Havana, Castles and Forts of its Jurisdiction, Year 1719).[40]

The administrative measures Pedro de Rivera suggested became official ordinances in 1729, with the first reglementary dispositions for the northern presidios. In them, Rivera clearly set up the basic organization principles, such as the granting of commissions to the officers, the soldiers' rotations, the prohibition against using the troops for personal matters, the procedures of the military courts, the manner in which the neighbors would collaborate with the presidios' forces, the obligations of custody, the establishing of set prices for the garrisons' supplies, and the prohibition of the enslavement of Natives.[41] In other words, Rivera established—at least on paper—the rational principles of modern management for the armed forces in northern New Spain. The most important underlying objective, to save money, was achieved by reducing the expenses by 178,000 pesos, that is, by 40 percent.[42]

Nevertheless, the measures suffered from a great defect: They did not reflect the conditions in which the northern presidios really operated. The presidios' new rules were based on those of Cuba, which were envisioned for naval defense. This

CHAPTER 3

is particularly evident in Rivera's recommendation of reducing the San Antonio garrison under the argument that the Natives would be incapable of taking over the presidio. This measure showed how little Rivera, an expert in pirates, understood the kind of irregular war practiced in that region where depredation and looting by the hostile Natives—whose quick mobility and superiority in numbers the presidios' troops had to counter in the same measure—were the relevant factors and not a fort's defense from a frontal attack. The changes saved the royal treasury costs but did not translate into a better functioning of the local forces. Fortunately, even though the procedures had become official, many of them were almost never put into practice. Actually, there was no way of doing so since they came up against a harsh strategic and tactical reality. Thus the military organization in the northeast kept operating as it had done since the sixteenth and seventeenth centuries, although now debilitated by the diminished resources.

As explained earlier, thirty-three years later, the disastrous role of the Spanish defense against England in the occupation of Havana shook Charles III's empire and brought about the military reformation, mainly based on the Prussian system. In their reformist schematizations, the Bourbons only took into account the English threat, which was naval for the most part. But in the northern territories of New Spain, there also was the possibility of a military expansion by land of the English colonies in North America, which caused some alarm among the colonial authorities. Those colonies would soon initiate their emancipation from England, and their expansion would run toward Louisiana in the South and onto two vast tracts in the West. The first one comprised the territories neighboring those emancipated colonies. The Bourbons, however, were never aware of the main threat to the settlements to the north of New Spain from the second half of the eighteenth century onwards: hostile Natives, some of them displaced by the expansionism of the formerly British colonies.

Apaches—who belonged to the Athabascan linguistic family (originating from Alaska and western Canada)—were one such group. After a long migration, Apaches arrived in the region of New Mexico and Arizona between the ninth and thirteenth centuries. Their political unity was constituted by bands, which implied the absence of a central authority. This made it difficult for the Spanish authorities to negotiate with all the various Apache groups: while some would remain at peace, others might not accept peace. They were semi-nomads and depended on buffalo hunting and seasonal crops. In 1541, the Spaniards made contact with the Apaches for the first time in New Mexico. This is when Apaches adopted the use of horses and developed a great ability at horseback riding, which fit perfectly with their fighting tactic of hit and run. During the most part of the seventeenth century, they would raid the Spanish settlements and the latter's allies, the Pueblos.[43]

During the eighteenth century, they started a new southward migration because other, more powerful Indigenous tribes that used firearms were displacing them. In their constant migration, Apaches had never fully adopted the lifestyle of the Great Plains and their static farming hamlets, which turned them into an easy target during the harvests. Some groups migrated to the West, to New Mexico and Arizona, while others migrated to Texas and the north of New Spain. Among the latter were the Lipans, who would settle down in the region between San Antonio, the New Kingdom of León, and New Santander. This led to confrontations with the neighboring Spanish communities, mainly around San Antonio. In other words, the Lipan Apaches and the Spaniards in Texas were in an almost permanent state of war. There were some periods of truce and attempts to settle them down in missions, which all failed. During the first half of the eighteenth century, there were frequent hostilities that at times put the presidios' troops in a difficult position, but the Natives' factions were not sufficiently powerful to destroy places like San Antonio. The status quo changed drastically in the 1760s, when the Lipans started raiding ever further south, putting the Spanish presence in the region in danger. This is why the Marquis of Rubi described the situation as dire in his report of 1765.[44]

Comanches—at first enemies of the Lipans, whom they would dominate over time—undoubtedly were the strongest group of autonomous Indigenous people in the region. Comanches belonged to the Shoshone faction of the Uto-Aztecan linguistic family. Originally, they were hunter-gatherers from the area of the Great Basin (in the present territories of Nevada, Utah, California, Wyoming, Idaho, and Oregon). During the seventeenth century, Comanches incorporated the use of horses into their culture, which completely changed their lifestyle. The horses allowed them greater mobility, so they started moving into eastern Colorado and western Kansas. Once there, they began a new migration southward to have better access to the herds of horses and buffaloes, as well as to exchange firearms with the French. Around 1720, the Comanches arrived at the southern plains, and by 1760 they had reached New Mexico. There they established a lucrative trade of horses and captives, whom they would catch and enslave during their raids on other groups of Indigenous people and some Spanish settlements.[45]

CHAPTER 3

Comanches were not unified but rather formed numerous bands, which themselves could be divided into smaller units or united into bigger groups, depending on the objective of the moment. Five large bands that played a main role in Comanche history have been well documented; they constituted one of the largest and most powerful groups in a territory that would range from the Central Plains of North America to Texas and the vicinity of the Spanish colonial frontier. Around 1743, they appeared for the first time in San Antonio, apparently while pursuing their rival, the Lipans. In 1758, a force of two thousand Comanche warriors attacked and destroyed the Spanish mission for Apaches in San Saba, Texas. By 1770, Comanches had already settled in the Texan plains, and the Spaniards became aware that they were in danger in the face of the number of Comanches. At first, the Spanish population tried to reach peaceful agreements, but with little success, since Comanches considered the Spanish to be allies of their enemies, the Lipans.[46]

In 1780, the conflict had grown bigger. Comanches gained control of parts of Colorado, New Mexico, Oklahoma, Kansas, and Texas, with a population of around forty thousand people. They were a significant economic and military power and demanded access to pastures for their horses, land to hunt bison, and slave trading.[47] The growth in power of those two groups, Lipan Apaches and Comanches, during the eighteenth century put the towns of the northeastern borderlands in a difficult situation. San Antonio, Lampazos, Laredo, and San Miguel became small islands of Spanish presence in territory dominated by the nomads. They were unable to perform their function as defensive settlements with militia colonists that were supposed to stop the penetration of Indigenous people not subordinated to the Spanish power. Indeed, the scale of the tribes' infiltration made it difficult to surveil their movements. This put the tribes at an advantage since it gave them time to spy on the towns and attack the ranches to grab animals and captives, as well as to kill people. In addition, the Indigenous groups were familiar with the Spanish war techniques and would even be better armed at times.[48]

On the other hand, when the forces of the borderlands' townships tried to retaliate or defend themselves, the Indigenous war band would simply disperse into multiple groups, moving toward terrains of difficult access or into the immensity of the pastures. On the few occasions when they managed to locate the enemy *rancherías* and attack them, they only did so when using the forces of allied Natives. To make matters worse, it was impossible to reach peace agreements due to the large number of bands in which they were divided. Indeed, while some Apache and Comanche groups were at peace with the towns of the Spanish Crown, others spent their time attacking them. The frontal, open war situation was unsustainable, and in the long run the solution came from diplomacy: bribing the various lordlings of the tribes with gifts and attempting to divide them and put them at odds with one another. In the late eighteenth century, the Spanish authorities had to admit that their position was tenuous and that a bad peace was worth more than a good war.[49]

So during the second half of the eighteenth century, the Spanish authorities in the northern frontier found themselves forced to react to the aggressive penetration of Apaches and Comanches into the royal borderlands of the empire, which extended from the Gulf of Cortés, through Arizona and New Mexico, to the coast of Texas by Espiritu Santo Bay. The monarchy was forced to give in to the realities of the American frontier, and the direction of the Bourbons' military reorganization took a new direction. While they maintained a military organization appropriate for fending off a European invasion in the coastal regions and the heavily populated areas of central New Spain, they started to test alternatives devised to face the Comanche and Lipan infiltrations. In 1765, Charles III appointed the Marquis of Rubi inspector of the defenses of the northern borderlands. This trip began in 1765, required two years, and covered seventy-five thousand miles. Like Rivera earlier, Rubi traveled all over the interior provinces and returned to Mexico City in February 1766 after having inspected twenty-four military settlements. During his stay in the north, Rubi witnessed the danger that Comanches and Apaches represented for the Spanish colonization project. For example, in San Antonio, Rubi found the presidio in terrible condition because the growing Comanche attacks rendered life in the settlement difficult, and many houses had been abandoned. In his report about his trip, Rubi highlighted the need to improve the borderlands' military system.[50]

Rubi's observations crystallized the new regulations for the presidios in 1772. The new ordinances fomented an aggressive offense against "Indians." Like Rivera, Rubi underlined the need to homogenize the procedures and to improve the operative efficiency by coordinating the military operations, optimizing training, boosting morale, and modernizing the equipment. He had the original idea of creating a defensive line of presidios uniformly spread from California to the Gulf of Mexico. His reasoning shows the influence of the Enlightenment's ideas and the goals for the military organization the Bourbons were trying to achieve. In addition,

CHAPTER 3

Rivera acknowledged that such defensive planning was inspired by the fortification system that Tsar Peter I had implemented on the Crimean border against the Tartars. There was a significant difference with the second line of settlements for the naval defense of the coasts: the presidios did not need artillery because the hostile Natives never attempted a frontal assault onto fortified positions.[51]

Rubi also proposed to match the equipment, armament, and uniforms of the presidio's troops with those of their counterpart, the army of the mother country. He was not oblivious to the purely administrative aspect: he decided to establish a system of fair and consistent prices for the supplies, as well as to ensure regular payment to the presidios' troops.[52] With this model, he was able to save around 87,027 pesos annually.[53] Last but not least, since it was of the utmost relevance to impose the Prussian military model, based on the experiences on the European continent, the Marquis of Rubi tried to raise the levels of conduct, military instruction, and maneuvers. Using a fortification system in the fashion of the Great Wall of China proved to be a utopia, a task much more difficult than it seemed at first.[54]

Clearly, there is a significant difference between Rubi's actions and Rivera's ordinances of 1729. Rubi became aware that it was necessary to have a permanent supervisor who would ensure compliance with the new dispositions; hence, he created the post of comandante inspector* (inspector-in-chief) of the presidios. Lt. Col. Hugo O'Conor was appointed to the post in 1772. An Irish Catholic refugee, he had ascended in the ranks of the Spanish army. He started his career as lieutenant in 1751, and by 1762 he had reached the rank of captain and participated in the war against Portugal. O'Conor arrived in Cuba in 1763, where he was appointed sergeant major as part of the effort to modernize the colonial troops. He moved to New Spain in 1765, and from 1767 to 1770 he was the provisional governor of Texas, thanks to which he was familiar with the military peculiarities of the northern provinces. O'Conor embodied the prototype of the military officers who arrived at the northern borderlands during the time of the Bourbon reforms and were immersed in the rationalism of the time. He was extremely professional and well-trained in a European perspective of warfare, which was not always applicable to the fluid conditions of northern New Spain.[55]

---

* A sort of inspector general.

O'Conor was used to frontal attacks between the armies that wanted to destroy one another on the battlefield. Hence the emphasis on having a fortified post that could serve as refuge and barricaded position at once. Following the zeitgeist, O'Conor relocated some presidios to restructure the defensive line, and, in keeping with the aggressive military policies of the time, he led various expeditions against different tribes. By 1775, he had launched a general campaign against those in the northeast. For the first time, there was an inkling of coordination among the different garrisons of the Spanish forces in the borderlands.[56] It is difficult to appraise O'Conor's strategy since it was difficult to confront an enemy that was not always willing to fight and who only did so when it had the advantage or was cornered. Nevertheless, we must suppose that the punitive expeditions of the inspector-in-chief contributed to the military efficacy since they dissuaded the tribes from making incursions. So even if there were significant advances in the coordination of the military efforts, it was not possible to reach peace overall. The Indigenous incursions and attacks continued, but at least some groups sought diplomatic peace accords.

One of the most problematic areas to manage for O'Conor was the region at the limit between Texas and Louisiana, but not particularly because of insecurity. There, O'Conor closed the settlement-presidios of San Agustín de Ahumada and of Los Adaes because Louisiana had become a Spanish possession and those presidios did not fit into Rubí's defensive line. Their colonists complained about this measure and asked for permission to return to establish themselves in that zone. O'Conor refused because he thought those settlements only served as points of entry for contraband, something he had realized when he was governor of Texas. The colonists went ahead of O'Conor and convinced the viceroy, Antonio María de Bucareli, to reverse the measure. At the beginning, they created a new hamlet called Nuestra Señora del Pilar de Bucareli, but by 1779 the population moved east, founding the town of Nacogdoches. Just as O'Conor feared, the place became an important contraband center where the British provided firearms to various Indigenous groups.[57] Those incidents brought to light the political limits that the inspector-in-chief faced when the vecinos were at odds with him, appealed to the political center of the viceroyalty, and the latter agreed with them.

In May 1776, Charles III created the General Command of the Interior Provinces, thanks to which the governments of the provinces of California, Sonora, Sinaloa, New Mexico, Arizona, Texas, the New Kingdom of León, Coahuila, and Nuevo Santander ended up under the direct authority of the Crown, and the viceregal authorities ended up without any jurisdiction over the northern borderlands of New Spain. The viceroy opposed the measure and reduced the economic support to those provinces, which would very soon become a source of constant friction in administrative matters. The command was headed by a figure who held the attributes of a governor together with those of a general in chief, authorized to delegate functions due to the large distances of the territory. The man chosen for that task was Teodoro de Croix, nephew of the previous viceroy of New Spain, Carlos Francisco de Croix, Marquis of Croix. At the age of sixteen, Teodoro, of French origin, had started his military career as second lieutenant of grenadiers. In 1765, he arrived in New Spain as part of a group accompanying his uncle; a year later, he found himself in Veracruz, fighting contraband. By 1770, he had obtained the rank of brigadier and was in charge of supervising the viceroyalty's troops; he served as commander from 1776 until 1783.[58] Like O'Conor, de Croix embodied the new generation of professional officers who would be in charge of the administration of the northern borderlands.

The creation of the General Command was part of the Bourbon strategy to fortify the empire's periphery.[59] This new form of political order tried to improve the region's administration and promote economic growth. The authorities hoped to open new communication routes between the interior provinces since the various viceroys had been unable to promote the region precisely due to the lack of communication channels in such a vast area. According to the ordinances, the commander of the interior provinces had to focus his attention on defense and economic development. De Croix chose experienced military officers as his helpers for this enormous task. Those strictly administrative tasks would be sent to the local governments. In theory, de Croix should have had political and economic autonomy from the viceroy, but he had to keep him informed because he depended on him for the supplies.[60] The new form of administration, however, was more a matter of reorganizing procedures than a revolutionary measure. Concentrating the civil and military power—which was dispersed among the provinces' governments—could have been an efficient measure in a smaller territory. In truth, the Bourbons were hoping, maybe with the optimism of those who did not know the subject of his measures, that all the interior provinces would work toward the same objectives and act in a coordinated way under a common command. But it is also true that the north had always functioned under a system of politico-military leadership, so it remained to be seen whether the parts would form a whole or not.

THE BOURBON RATIONALISM VS. THE

BORDERLANDS REALITY

The loss of Havana also affected the inhabitants of the northeastern provinces of New Spain. As part of the military reforms, the authorities carried out censuses to learn the number of men over the age of eighteen available for military service in case of a war, as well as what type of arms and resources they had. Such censuses were the necessary prelude to the military reorganization, but a peculiarity would distinguish them: they did not involve the Indigenous population.[61] In February of 1768, the viceroy ordered the census to be carried out in the New Kingdom of León, and it counted about 1,577 individuals available for some type of armed service.[62] But the census does not indicate exactly what the authorities hoped to find. Given that the order had been received orally, it was subject to the free interpretation of the local authorities. The census revealed what the local population understood as military service in accordance with its traditions and values.

Some lists comprised the number of family heads and with whom and what they could contribute in case of a war, such as children, servants, arms, and horses. This setup was the traditional means of obtaining political rights through military service; those who were able to bring more men to the battlefield were considered socially important. This way of integrating the census reflected traditional forms of information in the matter, which had been inherited from the sociomilitary organization of medieval Castile. Furthermore, we must highlight that there were at least four women in the census, and it also describes what they could contribute since the medieval tradition indicated that women too could be part of the military participation scheme.[63]

Another example that shows the peculiar way in which the locals understood the military service is the case of the Tlaxcalans of San Miguel, where they set up two lists. One mentions the number of available vecinos, their social class, the type of arms, and the number of available horses. The other one is titled "List of the unmarried persons of eighteen years of age and over."[64] It indicates that for the inhabitants of that township, the individuals who were not the head of the family did not belong to the military service. This contrasted with the European point of view at the time, according to which all men eighteen years old or older were considered eligible for military service. Lampazos, which included a criollo segment in its population, acted in the same way as San Miguel: the local authorities set up a list of forty-five people, which was about the same number as there were families in Lampazos at the time. The list does not include any servant or children of the family, since the local authorities applied the traditions related to that matter to what the higher authorities had asked of them. As in the case of the Tlaxcalans, these vecinos only included people who, in the eye of the community, were worthy of a military parade. Neither did they include the local Chichimeca, maybe because the authorities did not want the Indigenous people to participate. But even here, although the Indigenous men did not appear on the list, the Indigenous military participation was a significant tradition in the northeast. Consequently, the inhabitants of that township had a distinct, if not contrary, understanding of who was fit and proper for military service.

On the other side of the Atlantic, the Bourbon authorities only wanted to know the number of men and their armaments who could serve in case of an emergency. They were thinking of an organization based on a rational accounting manual in accordance with the principles of the Enlightenment. The following year, the authorities tried to carry out another census, but this time they were more specific by requesting that "all the shop owners, other vecinos and inhabitants, without excepting the men servants nor any other person of any state, quality, or condition," to "state their armament, mounts, and other war equipment, and he who did not own any to present himself in person to be suitable for the service of our king and lord."[65] But this was an exceptional situation: the enemies of the Crown against whom they were preparing themselves were not French or British, but unruly Indigenous peoples.

Since then, the military organization of the northeast focused on the defense against the ever more frequent attacks by Apaches and Comanches, who ventured more to the south each time, so much that by 1770 the Spanish authorities were forced to act. The frontier settlements of Laredo and Lampazos were insufficient to stop the wave of incursions. After Rubí's propositions, the authorities of the interior provinces soon became aware of the necessity of accepting the help of the local forms of military organization. One of the main changes was the creation of a local defense plan in coordination with the local militia. From the 1770s onward, the Indigenous attacks in the area of Texas, particularly San Antonio, became more and more frequent; the region's defense was possible only because all the vecinos were involved.[66] In 1772, a Lipan Apache attack in Coahuila obliged the garrison of the New Kingdom of León and forty vecinos to mobilize. The same occurred in Laredo.[67] All the routes connecting the settlements of the northeastern province were under threat, which made it necessary to accept the establishment of permanent forces at the limits of the New Kingdom of León with Nuevo Santander and Texas. It also became obvious that the militias of vecinos required a permanent supply of arms, ammunition, and powder.[68]

The coordination started with the establishment of permanent units in Lampazos and Laredo, the first line in the face of the raids; they comprised militias of vecinos of the New Kingdom of León and Nuevo Santander, drafted by the governors of each province. In Lampazos, there was a force of twenty-five men whose task was to patrol the surrounding area; a similar force did the same thing in Laredo.[69] The local authorities had to inform the comandante inspector of the interior provinces of any incursion and provide full information about the number of attackers, their tribe, and the route taken.[70] Consequently, communication between the provinces in relation to the Indigenous attacks became more systematized thanks to the establishment of the military mail.[71] The governor of the New Kingdom set up permanent vecinos meetings to organize the territory's defense with the local militias. At those meetings, there was a defense plan where each settlement had to have sentries at strategic points such as mountain passes, river crossings, and any other access point for the attacking war parties.[72] The case of San Miguel de Aguayo shows how this defense strategy worked. In 1776, a group of Natives attacked a ranch on the outskirts of town, taking away various horses and one man captive. Right away, thirty Tlaxcalan militiamen rode out in pursuit. In the end, they did not manage to catch the other force, but the vecinos informed authorities of the direction taken by the rival squad.[73] On other occasions, the system worked, and the neighbors were able to intercept and repel the Indigenous raids.[74] The hamlets of Lampazos and San Miguel de Aguayo played a central role in this task thanks to the organized vigilance and the willingness to launch punitive expeditions known as *mariscadas*.[75] The Bourbon administration promoted this defense system anchored on the vecindarios, based on the premise that the borderland vecinos had the duty of providing military assistance. In theory, this was true, but in reality the military senior officers and the local vecinos had differing understandings of what the military defense was and how it should be carried out. Soon there were conflicts between both groups.

The European officers tried to reorganize the local militias with the aim of achieving an optimal use of the local resources. In their mind, using local assets was a way of saving resources for the Crown, the same policy that had already been previously applied in the Spanish colonies on the American continent. One of the advantages of the royal administration was that the vecinos of the northern borderlands were more than eager to participate in military service since they were motivated by their long history of Indigenous conflicts.[76] This was the fundamental reason why, from the very start, the viceregal authorities had large numbers of vecinos participating in the defense operations.

The Bourbon system was not free of misunderstandings, which would have negative consequences. The Bourbons mistakenly considered the militia forces to be of permanent service, when actually their members were part-time soldiers, just as it had been since the antiquity wherever there were militias. The inhabitants of the settlements agreed to colonize and defend their lands against invaders, a common practice in the borderland hamlets going back to the Middle Ages. Nevertheless, this popular vision of the settler-soldiers had its limitations. We have already mentioned the main one: the vecinos were only part-time militiamen since they had other daily occupations, such as earning their bread by cultivating the land or by raising cattle. Whenever they participated in a military action, the compensation for their efforts came in the form of loot, mainly horses, and the product of selling the Indigenous captives they enslaved. On the other hand, the Bourbon reformists kept thinking of the men who populated the borderland settlements as troops they could use as they pleased for defensive tasks, which would bring them many problems.

The scale of the pillaging by the hostile Indigenous people kept the Spanish settlements in the northern borderlands in a constant state of alert and evidenced the need to create permanent service forces. During O'Conor's general campaigns of 1775 and 1776, there were large numbers of vecinos involved.[77] These campaigns lasted more than four months, during which the mobilized vecinos' families found themselves without proper sustenance. The military commanders admitted that it was unfair to use the settlers in such long military campaigns because there was no one to maintain their families, work their fields, and care for their properties. In addition—and this was not a minor criticism—when they left for military action, their townships were left without surveillance and were hence at risk of attacks.[78] In San Antonio, for example, the situation became dire. The authorities complained that this settlement was in a "deplorable state, due to constant warfare, whose series of events made those inhabitants be insufferably subject to spending ten, twenty, and even forty days bearing arms, without having the possibility of requesting sustenance for their family in the meantime." The complaints continued, explaining the heavy load "of bearing arms, day and night, in contrast with the custom—respected up till then—where each individual participated at his own cost in such or such invasion."[79] Tradition and opposing needs came together to cause the failure of the Bourbon project of the vecinos' military participation.

The appointment of the vecinos as part-time soldiers became unsustainable because they could not be kept up. In the case of San Antonio, some settlers abandoned the settlement to go live in safer areas with less turmoil. The governor of Texas, the Baron of Ripperda, confessed that the vecinos' complaints were fair. Even while he backed up the claim that they needed to maintain their families, he also made it clear that he did not have enough regular soldiers of the presidio to carry out his military tasks without the help of the local militias.[80] The limitations affecting the local population in the performance of the imposed defensive tasks were not unique to San Antonio. The Laredo area, too, faced a similar problem:

> Those vecinos who serve by providing, at their expense, supplies, horses, and arms; and others who due to their needs do not have it, run the risk of holding themselves up with venison, rats, or field roots, and when the situation makes it impossible to hunt or to request food, they run the risk of dying of hunger, and this, with nothing more than defending the settlements and their properties, or in the case of he who does not have such, to fulfill the obligations [of military service].... They end up wasting away completely due to the constant exhaustion, be it of containing the "Indians," be it [helping out] the detachment, or be it in the campaigns.[81]

In the northern region of New Santander, the permanent use of the militias became unsustainable due to the frequency and intensity of the incursions. The New Kingdom of León faced a similar situation. Like Laredo, the settlement of Lampazos was incapable of facing the growing number of raids on its own. It was impossible to surveil the whole territory and at the same time complete the agricultural tasks. Because of this, the governor created a force of twenty-five men who were permanently stationed in Lampazos and whose duty was to patrol the province and prevent the Lipan attacks. This force was integrated by vecinos who were rotated monthly.[82] This was the right measure, given that this force could be combined with the sentries of various settlements and their vecino militias in case of emergency. To solve the problem of how to maintain the permanent militia force,

CHAPTER 3

they turned to what the law had to say: it provided that the defense in the face of the "Indians" was at the expense of the vecinos of the borderland settlements.[83]

In September 1774, the Bourbon authorities ordered the vecinos to take upon themselves the cost of the force; they had to be responsible for paying, arming, and supplying it. In the Bourbon logic, the payments had to be done in accordance with the ability of each vecino to pay. According to the governor, all the vecinos agreed to comply with those orders, but two months later, they had not contributed anything.[84] The governor requested resources from the viceroyalty to set up an official fund for that force, but the answer kept being delayed. In the meantime, the force of twenty-five men was left to its own devices, without resources to pay its own sustenance. In January 1775, the governor requested another meeting with the representatives of all the vecinos to find a solution. He wanted to reach an agreement where the vecinos would in some way take the cost upon themselves, because "it was not fair that the only the poor would bear that weight, which is that of each and every one; they had to lighten it for them, providing money for their subsistence since they take over from them the personal work and risk to which they would be exposed."[85] Thus, the view of the Bourbon authorities in the matter were totally opposite that of the locals.

The northeastern region's vecinos saw the problem differently. They were used to fulfilling their defense obligations by serving in military actions and not by financing a garrison. Such service was not continuous, but rather intermittent and always in cases of emergency. But the attacks became dramatically more frequent, which led them to be more active in the territory's defense. Again, the governor called a new meeting to discuss the issue,[86] where he once more requested resources. In response, the vecinos suggested the creation of more defensive settlements that would act as a barrier. One of them could be set up in Catujanos, a vast plateau close to Lampazos; the other places they suggested were in similar locations. In the vecinos' mind, this was the logical way of pacifying an area since it had been the pattern of colonization and conquest during the two centuries prior to the Spanish presence on the American continent, a vision with roots in the Reconquista that now collided with the Bourbon regime's rationality.[87]

The authorities definitely refused to agree to that plan, arguing that the suggested locations belonged to other people and that reassigning them would cause many problems between the various jurisdictions. The viceroy was strict and said the vecinos had to comply "with the expense they had taken upon themselves by settling down" in the borderlands. The latter, however, still did not pay anything, and the issue came to a dead end.[88] In 1776, the governor tried once more to defend the settlers' point of view, alleging that the provinces had suffered a fever epidemic and therefore were not in a position to pay for a garrison. Again he suggested the creation of a special defense fund that could come from one percent of the income received through other taxes.[89] The viceregal authority rejected the proposition and threatened to force the vecinos to pay for the defense by any means in its power.[90] The warning was categorical: "if you cannot comply with this specific obligation and responsibility that correspond to the land that you own, you should sell it immediately to whomever . . . warning you that, by the very fact of not doing one or the other, they will be taken away from you and allotted to someone else." According to the Crown, even the clergymen had to pay and contribute to the defense.[91] In the end, this kind of administrative imposition did not work, and the authorities understood that they had no other option but to cooperate and use the vecinos' traditional defense structures.

In 1778, the viceroy authorized those borderland communities that contributed with sentries and punitive raids to be exempt from paying for the permanent force. San Miguel de Aguayo and Lampazos were immediately included in this category. In other words, the viceregal authorities consented to the pre-existing military structures.[92] Simultaneously, the Spanish authorities started to promote the traditional annual military parades of July 25, the feast day of Saint James the Apostle, a well-ingrained custom of the region going back to the beginning of its colonization. The governor pointed out that no matter how big the changes in the military organization, they would not suppress this tradition, which had a practical and vital function in the community, and that it was the duty of all the vecinos to participate in it.[93] In this way, the Crown incorporated the structure of political rights and military participation into its institutional efforts to reform the military and to ensure the defense of the northeast.

Even though the interior provinces were administered as if they were a single, homogeneous province, actually there were significant cultural differences between them, which made it difficult to coordinate the defense. This was particularly evident in the case of San Miguel's Tlaxcalan militia, whose members had always performed their defense duties. The governor even referred to that Indigenous militia as "one of the best garrisons that these frontiers count with."[94] But the community had disputes and rivalries with the neighboring settlements, maybe because they had privileges that the majority of the other Indigenous and Spanish groups did not enjoy. Therefore, the governor of the New Kingdom of León had

CHAPTER 3

to hold separate meetings with the Spanish communities and the Tlaxcalans for military issues.[95] Hence the logistics of a coordinated defense plan were complicated, but the authorities had to accept and yield to the local procedures if they wanted to achieve anything.

Another matter the Spanish authorities had to accept was that if they wanted an efficient defense force, it had to be adequately supplied with weapons and provisions, and that rather than imposing that responsibility upon the influential vecinos, the Crown should pick up the cost. This is why the colonial administration started arming the local forces. The governor of the New Kingdom provided the vecinos' militias with two hundred swords, two hundred muskets, and two hundred lances.[96] He also set up a regular supply of subsidized gunpowder.[97] The governor of Nuevo Santander, Lt. Juan Miguel de Zozaya, reasoned likewise, given that there were many vecinos who had no weapons nor horses and were in no position to obtain such things.[98] Therefore, the governor requested muskets and pistols to arm his militias because, even though some settlers had the resources to pay for them, there simply were no weapons available. In addition, they started setting up weapon warehouses in the province for use in the settlements.[99] Finding solutions for the economic needs the vecinos confronted when they were performing their military duties was a pressing matter, so the governor of Nuevo Santander offered that each militiaman should receive four reales for each day of military service. This measure proved useful to the defense by lessening the needs of the families of the men involved, and so did paying for weapons, horses, and provisions.[100] In the end, the governor authorized the area's vecinos to go out and gather wild horses to sell them and be able to buy armament.[101] Thanks to all these measures, the Crown was incorporating the local traditions where a person of resources would take upon himself the political command of the area thanks to his skill for organizing and upholding its defense. Now, instead of powerful individuals, the colonial administration took upon itself the obligation of arming and sustaining the vecinos' militias through some form of institutional paternalism, an important precedent for the development of the modern state in Mexico after independence.

Due to the limitations of the defensive apparatus based on militias of vecinos, the reorganization of the regular units in the northeast became a pressing matter because of the growing pillages. A quick look at a map of the course taken by the raids clearly reveals the relevance of Laredo and Lampazos in the defense of the communications between the interior provinces in the northeast. Already in 1782, the militia garrison stationed in Lampazos had been converted into a permanent unit of the Spanish army, and the number of its soldiers rose from 25 men to 116.[102] The same thing happened in Laredo, where the regular unit reached 50 members and two years later it had grown to 100.[103] As for the presidio of San Antonio, its troops also grew; the garrison went from 21 to 118 soldiers.[104]

Although the permanent army unit was paid with resources from the Crown, its troops were recruited from among the region's settlers because, for the colonial authorities, their incorporation was simpler than that of men foreign to the area, and what is more, the locals had the necessary experience to find the Indigenous rivals. In combat, nothing unites more than common experience; by recruiting locally, the local interests found affirmation through the inhabitants' common defense, which would have long-term political consequences. Local recruitment was the main characteristic of those militias, more than that they supposedly were regular troops. This definition was only true on paper, and as far as the mentality was concerned, it did not make those troops loyal to the colony's central political power. They were not subjected to formal military training, or at least not in accordance with the norms current in eighteenth-century Europe. The warfare skills of those soldiers—being able to ride on horseback, use weapons, and survive in a tough environment of extreme climates—were skills that most of the region's vecinos possessed and the officers lacked, even though they were professionals coming from the mother country or the city of Mexico.

In this context, the arrival of inexperienced officers lacking all knowledge of the local ways of life and combat caused problems and conflicts between the men of the presidios and the recently arrived officers. The Bourbon authorities showed their preoccupation with the way the officers of the region interacted with the soldiers. An administrator even came to write a series of instructions about what the protocol should be: "the subordinates [local officers] should not be allowed to socialize with the presidios' soldiers ... but rather they should make themselves be obeyed and respected as such officers; and they and the soldiers should not call one another 'buddies'; rather the way of addressing one another must be sir and soldier; neither should they eat, drink, or play together."[105] Such a rational but aristocratic concept of the officer did not get along well with the customs of the rough borderland inhabitants. These ordinances even forbade presidios' soldiers from settling down as vecinos in the areas they served. The military authorities referred to the local officers of Nuevo Santander as "useless, ignorant, and extremely prejudiced,"[106] and put into effect physical punishments such as the "ramrod runs," that is, having an individual walk between two lines of men while they hit him on the back.[107]

CHAPTER 3

According to the European precepts of social order, the troops should have been organized within the framework of strict discipline so that the soldiers could be directed like robots on the battlefield. The officers would behave in accordance with their social status; coming from the elite, like the nobility or bourgeoisie, they were expected to maintain a certain distance when interacting with the troops. In essence, they were officers and gentlemen. But the reality of the borderlands was distant from the wishes of the General Staff; what the officers considered inappropriate were traits in the frontier culture that had been accepted for the past two or three centuries. The way the northeasterners behaved would have been acceptable in any European army of the sixteenth century but not of the eighteenth. In other words, compliance with the social behavior expected by the civil and military administrators in Mexico and Madrid was impossible in the borderlands. The same thing happened with regard to the combat deployments: A military engineer who was visiting Texas around that time said that the local soldiers were lacking military training, the officers were not used to giving orders, and in combat there was no formation, which led to a chaotic exchange with the enemy.[108] Obviously, there was a different evolution when deploying. On eighteenth-century European battlefields, the combats were bloody, and, on a large scale, the opponents would fight under the implicit rule established by the Prussians that the maneuvers had to be planned ahead and precise. This implied a prior understanding that both armies had accepted the Prussian rule. To accomplish the Prussian level of precision, the European armies had undergone a long transformation over a century, a process that had been absent in the warfare needs of the northeastern frontier since the Indigenous forces were not going to respect and incorporate the Prussian combat rules.

The raid-based warfare experienced by the borderland inhabitants was less direct and on a much smaller scale than the European conflicts. Frontier forces fought well if one considers that their tactics responded to the challenges of an irregular conflict. A more balanced view shows a different perspective. According to Alexander von Humboldt, who was familiar with the European wars, the presidios' troops were:

> exposed to continuous fatigue. All the soldiers are natives of the northern part of the kingdom of Mexico; they are mountain people of tall stature, robust in the extreme, and as accustomed to the ices of winter as to the ardors of the sun in summer. Constantly under arms, they spend their lives riding on horseback, and make marches

of from eight to ten days across desert sands, carrying with them no provisions but corn meal, which they dissolve in water when they find a spring or puddle on their way. Some educated officers have assured me that it would be difficult to find in Europe a troop lighter in its evolutions, more impetuous in combat, or more accustomed to privations than that of the presidios. This cavalry cannot always prevent the incursions of the "Indians," because these are enemies who know how to take advantage with great cunning of the slightest unevenness of the terrain and have been accustomed for centuries to all the tricks of guerrilla warfare.[109]

Humboldt's observations show that the local troops in the north were not at all bad, for they were adapted to the ways of fighting in the region as well as to the environment, and that despite its climatic extremes they could survive in it without diminishing their effectiveness. There was animosity from the European-trained officers, who did not know how to wage war any differently from the way they had been trained. Their aristocratic pride prevented them from seeing the surrounding reality and learning what the locals had learned two centuries before: you fight according to the enemy's skills, or you are lost.

During the 1790s, the Bourbon administration tried harder to impose its concept of discipline on the troops and militias of the northern borderlands, since they perceived that instability in Europe endangered the colonies in America. In this decade, another threat arose: the newly independent British colonies in North America soon began to show an expansionist tendency due to immigration from Europe. With this body of concerns as baggage, Félix María Calleja arrived in the northeast in 1795 as the region's commander. Calleja (1755–1828) was an officer with extensive experience; he was one of the officers who arrived in New Spain with Revillagigedo in 1789. He had begun his military career in the failed expedition to Algeria and had also participated in the siege of Gibraltar (1782) and in Menorca. From 1784 to 1788, he was the studies director at the military college of Puerto de Santa María. In New Spain, he inspected the regular forces and militias in Nayarit and San Luis Potosí during the biennium of 1792–1794.[110] In 1795, he was in charge of supervising the forces of the New Kingdom of León and Nuevo Santander, where he counted a total of 4,500 men.[111] By 1799, he was commanding the tenth brigade of San Luis Potosí, which he led in several actions in defense of the northeast, including Texas.

CHAPTER 3

Calleja was a living example of the way of thinking and acting and of the peninsular officialdom's priorities in the late eighteenth and early nineteenth centuries. He had fought on several occasions against the English, so he was more concerned with organizing defenses against Spain's imperial rivals than with Indigenous raids in the region. For the latter, which he could not completely ignore, he suggested a more aggressive policy, always on the offensive, and suspending the ridiculous and ineffective policy of buying peace through gifts and payments to the hostile tribes. It was the way European absolute monarchies acted to resolve their internal affairs: the prompt and total elimination of any opposition, something difficult to achieve in the borderland context. Calleja thought that the defense of the northeast by the local vecinos had been performed "with little method."[112] He went so far as to describe the northern provinces' inhabitants as "cowards by nature and customs and out of selfishness and relaxation they ignore that they have a homeland."[113] Finally, Calleja pointed out that "only armed and united will [the vecinos] be able to defend themselves from the many enemies, interior and exterior, that harass and threaten them, notwithstanding they do not foresee those that may come to them from the coast [the English], more fearsome thanks to their discipline, enterprises, and ideas."[114] Calleja, a product of the European military academies of the eighteenth century, despised the organization of the northeast's local defense even though its inhabitants had remained in a constant state of war for the past two hundred years under ideas and concepts that came from much further back. This was more than just a disagreement between the European military elite and the local traditions: It was a clash between Bourbon modernism and frontier medievalism.

Calleja's antipathy toward the northeastern military organization was most evident when he supervised the garrisons at Laredo and Lampazos. He found the force stationed at Laredo reasonably well organized but described the troops' instruction as unmethodical and slow in orderly evolutions. He recommended that they learn battle formations. According to Calleja, Major Ramón Díaz de Bustamante was industrious, brave, and fair but had "little talent and instruction."[115] In contrast, the Lampazos company's evaluation was that it was a complete disaster. Calleja found the garrison's finances in large deficit due to poor administration. To make matters worse, the troop was "badly dressed, lacking uniformity, and with very few minor garments, it has no instruction, nor discipline"[116]; "they look like a company of comedians"[117]; the "sergeants, corporals, and soldiers ignore most of their duties and fulfill with slovenliness the small one they have"[118]; the subordination of the soldiers to the officers "is the effect of pusillanimity."[119] Calleja blamed the governor of the New Kingdom of León for the lack of concern for the Lampazos garrison, even prosecuting his lieutenant, Juan Ignacio Ramón, for alleged abuse of power, immorality, and corruption. Calleja's attitude demonstrated that his views of military discipline were completely opposed to those of the northeastern military. The behaviors he criticized were in reality the product of values and attitudes enduring from another era that he neither understood nor cared to understand.

Calleja's displeasure with Juan Ignacio Ramón perfectly represents the clash of values between the centralized administration and the local elites. Juan Ignacio belonged to the family of regional notables, the Ramóns, who had settled in the northeast in the seventeenth century. His great-grandfather, Diego Ramón, had accompanied Alonso de León in the first entries into the territory. Juan Ignacio's grandfather, Domingo Ramón, founded the first settlements in Texas between 1717 and 1719. His father had been an ensign in the presidio of San Antonio, and Juan Ignacio had served in different garrisons and participated in the expedition of Teodoro de Croix in 1777. His military experience was ample because despite his age, he had participated in many battles against Apaches, so his knowledge of borderland military affairs could not be doubted. In spite of—or maybe because of—all this, Calleja, who had arrived without knowing the peculiarities of the region, formed a negative opinion of the officer. He described him as "little applied, ignorant of any other service than that of following the 'Indians.'"[120]

Since his arrival on the American continent, Félix María Calleja showed an inexplicable disdain toward the local officers.[121] Those of Lampazos were no exception, as he said that "the officers [of Lampazos] ignore most of their obligation."[122] In the end, the trial against Juan Ignacio found him innocent of the charges brought by Calleja. All of Calleja's negative opinions about the northeastern officers make it clear that for this representative of the colony's central authority, there was only one priority: the imperial enemies of Spain. Like his superiors, Calleja attended more to a latent threat than to the real threat posed by Native incursions. This dissent over defensive dispositions was of great importance to the local elites, for it would translate into the conviction—which would transcend the times—that any central authority tended to ignore local interests and defense needs.

Félix Calleja was not entirely wrong in believing that external powers were a risk to Spanish permanence in the northeast. In 1783, the English colonies in North America achieved independence from England, becoming a new player that immediately entered the game of territorial expansion in the hemisphere. In 1800, viceregal authorities learned that the North American adventurer Philip Nolan was planning an invasion of Texas. The northeastern military units mobilized, including Calleja's Tenth Brigade, and in March 1801 entered Nolan's camp near Nacogdoches in Texas. The tiny invading troop of twenty-eight men was destroyed, but the event reinforced the conviction of the danger of invasion. The worries of the Spanish authorities grew when, surprisingly and through secret negotiations, Napoleonic France sold the province of Louisiana to the United States in 1803. The Spanish considered Louisiana to be an area of territorial security between New Spain and the nascent United States. The sale came as a surprise to the colonial authorities when the boundaries between Louisiana and Texas were not clearly defined.[123] This inevitably led to an increase in military forces in the region.

Military reorganization thus became a matter of extreme importance for Spanish security in the area. In 1806, the authorities organized a force of seven hundred men recruited from the towns of the New Kingdom of León and Nuevo Santander.[124] They also mobilized units from Coahuila, as well as fifty men from the Lampazos company, including Juan Ignacio Ramón. By 1810 in Texas, there was a combined force of 1,103 men, of which 293 were from the New Kingdom of León and 373 from Nuevo Santander. In San Antonio alone, there were 718 men between soldiers and militiamen.[125] These troops were organized to prevent an invasion and not to fight the region's Natives.

The number and objectives of this force were something never before seen in these borderlands: its assembling had been done by forced conscription and not as volunteer militia. The wives of many of these new soldiers complained for months and years that they had no way to support themselves since the army never paid them their husbands' salaries. Most of the draftees were poor and viewed such prolonged military service with animosity.[126] There are some records of payments, but the soldiers were irregularly paid. Calleja, who administered this force, called this information exaggerated.[127] But exaggerated or not, it was a fact that this was not the traditional military service to which the settlers were accustomed. For the first time, the northeastern vecinos were involved in an imperial conflict that they did not feel was their own business. Despite the scarcity of resources, the military authorities planned to expand this military structure. In 1809, the military commanders and governors of Texas, Coahuila, and the New Kingdom of León held a meeting in San Antonio. Their objective was to agree on a defense plan for the northeast in case of an invasion, and when laying it out, they requested more infantry and artillery troops. They saw in Lampazos a recruiting vein and demanded that it become a military canton of 825 infantrymen and 500 cavalry soldiers.[128] The plan never materialized because in September 1810, the independence movement broke out in Dolores, which would immediately change priorities.

THE CATACLYSM OF THE WAR OF INDEPENDENCE

The War of Independence of Mexico began as a social outburst in the Bajío region in September 1810 due to the confluence of several factors: an economic crisis, resentment toward the reformist measures of the Bourbon regime, and a power vacuum caused by the *vacatio regis* provoked by Napoleon when he deposed the Spanish monarch, Ferdinand VII. The movement initiated by Hidalgo was a social uprising and would lead to restoration movements when the privileged classes took matters into their own hands and reacted against the ideas of the French Revolution promoted by Napoleon. The effects of the independence movement were soon felt in New Spain's northeast. The military commander, Félix María Calleja, who went from being the organizer of the borderland imperial defenses to being required by the viceregal authorities for other tasks, soon found himself fighting the insurrection in the center of the viceroyalty. On September 22, he asked the governors of the New Kingdom and Nuevo Santander to gather their provinces' regular army units and militias and send them to reinforce the royalist army. While Calleja was waiting for these troops, the independence forces were advancing from San Luis Potosí toward the interior provinces. The governor of the New Kingdom of León, Manuel de Santa María, was unable to obtain even half of the 250 militiamen required, and of the regular force of Lampazos, theoretically composed of 100 men, there were only 23 ready to march to Calleja's aid; even worse, they were poorly armed and without resources. In Nuevo Santander, Governor Manuel de Iturbe was more fortunate as he obtained 250 men, between regulars and auxiliaries, although also in terrible condition and poorly armed. The Nuevo Santander forces marched on October 21, but they stopped in Tula, in the limits of the province of San Luis, where many deserted. Those of the New Kingdom would not march until November 11.[129]

Consequently, by November 20 the important plaza of San Luis had fallen into rebel hands. It was the richest city in the region. The military budgets of the provinces of the New Kingdom, Nuevo Santander, and Texas depended heavily on San Luis, and therefore their military capabilities were affected by the loss of that city to the insurgents. At the end of November, relief forces sent from the northeast returned to their home provinces. While this turmoil was ongoing, inaction, poor communication, and lack of coordination damaged the royalist

CHAPTER 3

cause. Once again, Calleja ordered the various governors of the region to gather troops in Coahuila, Nuevo Santander, and the New Kingdom of León. There were many rumors and misinformation; there was no certainty of anything other than the invitation of the insurgent forces in San Luis to join their cause. Capt. Juan Ignacio Ramón, commander of the Lampazos garrison, is an example of a figure who joined the insurgent cause thanks to the chaos in the royalist ranks. Toward the end of December, the insurgents calmly entered Coahuila and the New Kingdom of León, and at the beginning of January they took the capitals of Saltillo and Monterrey. They took these cities without firing a shot because the movement caused many royalists to desert and join them.[130] The same thing happened in Texas. On January 22, the mayor of San Antonio, Francisco Travieso, together with Capt. Juan Bautista Casas and Ens. Vicente Flores, organized a coup to overthrow the royalists. They convinced the troops stationed in San Antonio to join them, and they imprisoned the military commander and governor, José Manuel Herrera.[131]

Soon, though, the balance in the conflict began to shift. The rebel army suffered important defeats at the hands of Calleja in the center of New Spain, and the remnants of the insurgent force tried to retreat north but were doggedly pursued. On March 1, a counterrevolutionary council organized by some neighbors took control of San Antonio. The same happened in the New Kingdom of León and Nuevo Santander. By the end of March, the northeast was again in royalist hands.[132] During the summer of 1812, however, Texas would again suffer a rebel invasion led by the insurgent Bernardo Gutiérrez de Lara. Because his army also included Anglo-American militias, he had the support of the United States government. In April 1813, they took San Antonio, and things became more radical, as Gutiérrez de Lara's forces literally lynched the governor of Texas, Manuel Salcedo, as well as the former governor Herrera and fifteen other officers.[133]

The royalist reaction would be just as bloodthirsty. Joaquín de Arredondo*, a Spanish officer stationed in Veracruz and a friend of Calleja, was the man chosen to deal with the Texan rebellion. In June, he arrived in Laredo and dedicated himself to accumulating reinforcements. Meanwhile, Gutiérrez de Lara faced serious problems in maintaining the leadership of the insurrection. He was deposed by José Álvarez de Toledo, who had the support of the Anglo faction. On August

---

* We will discuss Joaquín de Arredondo in more detail further down in this chapter.

18, the royalist Arredondo faced the Texan rebels in the battle of Medina, on the outskirts of San Antonio. The rebel forces had about 1,400 men, while Arredondo had about 1,800. Arredondo's plan was to lure the rebel army into an ambush. The royalist commander let one of his cavalry units approach the insurgent force and call their attention with gunfire, then pretend to flee. The insurgent force took the bait and went into the place chosen by Arredondo to give the death blow. There the royalist artillery pounded the insurgent positions while Arrendondo's infantry hit the center of the rebel army's line with lively musket fire and a series of movements clearly of Prussian style. Finally, when the insurgents dispersed, Arredondo's cavalry took pleasure in sabering them. This was probably the first battle with modern European features in the history of the northeast. Not even the presidios'"regular" soldiers were familiar with fighting in this manner. From their skirmishes with the Native Americans, the local inhabitants were accustomed to hit-and-run raids. Arredondo deployed his infantry, cavalry, and artillery forces with great efficiency; in his war report, he would report that when he took the field, he counted close to a thousand rebel corpses fallen in battle. After the encounter, Arredondo stopped behaving as a soldier to move on to the nefarious political tasks of retaliation to set an example. He executed 122 prisoners and then ordered his cavalry to pursue the rebels who were trying to flee to Louisiana, causing 24 casualties.[134] After his victory, Arredondo became the de facto governor of the provinces of Texas, Coahuila, Nuevo Santander, and the New Kingdom of León.

Joaquín de Arredondo remained the absolute sovereign of the eastern interior provinces from 1813 to 1821, during which time he ruled with a ruthless but effective style, so much so that some historians have categorized him, in an ironic tone, as one of the two viceroys in New Spain.[135] Arredondo was a professional army officer whose career had begun in 1787 when he joined the Royal Guards. He fought against the French army in the Rousillon War in 1793 and against Portugal in 1802. He was later transferred to the American continent, where he was promoted to colonel and commanded the Veracruz Line Battalion in 1810.[136] After crushing the rebellion in Texas, he implemented a series of draconian measures in the region, such as prohibiting the carrying any type of weapon, an act that, in an area that was permanently threatened by Indigenous attacks, was a death sentence. He also prohibited talk of revolution and established the forced recruitment of the population.[137] Arredondo represented the apogee of the reforms of the Bourbon military policies that had been initiated by the Bourbons and that Calleja had tried to impose in the northeast beginning in 1795. The changes

Arredondo sponsored were those devised by Calleja: to organize the defense against a possible invasion from England or the United States and to downplay the importance of the Indigenous incursions. In contrast to his predecessors, Arredondo was the first strong figure to concentrate all the power in the region. In a certain way, he was a prelude to Santiago Vidaurri, although the latter, being in the liberal republic, would base his power on the population's consensus and constantly resort to elections.[138]

The polarization of the local elites was a consequence of Arredondo's arrival, a process that had begun with Calleja's arrival in the region in the 1790s. An example of this was Juan Ignacio Ramón, commander of the Lampazos garrison and veteran of the Indigenous wars in Coahuila and Texas. At the beginning of the insurrection, Ramón was in charge of preparing the defenses of the New Kingdom against the rebel forces, but soon he changed sides when some of the leaders of the insurgent movement communicated with him. Ramón was eventually captured by the royalists and executed. He was one of the few officers of the northeast who changed sides and was not pardoned, perhaps to set an example. This is a typical case of how the independence movement affected the local elites and the positions of military and political leadership in the region. The extreme cruelty is evident: Juan Ignacio Ramón's properties were confiscated and publicly auctioned. Evidence of the elite's polarization is that one of the bidders to acquire Ramón's properties was Juan de Zuazua, father of the future liberal general Juan Zuazua, Vidaurri's ally.[139] The old Zuazua had a privileged position in the regional elite, particularly in Lampazos, because he was in charge of the monopoly of tobacco, games, and stamps, besides being the postmaster.[140] He was against the independence movement and denounced any presumed insurgent to the authorities. Old Zuazua was a person of political influence and a member of the local militia of Lampazos, one of the town's best armed vecinos.[141] Zuazua perfectly represented the integration of the political and military dimensions, a pattern that began then and that would characterize the regional political development practically until the failure of Maximilian's empire in the 1860s.

Another regional figure, Andres de Sobrevilla, exemplifies a pattern similar to that of Zuazua Sr. Born and raised in Lampazos, when he was of age he joined the town's garrison under the command of Juan Ignacio Ramón and deserted with his chief to the insurgent side. Sobrevilla, however, had doubts and rejoined the royalist forces in Laredo. He would later assume command of the Lampazos company and was a distinguished leader of the Lampazos community during the nineteenth century.[142] As can be seen, the War of Independence altered the local leaderships, displacing some of the old elites with new characters. In other cases, the same people remained in their privileged positions. The old order, which consisted of individuals with resources and power dominating the political and military positions in local leadership, would prevail.

Not only would the local elites be affected by the War of Independence, but the role of the communities would also oscillate according to the particular circumstances of each collective.[143] The Tlaxcalans of San Miguel de Aguayo, for example, responded by giving their full support to the royalist authorities. It was one of the few communities that mobilized quickly in 1810 and gathered a force of forty-three volunteers.[144] Even during the brief hour of revolutionary fervor, the Tlaxcalans refused to join the rebels. Something similar happened in Laredo, where the regular garrison remained loyal to the royalists, as did the rest of its population.[145] The military commander of Laredo, Ramón Díaz de Bustamante, assumed a leading role in the operations against the insurgents in the region.[146] In Lampazos, things were no different. While it is true that many of the military personnel stationed there momentarily embraced the independence movement, most of the garrison was far away from Lampazos at the time of the insurgency's arrival in the region. In addition, the civilian population stayed away from incitement to join the emancipation movement. The majority of the population had no direct involvement in the movement. In San Antonio, in contrast, things were very different and reached extreme violence. The participation of Anglo-American mercenaries escalated the situation to the point of executing the governor and several royalist officers. Arredondo's reaction was equally brutal. In short, there was division in the northeastern region; not everyone supported independence, and there were changes of opinion and shifts of sides depending on the circumstances. In general, the reactions of the local populations were pragmatic and always in accordance with their immediate needs. Even so, these comings and goings activated changes in the region. The arrival of Arredondo would notably accelerate the enforcement of what the Bourbons had been trying to implement since 1790 in the northeastern territory.

What Arredondo actually changed was the nature and orientation of the local militias. As we have already mentioned, these had a long tradition of rational preparation for the armed conflicts with Natives. Since the end of the eighteenth century, as noted above, the Bourbons had tried to transform them into a force able to face an invasion. The independence movement, however, came to complicate the choice between internal and external warfare since it posed a serious threat to the colonial administration, especially in the first months of its development. Consequently, the dilemma was dissolved, and the civil and military administration was faced with the problem of organizing the militias and preparing them simultaneously for internal and external threats. The authorities thus devised the creation of Urban Patriots companies.[147] In 1815, the community of San Miguel de Aguayo was asked to organize an urban sapper company of sixty men.[148] They were supposed to be an auxiliary force, although very different from the traditional militias. The sapper units acted more as manpower for the army engineers, although this did not exclude their use in combat in exceptional cases. Arredondo had little esteem for the Tlaxcalans' military skills, perhaps because they were Indigenous and army officers had always felt contempt for this type of unit or because he did not consider their previous military experience in the wars against Apaches to be useful. Whatever the case, the best and most effective troops of the previous years were left aside.[149] Another novelty Arredondo introduced was the pyramidal structure of the military command, which granted it the power to dispose of these forces at will. The volunteers signed an enlistment contract "to serve as soldiers for ten years."[150] At the moment of signing, they were made aware of "the penalties for lack of subordination and respect for their superiors, being warned that no apology will serve as justification."[151] The new command structure radically changed the patterns of behavior and local military relations. The region's inhabitants found themselves abruptly submerged in the dynamics of the absolute monarchy of the mother country, according to which the Crown authorities could use the local militias as an available resource for external conflicts or internal uprisings.

The military system imposed by Arredondo tried to use the old structures of military service. The authorities continued to use the concept of borderland vecino, which, according to tradition, obliged settlers to defend their lands, an inheritance from the Middle Ages. While the inhabitants understood this obligation as synonymous with fighting the Native Americans, the authorities used it to strengthen the regular forces. Consequently, there were many misunderstandings and problems. In 1819 in Lampazos, the military commander ordered the playing of *generala*, a military melody that called for a general meeting. To the officer's surprise, no one showed up because no one in the town had ever heard this type of tune or had any idea what it meant. In a fit of anger, the commander, arrogant and ignorant, threatened them with the death penalty if they again refused to give military service.[152] Clearly, the local and external traditions of armed service caused confusion. The harsh military discipline imposed by the commander in office attributed the action to cowardice when, in reality, it was a lack of training in the new ways of conducting military affairs.

One of the harshest impositions was the blood quota in the form of forced levies among the settlers. The levy was rejected and was difficult to enforce because the people enlisted in this way were used as cannon fodder in the regular army. This was the case of Cándido Sánchez, a native of San Antonio who was assigned to the second company of the Veracruz Line Regiment, Arredondo's most important unit, but deserted immediately after being recruited.[153]

Arredondo's changes had serious consequences for the subsistence of the population because there was simply a shortage of labor for agricultural work. In San Antonio, a company of eighty to two hundred men was ordered to be formed, which affected the productive cycle of the fields in the region, ruining ranchers and workers.[154] The commander in charge tried to levy economic exactions to sustain the army, but, given the disastrous economic situation, it proved impossible to collect them.[155] This particular measure was so drastic that it depleted local resources.[156] In some cases, the troops looted whatever they could find of livestock and seeds.[157] The situation became so desperate that at one point the army allowed some of its militia troops to return temporarily to work on the ranches with the obligation to return later to their units.[158] The population asked, unsuccessfully, for the abolition of military service under such conditions. The situation in San Antonio shows how the changes imposed by Arredondo affected the local population without resolving the main military concern of the vecinos: the eternal conflict with the Indigenous peoples.

As a consequence of the defenselessness in which the residents of the northeastern towns were left, Apache and Comanche attacks became more and more frequent.[159] The few troops who were supposed to help contain them had no resources, ammunition, or horses and, according to one witness, were in rags.[160] As a result, some residents began to abandon the northeastern settlements because of the dangers posed by Arredondo's military changes. Some reports indicated that up to two-thirds of the settlers left Texas.[161] Nevertheless, the remaining settlers organized themselves as best they could and continued to defend their properties.[162] Thus the organization of local defense according to traditional ways persisted throughout this difficult and painful decade.

The second half of the eighteenth century and the first two decades of the nineteenth century brought important changes for the inhabitants of the northeastern borderlands. The Bourbons imposed a new administrative model in the American colonies, which implied the imposition of a centralized state aimed at making tax collection, censuses, and military service more efficient. Although this model began during the sixteenth century in Spain and in the large urban centers of the Americas, the population of the peripheral northern areas was accustomed to greater autonomy. This autonomy was, in part, a product of the persistence of certain medieval traditions that had been the mainstay of the Hispanic presence in the region since the sixteenth century. It is unsurprising, therefore, that the two forms of administration came into conflict. In essence, they represented two differing thought systems: the Spanish preconquest traditions, which persisted, and the new administration, which enjoyed a more "refined" character. In addition, the region began to have strategic importance in the expansionist geopolitics of Great Britain, France, and, soon after, the United States, and this was in addition to a tremendous migratory and expansive wave of warlike Indigenous groups such as Comanches and Apaches, who became more powerful than any European power in the area. It was to be expected, given the above, that local traditions of military organization would be strongly affected. Eventually, the Bourbon authorities realized that they needed these traditions and leadership to exert any control over the region. Perhaps the most significant change in this whole process was the generation of a sense of regionalism that went beyond the communities' localism, but the changes were limited. The different threats ended up strengthening the local values, and the persistence of certain conditions made the traditional system grow stronger and demonstrated the limitations of the state's ability to assert its authority. This period marked the beginning of the emergence of regional opposition to military administrative changes from the center. The issue became a problem that would grow throughout the first half of the nineteenth century, except that now, instead of confronting an absolute monarchy, the local traditions of military organization would declare war on the republican administration of a new nation that would bring further changes and challenges to the warfare medievalism of the inhabitants of the northeastern borderlands.

CHAPTER 4

The Era of Nationalism

After three hundred years, New Spain ceased to be a Spanish colony and became an independent state. It abruptly became a nation occupied with complex organizational problems, such as devising a novel regime with forms of political participation, definitions of citizenship, and an administrative organization in which the inhabitants and their leaders lacked experience. After the brief and unsuccessful experiment of a constitutional monarchy, that of Agustín I, the newly independent country adopted the republican regime in a constitution of 1824, extremely decentralized and contradictory in many of its precepts (for example, freedom of thought but with a single religion). When the constitution's authors wrote it down, the echoes of the French Revolution were resounding in their heads, which is why they paired federalism with the power of the states to constitute their militias, following the example of the French Garde Nationale. In principle, these state armies could be called into service outside their states under national command, but this required the explicit permission of Congress. For that matter, the army thus integrated would be known as the Milicia Nacional (National Militia) and later as the Milicia Cívica (Civic Militia). In theory, it would be a national force of citizens in accordance with the French ideal.

THE FIRST REPUBLICAN STAGE

The origins of nineteenth-century republicanism in Mexico lie in earlier political experiments of the Spanish empire, which culminated in the Cadiz Constitution of 1812. This constitution would not have been possible without the invasion of Spain by the Napoleonic army in 1809. When Napoleon overthrew the Bourbons, it created in the minds of most Spaniards (except for the Frenchified minority)

CHAPTER 4

that there was a power vacuum, a vacatio regis to say it in the Latin of the time. The effects of this vacuum have already been studied in detail by other authors,[1] but it is worth highlighting two central aspects: First, the juntas were immediately called upon to assume sovereign authority under the assumption that in the absence of the king, the sovereignty that the subjects had given him returned to them; and second, that the opposition to the French was translated into an attempt to transform the absolute monarchy into a constitutional one, taking advantage of the opportunity that the political moment of Spain offered. Hence, the Constitution of Cadiz, which, although it was in force only for a short time and with lapses, was the first constitution to take effect in the Spanish Americas. And those moments of being in force were enough to introduce great and transcendent institutional novelties in the colony. This effect was notable in generalizing the ayuntamientos (town councils) to practically all the townships and converting the subject into a resident-citizen.*

It is worth mentioning a third great novelty about citizenship (although different from the current one, given that it was defined on the basis of vecindad)—perhaps the most relevant one since it would pave the way for the subsequent arrival of the republic after the consummation of the independence of the colonies—and that is the elections of representatives, first the deputies to the constituent Congress of Cadiz and then to the ordinary courts that emanated from it. The convening of courts was indeed the expression of an old tradition dating back to the kingdoms before Habsburg Spain, which had assemblies in front of the royal power. In the case of the Congress of Cadiz, however, modern novelties were at play since the integration of political representation was not stratified, as had been the medieval custom. Instead, it was carried out through practically universal male suffrage. Even if its creators had intended to exclude the castas in the American lands, this was not obeyed, and whoever wanted to vote did so thanks to a liberal interpretation of the electoral rules by the polling places dominated by the criollos. A broad representation was in the latter's interest since a political dispute existed between them and the Spaniards by then. Taking advantage of the Bourbon reforms and desire to control, Spaniards had held in check the most important political posts in the colonies, particularly New Spain,

---

* The Cadiz constitution made the ayuntamientos autonomous. The charges were elective and made possible the political participation of broader sectors of the population.

the most prominent and important part of the overseas territories. Thus, in a brief period, the Americans found themselves with a treasure of political and institutional novelties that opened previously unimagined paths. The Cadiz Constitution brought to the American lands not only the extension of the town council and universal male suffrage but also the concept of citizenship, the control of political power through its division into three branches (a legislative one—the courts (las cortes)—the king as head of the executive, and a judiciary one independent of the executive), and some developing rights such as freedom of the press (although limited, since it was conditioned on the preservation of the Catholic religion, the protection of public morals, and the integrity of the reputation of third parties). Another crucial institutional contribution was the provincial deputations, which proliferated throughout New Spain within a few years. They were elected bodies that did not have legislative functions but had administrative ones, mainly related to public works. Despite the limitations, the provincial deputations contributed to the downward extension of the frequent voting practice and the custom of having some type of representation taking roots in the regions, which would later form the states of the republic.[2]

A matter that remained unresolved in the Cadiz Constitution was parity in representation between the mother country and the colonies for the integration of the ordinary courts, despite the fight that the American deputies, led by the northeasterner Miguel Ramos Arizpe of New Spain, put up in the constituent assembly. Compared to the metropolitan provincial deputations, the Hispano-Americans were underrepresented in the constituent and the ordinary courts. What would have happened if equal representation had been accepted according to the number of inhabitants? Would the empire have been dissolved anyway? But whatever might have happened, the fact remains that the few Americans who attended both the constituent and the subsequent ordinary courts would acquire sufficient experience to initiate the parliamentary lives of the nascent American republics. At least in what became Mexico, there were prominent veterans of the Spanish courts maneuvering and achieving compromises so that the inherited political unity would not be dissolved by the onslaught of a growing sovereignty of the regional proto-states, whose elites were rushing to write local constitutions before the Mexican constitution of 1824 bore fruit. Ramos Arizpe stood out in this work by pushing for the approval of a prior act on what the constitution would contain to guarantee broad political autonomy to the regions and their notables in the form of the first Mexican federalism.

CHAPTER 4

Barely a decade before the culminating moment of the constitution of 1824, the political situation in Spain and the colonies had become excessively fluid; too many contradictory events converged to create an atmosphere favorable to independence by the beginning of 1821. The war in Spain became too onerous for Napoleon, who was pressed by offensives in the rest of Europe. Forced to withdraw his forces precariously spread throughout the peninsula, Napoleon signed a treaty with Ferdinand VII, returning to him the crown that, for a short time and with much labor, had been held over his head by Joseph, his brother. Suddenly, El Deseado* (The Desired One) was back, and, whimsical and erratic as he was, he soon found it difficult to cope with the limiting institutional burden developed by the constituents of Cadiz and embodied in the constitution. Hence as soon as he set foot in the palace, he began to conspire against it to restore the absolutism he felt more comfortable with. He dissolved the courts in 1814 and declared the Cadiz Constitution nonexistent. But Col. Rafael de Riego would restore it: he rebelled in 1820 amid the revolutionary wave that shook all of Europe, forcing the reluctant Ferdinand to become a constitutional monarch once again. After the coup, the Liberal Triennium began. Still, so many ups and downs would discredit the metropolitan institutional framework in the colonies, and not even the government of the Liberal Triennium would be able to prevent their emancipation. Thus, in the midst of pronouncements, shouts of gathering, and punctilious manifestos, the first half of the 1820s would see in rapid succession the independence of the colonies and the emergence of new countries through revolutions led primarily by criollo militia chiefs who had previously supported the royalist cause. In February 1821, a royalist officer, Agustín de Iturbide, proclaimed an independence plan for New Spain known as the Plan de Iguala (Plan of Iguala). With its subsequent additions to the treaties of Cordoba, it was instrumental, as one would say nowadays, to the transition from colonial status to that of a new state for which the constitutional monarchical formula was proposed. Consequently, the Constitution of Cadiz was declared in force insofar as it did not oppose the latest state of affairs, that is, independence. Its use would be prolonged until Mexico could write its own constitution. Iturbide quickly gained powerful support, and on August 24, 1821, the last viceroy, Juan O'Donoju, recognized Mexico's independence by signing the treaties of Cordoba, which Madrid would not recognize.³

---

* Fernando VII

The plan and treaties foresaw the surrender of the Mexican throne to Ferdinand VII or any of his relatives, which was rejected. The reason why—and following the line of argument of those founding documents—a criollo dynasty would have to be improvised, and Iturbide was in the front of the line to try to do it. For the time being, Iturbide would head a provisional government as regent. From this position, Iturbide attempted to reorganize the army and the treasury with new tax burdens and strengthen the government against the powerful elites of the provinces. Notwithstanding the proclamation as emperor by the military on May 18, those actions would alienate him from the deputies of the First Constituent Congress, who, after all, represented the regional and local notables. Among other measures, it proposed to limit the functions of the provincial deputations, which opposed the new taxes. The congress never got down to work on the new constitution—which would have given an institutional framework to Iturbide's moderate monarchy—but rather dedicated its time to discussing ordinary legislation, debating inanities, and providing shelter to the conspiracies of the republicans, who were not many among the deputies but were very effective as propagandists. Tired of the delays and parliamentary conspiracies, Iturbide dissolved the congress in October 1822. By February 1823, the emperor had lost the support of a large part of the army, which soon, anticipating a coup, proclaimed the Plan de Casa Mata (Casa Mata Plan) that called for a constituent congress and put an end to the monarchic option as a form of government.[4]

With the end of Iturbide's reign and no political system or constitution in place, there was a danger of fragmentation among the former provinces and the now sovereign territories. The autonomist euphoria led to an extremely federal constitution. In January 1824, the constituent congress published the new constitution after no small amount of work. Much more decentralized than the U.S. federal system, Mexican federalism looked more like a confederacy, granting extensive powers to the states and few to the federation. This would lead to the central government's political and financial crisis, marked by the indiscipline of the political class, which soon polarized into the Scottish (conservative) and York (liberal) groups, according to the lodges to which these political factions belonged. The federal government became subject to the whims of the states insofar as it was fiscally dependent on them. This was because of the federal contribution to which the states were supposedly bound by the constitution, an obligation they did not always fulfill. The federation was also limited in federal matters in the sense that, as with the taxes, it depended on the "blood quota," that is, on the contribution of conscripts by the states in the measure of their population. In other words, the sacred constitutional text had enshrined a weak national government with no real income to pay for its debts or an effective military defense. This had disastrous consequences since it established a national government that sought loans that were granted on unfair terms and kept it in chronic debt. By 1831, Mexico had a debt of thirty million pesos, representing three times the federation's annual income and 10 percent of the gross domestic product. In 1832, the government had to declare a moratorium on payments, which further limited its already reduced capacity to manage the nation. In addition, the national economy was also in crisis, as the once-thriving mining industry was virtually destroyed during the War of Independence and had yet to recover. The agricultural sector was profitable, but poor communications limited the access of products to the market. The federal government had to absorb more debt, with interest rates reaching 300 percent annually.[5] What is more, an army took a large share of the budget since its chiefs and officers were convinced that they were the guarantee of the country's independence, and Barradas's failed attempt in 1829 to disembark on the Gulf Coast to try to recover the lost colony was proof of this.

The conditions of early Mexican federalism inevitably led to a political crisis. The second president, Vicente Guerrero, resigned due to opposition from some army sectors. The vice president, Anastasio Bustamante, began a series of reforms to strengthen the federal government. One of the main issues was to fix the disorder of the state treasuries, so the federal administration imposed strict supervision and, in some cases, took over their administration. It also tried to improve conditions for the federal military. But just when it seemed that the problems would be solved, even more chaos was generated by the debut of the indispensable Antonio López de Santa Anna, who spoke out against the government and called for a change in the cabinet. The state of Zacatecas, with five other states, led an armed revolt against the federal government, using their state militias. Bustamante used the army to defeat the rebellion, but despite that, the government was already bankrupt, and the military had suffered throughout the decade from a lack of funds, trained officers, and corruption. When Santa Anna was elected president in March 1833, he faced a new coup and spent most of the year leading the armed forces instead of fixing the administration. The first decade of Mexican federalism (1824–1834) was one of serious problems mainly due to the excessive autonomy of the states. It would also transform the country's military organization.[6]

THE ZEITGEIST OF A MARTIAL CITIZENSHIP

The new liberal-republican and federalist order of the first half of the nineteenth century derived much of its ideological background from the Cadiz Constitution of 1812 since it had incorporated, in turn, a good part of the ideological framework that characterized the French Revolution, whose principles eventually transformed the face of absolutist Europe. One of the peculiarities of that revolution was the transformation of French subjects into citizens. And a peculiarity of that citizenship was its component of military service: the militia citizen, the Cincinnatus who tills the land or works in the workshop with the rifle at his side, waiting for the besieged homeland to call him to the ranks to defend it. This example was the principle based on the revolutionary fervor of the end of the eighteenth century that the first agitators knew so well how to ignite and incite. That revolutionary fervor and militia interpretation would impact the nation-states' military organization during the nineteenth century. In the 1790s, the French revolutionary regime, besieged on all sides by the absolute monarchies that would end up forming a formal alliance against the state born of the French Revolution, was forced to invent a military organization, in keeping with its circumstances and the revolutionary discourse on citizenship, to be able to confront its enemies in the rest of Europe. In 1789, the French Constituent Assembly decreed that "every citizen must be a soldier, and every soldier must be a citizen."[7] A simple phrase but of great significance. In 1793, the French authorities imposed the *levée en masse* by decreeing that all French people would serve the national war effort according to age, gender, and abilities until the expulsion of enemies of the republic from the national territory. This decree called all unmarried males between the ages of eighteen and twenty-five to the ranks, assigned women to tasks such as bandaging and sewing tents, old men to publicly encourage patriotic fervor, and children to collect saltpeter to make gunpowder. It is a lyrical passage, it is true, and it is more appropriate to a poem than to a parliamentary discussion. Still, it exemplifies the tone and orientation of the policy of mass conscription. By the end of that year, revolutionary France not only had an army of half a million men, but a new social pact had been established whereby citizens were directly involved in national defense.[8]

Prior to these developments, during the eighteenth century, war in Europe was an enterprise limited in scope, ideology, and military objectives. In wars of

CHAPTER 4

succession to crowns or of limited territorial irredentism, no ideological or national motivation drove them outside the interest of the reigning houses in conflict; monarchies waged wars with small armies of professionals and mercenaries, sometimes of different national origins, who enlisted and fought for pay and booty. The novelty introduced by the imaginative French revolutionaries of the first hour, with the leveé en masse, the mobilization of all the resources of a France in danger, would transform the way of waging war. Suddenly, the enemies of France found that it could mobilize five hundred thousand men on the battlefield, and soon after, between 1800 and 1815, an army of about two and a half million men was integrated, perfectly armed, and motivated. In comparison, the other nations' military strength was significantly smaller. The traditional armies of Prussia, Austria, and Spain were quickly overwhelmed, and the balance of military operations changed abruptly and radically. A nation of citizen-soldiers successfully took the offensive and came close to imposing its hegemony on Europe.[9]

Prussia was the first to react to the new state of military affairs by decreeing that national defense was a universal obligation of its citizens. The conscription law of 1814—which created a military service force called Landwerh, similar to the French Garde Nationale—made all subjects eligible for military service who were not in the regular army, and the troops integrated into the Landwehr elected their officers. Only in this way was Prussia able to have a force of six hundred thousand men that, with the assistance of other armies, would end up defeating Napoleon in 1815.[10] Toward the end of the first decade of the nineteenth century, the European military found themselves faced with the novelty that the praxis of war had changed; it implied thinking differently not only about strategies and tactics but also about the very integration of armies, which henceforth could not be sustained without military service. Paradox of paradoxes, the nations that defended absolutism and the traditions of the Ancien Régime ended up accepting the concept of the citizen of the French Revolution to maintain a military force capable and sufficient for the mass wars that were to characterize the warfare scene from 1870 until the end of World War II in 1945. The French Revolution had created a symbiosis between national identity, political participation, and military engagement, the sole purpose of which was to give France strategic and tactical superiority on the battlefield. Wars would no longer be what they had been—minor, chess-like clashes—but mass armies would break through, and nationalism and the purpose of total victory would drive wars of annihilation.[11] In the face of these qualitative substance changes, all other European nations would follow suit, including Spain.

For Spain and its overseas territories, the Constitution of Cadiz represented the adaptation to the novel understandings of citizenship: political rights and military obligations. Like the ordinances that created the Garde Nationale or the Landwehr, the Spanish constitution laid the foundations for the National Militia of 1814.[12] This was a fundamental change in the structure of the Spanish defense forces, as the new National Militia was different in its structure from the previous provincial militias established during the time of the Bourbon reforms and conceived under the criterion of having an auxiliary army, a sort of second-order extension of the regular forces. Like in the French case, the National Militia had to guarantee the existence of the nation-state conceived by the constitution. The process of constituting the new militia was interrupted in 1814 by the absolutist coup d'état of Ferdinand VII. But in September of 1820, after the restoration of the constitution, thanks to Colonel Riego's *pronunciamiento*, the National Militia became an official military organization in New Spain.[13] According to the secondary legislation issued by the courts, the militia was to be composed of inhabitants of each province, depending on the population and circumstances. Recruitment was open to every citizen between the ages of eighteen and fifty willing to enlist and pay for his uniform. They would elect officers and noncommissioned officers by majority vote. The militiamen would enjoy military privileges, but only during the time they were on active duty. The governors or commanders of each province would be the ultimate leaders of the organization. Although established in an ambiguous manner, the town councils would be responsible for the integration and organization of this militia.[14]

The law provided that the National Militia could only install itself in provincial capitals and districts. If they wanted to organize their militia, municipalities other than the above had to ask permission from the government. Even so, the new military organization spread rapidly. Barely forty days after it had been established as law in New Spain, the townships were already organizing their National Militia units and substituting these forces for the old provincial militias. What advantage did the townships' authorities see in the new military organization? The town councils ceased to be mere collectors of war taxes and, for the first time, became a military authority, something totally different from the defense structure headed by the regular army. The viceroy tried to stop the process of militia formation by insisting on prior permission to organize them. He pointed out that only citizens with their rights in force, able to pay for their uniforms, and with military instruction could be part of the National Militia. In addition, he ordered that the structure and organization of the old provincial militias should not be affected, nor should the collection of war taxes, and that only the political intendant of each province could command these forces. But from the results, it seems that no one paid any attention to the viceroy, and the process continued. Even in Spain, there were modifications to this first phase of regulations, making conscription mandatory for all males of serviceable age, eliminating the judicial exemption, and stating that officers "shall conduct themselves as citizens commanding citizens."[15] These guidelines represented a major departure from the regular army. Among the characters who modified these regulations was Miguel Ramos Arizpe, who was originally from the province of Coahuila and knowledgeable about conditions in the northeastern provinces. Nevertheless, the authorities never put into practice those measures in New Spain.[16]

The new organization of the National Militia overturned the armed structure of the old regime in New Spain. That the duty of organizing and administering the militias fell to the town councils represented a great political change whose scope no one could even imagine. This was also a way to avoid paying military taxes to the central government, which had become a great burden for the communities. But it was not all smooth sailing with the new military institution. Due to the War of Independence, the royalist forces were forced to impose onerous levies on the towns to sustain their provincial militias. The emergence of the National Militia did not mean that it was made up of solid military units since most of its members had neither training nor weapons. In any case, the militia helped the inhabitants of medium and small municipalities to organize themselves and avoid paying taxes. It is here where the most critical change lay: the central government was no longer in charge of this new military branch. Now the town council of each town was in charge of its own armed force, and the cities and towns used the militia as a legal tool to maneuver against the viceregal authority. The townships no longer had to provide men for the levy of the royalist military forces nor pay extraordinary contributions for their maintenance. The burden of paying for troops, building fortifications, and buying uniforms and weapons during years of war had disappeared. Thus the National Militia added a new element to the traditional axis of tension between center and periphery: if until then this tension had lain between viceregal authorities and authorities of the intendancies, now it added the municipal dimension with the burden of all its claims, armed with its ragged but important militias.[17] Both elements—municipality and militia—were a generous contribution of the Cadiz Constitution to the American lands.

In the northeastern provinces, the implementation of the National Militia began in 1820. The royalist commander, Joaquín de Arredondo, ordered towns

THE ERA OF NATIONALISM

to assemble companies to form this militia organization in October of that same year.[18] As in the rest of New Spain, the development of the companies was rapid, and they were fully established by December 1820. San Antonio de Béxar, for example, quickly established a company of sixty-five men.[19] The town councils organized the companies according to the ordinances of April 1820.[20] The early Bejareño organization followed the same pattern of rapid organization that prevailed throughout the viceroyalty: since the inhabitants could no longer afford war contributions, they avoided them by volunteering for military service. That volunteering was done to avoid taxation is obvious because, at first, only infantry units were formed, which were inappropriate for fighting nomadic Natives. Also, there were no more insurgent rebels in the area by this time. Forming an infantry unit was more of a legal tool to defend against abuses of authority than a way to fight Apaches. In fact, only a few individuals from the local National Militia companies pledged to arm themselves because most did not have the resources to do so.[21] Being cautious, the town council of San Antonio asked whether the former provincial militia should be integrated into the new corporation or be extinguished.[22] We do not know what the answer was, but the whole scenario suggests the autonomy of the locals over the political-military order that the Bourbons had tried to impose during the second half of the eighteenth century. Supporting this thesis is the fact that the provincial councils had forbidden the members of the town councils to serve in the provincial militia.[23] Therefore, the local authorities were trying to distance themselves from the military measures imposed from Mexico City. The inhabitants of the area showed that the pre-existing culture of political participation through military service was congruent with the new tradition imported from the French Revolution by way of the Cadiz Constitution.

The National Militia would continue to function after the Proclamation of Independence in 1821. In the northeastern zone, the different forms of militia were of great importance due to the communities' long tradition of having their own units. The process of militia reorganization, initiated in 1820, continued in the region, and the town councils remained in charge of the institution. In 1821, ordinances were issued that positioned the National Militia as an important instrument for establishing internal security and maintaining public order.[24] During the early days of the Mexican empire, it was considered an inclusive institution in which the entire "neighborhood" was to be enlisted.[25] Furthermore, whether it was thought of as such or not, it remained a means of national political socialization. The category of citizen, a novel concept contributed by the Cadiz Constitution, came to synthesize the new concept of resident-citizen with the

CHAPTER 4

tradition of the vecino as a defender of the community to transform him in the political imaginary of the time into an armed citizen defender of the nation. This evolution was reflected and evidenced in the provisions on the militia organization in different places; for example, those related to San Miguel de Aguayo of October 1821 stated that "being citizens all the natives and inhabitants of this America, any individual capable of taking up arms may enlist in the National Militia."[26] This clarified the way for the integration of the political and military obligations of the resident-citizen.

The feeling of national identity was also something new in the provinces of Texas, Nuevo Santander, and Nuevo León. In these territories, the National Militia was seen as a good way to carry out a national ideal through rapid political socialization. For example, in the provisions referred to earlier, the National Militia of the area was to be a tool for "good harmony with the town councils . . . and neighborhoods, by inspiring these with the knowledge that has the love of country, and the other knowledge that is required from every citizen for the political and civil liberty of the nation."[27] The implicit purpose was the merger of the neighbors and the local government into a single political entity at the service of the nation. Although the subject should be the object of another study, we must point out here the birth of the political current of municipalism, which will find itself uncomfortably located on the most important axis of tension in the relationship between center and periphery. The towns of the northeast formed their militia companies according to their number of inhabitants. That of San Antonio consisted of sixty-five men; that of San Miguel de Aguayo one hundred; and that of Lampazos twenty-nine. Although there are no documentary records of Laredo on the subject, it is likely that it formed its own.

The authorities during the brief reign of Iturbide tried to use the militia officers as propagandists of the new national ideal. The provisions they issued for organizing the militias in the region pointed out that the town councils should propose as officers "the individuals who have shown themselves to be the most devoted to our cause."[28] At the same time, these officers were to be chosen from among the rest of the citizen-soldiers to ensure greater cohesion and loyalty among the local force.[29] The method of selecting their leaders was not unlike the way these communities had done since their founding: their political leaders were chosen primarily for their ability to organize and sustain armed defense. Hence it seemed more like a continuity of the old system than the imposition of a new law. It is difficult to determine the sequence of causality here, whether the authorities, in applying general militia provisions at a local level, accepted the traditions or whether these simply coincided with what they were mandating.

But, since local elites were and would remain in command in the regions and towns regardless of political regime changes at the national level, they most likely acted in accordance with their traditions in all matters of public affairs. For example, the Tlaxcalan town of San Miguel organized the election of officers and sergeants of its local National Militia force after complying with the enlistment protocol as ordered. The individuals chosen had the appellation of Don, which meant that they came from a stratum of certain means and were defined as "republican residents." That was the case of Second Lt. Don Bartolomé de la Cruz or Sgt. Don Leandro Zamora.[30] This new order incorporated the traditional category of vecindad as a residence, an adaptation to the new circumstances. San Miguel de Aguayo was a community that defined itself for more than a century as a Tlaxcala Indigenous town and an armed force allied with the Spanish crown, thus managing to preserve the privileged status it had enjoyed practically since the Conquest. Now it defined itself as a republican entity, but it is unlikely that this "republicanism" referred to the North American republicanism or that of the first moments of France after the Revolution; more likely, it was anchored in the very ancient concept of the Roman Republic, which is more in line with the image of Cincinnatus, a republican and militia resident who defends the integrity of the community and its political rights by force of arms.

The towns used the militias in a way that helped their interests or those of their neighbors in particular contexts. The town council of San Antonio ordered the provincial militia units to join the National Militia.[31] In Lampazos and San Miguel, the authorities ordered exactly the same.[32] Incorporating the militia forces under the administrative and political control of the municipalities caused problems with the regular army since deserters from the line troops enlisted in the National Militia to protect themselves, and the army demanded in vain their reincorporation into its units.[33] Another way in which the populations asserted their priorities was by determining the nature and objectives of the new militia. In central Mexico, this organization was thought of as an instrument to repel a possible invasion and, therefore, as the most effective means to preserve national sovereignty. That is why most of its units consisted of infantry. In Lampazos they refused to do so and instead formed a cavalry unit because "it is convenient for their defense since infantry is useless for these borderlands."[34] This is undoubtedly one of the most important points in the militia development of the region, in fact a

CHAPTER 4

turning point. Despite being a borderland, the danger is not perceived as coming from the United States, a distant country in formation with its own problems of internal articulation in those years. Even less is it perceived as coming from Europe, with all countries engaged in wars and the mother country engrossed in the internal aftermath of the Napoleonic invasion. The perceived danger was immediate and daily: the insecurity caused by Natives. This was a tangible reality that left dead, wounded, and kidnapped people and that damaged property. Symptomatic of this was Lampazos, an outpost against Indigenous incursions and the first line of defense for the rest of the region, which adapted the militias to the weapon most effective to counteract the incursions: the cavalry. Lampazos thus establishes the fundamental principle of any militia: it must serve the community according to the dangers of its surroundings, or it is useless. This principle will be a determining factor in all efforts to organize militias or national guards in the region.

THE CREATION OF THE CIVIC MILITIA

In 1823, Mexico ceased to be an empire and became a republic. The change of government also brought changes in the organization of armed forces. Concerning the militia, the most important one was the change of name from the National Militia to the Civic Militia. It was thought inappropriate for Mexico, now a sovereign republic, to have the same military institution as Spain, or at least one with the same name. This was a principle of national affirmation, which always begins with the names of institutions, but it was also an attempt to ground republicanism by emphasizing the civic character of the militia. Since the militia was civic and this refers to the citizens, it is worth clarifying at the outset. The Federal Constitution of the Mexican United States, sanctioned by the Constituent General Congress on October 14, 1824—such was its official title—did not define citizenship, nor did it establish requirements to be a Mexican citizen. The law referred the matter to the federated states and their respective constitutions; one was a citizen through the federated states. The Constitution of 1824 reserved to the General Congress only the power to issue letters of naturalization of foreigners, which created the nonsense: While the states defended citizenship based on vecindad (one was first a citizen of a state and then a Mexican), the federal constitution created a category of citizens without territorial adscription, the naturalized foreigners. The constitutions of Coahuila-Texas and Nuevo León established citizenship with strict adherence to vecindad, both for Natives and foreign-born citizens who settled in Mexico. In this way, the Cadiz legislation reaffirmed, updated, and transmitted an old tradition to American territories. The provisions related to the militia, already republican, had to define another of the essential features of citizenship, minimum ages with militia obligations, an aspect that normally remained in the air as much in the constitutions as in other secondary state legislations. The Civic Militia included all male citizens between the ages of eighteen and fifty.[35]

The militia not only trains but also socializes politically through martial rituals. After each town approved the local integration of the Civic Militia, the following Sunday the militia members were to have an assembly to swear political and military loyalty to the Mexican nation. As part of the ceremony, the assembly celebrated a mass where the priest gave a sermon alluding to civic duties. Once they had sworn allegiance, the force members swore again, now before God, to fulfill their patriotic duties to the nation. Finally, each battalion had to have a flag with specific characteristics, such as the use of national colors and a shield displaying phrases such as "Religion, Independence, Union" or "Mexican Constitution." The Civic Militia used religious and national symbols to spread its republican orientation.[36]

At the national level, federalism became more decentralized throughout the 1820s. In 1827, the Mexican government reformed the Civic Militia by making service compulsory for all Mexicans. In 1822, the rules only allowed access to an exclusive number of wealthy people, but now all male inhabitants were required to do their service, which caused the numbers of this organization to grow rapidly. This incorporated the levée en masse concept of the French Revolution and the Napoleonic period used since then throughout Europe. The Civic Militia continued to use the system of electing officers through voting by the troops, making it an instrument of popular representation. The spirit of the 1827 regulation, however, made the militia voluntary and not compulsory. Some states ignored this fact and recruited troops in the same way the army did. The states also adopted criminal codes for militiamen and regulated the manner of recruiting and the prerequisites for the officer corps. Federalism used the Civic Militia to its advantage.[37]

There was another fundamental change: parity of the Civic Militia and the regular army in arms and organization. The militia would include cavalry, infantry, and artillery units the same as the army. The rank and grade of its officers would be the same. The orientation of the civic institution had changed radically from that of 1822. Before 1827, it was thought of as an internal security force, and its regulations made it look more like a police force than an army for battles. Its duties were reduced to tasks such as providing guards and security patrols, apprehending deserters and criminals, and escort duties. Therefore, unlike the federal army, the Civic Militia was not composed of units whose main function was to carry out warfare. This would change when the Spanish monarch, Ferdinand VII, called for the "reconquest" of the independent colonies in America, which led Mexican authorities to strengthen the Civic Militia to reinforce the national defense. The problem was that this only became an instrument for the regional elites to support their own agenda rather than the national one, which led them to go against the army.[38]

During the 1830s, the national administration tried to reduce the autonomous prerogatives of the Civic Militia. The government headed by Lucas Alamán (1830–1832) promoted a military reform to demobilize the formidable Civic Militia and to try to reinforce the army by providing it with better armament and competent officers and by improving its recruitment. These measures sought to subordinate the action of the militia to the regular armed forces, and some elites who feared a social explosion partly supported them. The federal government wanted to return the civic units to the role of internal police force. This is why the local governments abolished the prerogative to elect officers. The popular classes, such as the day laborers, were discharged from the institution. In January 1835, the government of Gen. Antonio López de Santa Anna presented an initiative to abolish the Civic Militia altogether, which ended up not being approved. Instead, the National Congress decided to decree that there should be only one militiaman for every five hundred people. The state of Zacatecas, which had the largest Civic Militia units in the country, sustained by its rich mining production, opposed this measure. Consequently, Santa Anna marched to confront these militias, which he would end up crushing in May 1835. In this way, the conservative governments managed to destroy the institution.[39] It was not until the war with the United States that the militia was reinstated in 1846, but now under the name of Guardia Nacional (the National Guard).

THE ERA OF NATIONALISM

THE LOCAL REINTERPRETATION

OF A NATIONAL INSTITUTION

During the 1820s, the governments of Nuevo León, Tamaulipas, and Coahuila-Texas* created their constituent assemblies as part of the national federalist organization. These assemblies incorporated the concept of the Civic Militia into their local constitutions. They established the nature of this institution: a force to protect the state from external threats as well as to take charge of public order. The governor was made responsible for this force by being designated as the supreme commander by operation of law. These three states agreed to use the nationally established rules for Civic Militias.[40] It did not escape the attention of the authorities of these states that the nascent republican regime could have enemies since, among the national political class, there were not a few with conservative tendencies and monarchical nostalgia. Therefore, they counted on the Civic Militia to defend the republican and federal regimes from their possible enemies, granting them special privileges. For example, the government of Tamaulipas decreed that all residents had to register their weapons, and those who failed to do so "would be considered suspicious to the government." Members of the Civic Militia, however, were exempt from this measure.[41] This was a way in which the regional authorities privileged the militia as a tool for propagating republicanism.

After 1823, local communities began to organize themselves according to the legal framework of the Civic Militia.[42] In some instances, this organization was done with great care. For example, the Provincial Council of San Antonio had an extraordinary session just to read the militia ordinances.[43] The northeastern communities established their local Civic Militia companies based on their population: San Antonio organized two companies; Lampazos a force of 46 men; Laredo a company of 88; and San Miguel another of 103.[44] The Civic Militia became an integral part of the towns' defensive organization throughout the decade. Militia records and journals appear during the 1820s and 1830s. It was an important issue because the entire region fell into disorder caused by the remnants of the

---

*   The New Kingdom of León became just Nuevo León, Nuevo Santander became Tamaulipas, and Texas formed a single entity with Coahuila.

CHAPTER 4

independence movement, primarily highway robbers. By 1823, the civic forces of each northeastern state were employed to patrol and apprehend criminals and gradually became a police force under local command.[45]

But the establishment of the Civic Militias brought political consequences that may have been present in the minds of the deputies of 1824. First and foremost, they meant autonomy from the federation since the members of the militia were exempt from being recruited into the permanent army.[46] This, together with the fact that they served only in the locality, made the militias attractive for military service without the fear of being transferred to another place, given that they did not fall within the contribution of men that, in principle, the states were obliged to contribute to the federal army.

The autonomy of the militias was something serious and was not limited to the paper that consigned it. This autonomy would provoke confrontations with other authorities. In 1824, San Antonio's city council received an official notification from the Provincial Council, which instructed that the captain of the Civic Militia, Don José Salinas, should be removed from his post. The city council only notified Salinas but refused to enforce this order, arguing that it was not within its attribution.[47] The Provincial Council threatened to fine the city council if it did not comply with the order.[48] In the end, the latter gave in and argued that the misunderstanding was due to a lack of knowledge of the militia's rules.[49] Consequently, the city council issued the order to withdraw the commission to the detriment of Salinas. The company that Salinas commanded had a meeting with their new officer in charge, Manuel Iturri Castillo. There, other members of the militia, corporals José María Morales and Luis Carbajal, refused to comply with the order deposing Salinas and refused to recognize Iturri as their officer, accusing him of punishing the militiamen and calling him a "Borbonista," an implicit accusation of being pro-Spain, a severe charge given the republican fervor of the time. In addition, they led a group of twenty men, including officers, sergeants, corporals, and civic soldiers, to protest against that measure. They argued that they had chosen José Salinas as their captain and that only they had the right to depose him. Therefore, they were not willing to follow orders from a different officer.[50] The situation reached the point where there was no authority capable of enforcing the measure. In the end, the Provincial Council had to ask the regular army to provide troops to subdue the organizers of the revolt. Due to the scandal, San Antonio's city council disbanded the Civic Militia's two companies and reorganized them.[51] To prevent recidivism, the Provincial Council sent copies of the militia ordinances to avoid future mistakes.[52]

The militia organization was adopted, but at the same time it was modified by the inhabitants of the northeast to meet regional needs. Its regulations stated that those who could be recruited should have their own means of subsistence and that day laborers should not be recruited into the militia. In Lampazos, there were complaints that it was difficult for someone from that town to belong to the institution under this classification. The town council requested that the rule be modified because only a few neighbors had the required wealth. There were even men who had the necessary resources but no servants, which meant that they had to work for themselves and lost income when they served in the Civic Militia. The town authorities pointed out that "there are quite a few individuals who can serve the nation with arms when necessary, but these are wretches who support themselves with their personal labor, and the day they find nowhere to work, they do not eat."[53] In any case, the town council pointed out that such people were part of the local Civic Militia even though that the constitution and federal laws prohibited it.[54] The local tradition of serving in emergencies was enforced over national laws because the borderlands were always threatened by Indigenous attacks.

Similar situations presented themselves in other places, such as the town of San Miguel, where its authorities expressed similar concerns. They asked that training exercises be held every eight days instead of daily so that the militiamen could participate in the wheat harvest.[55] San Miguel's authorities mentioned that most villagers were poor and without any assets. They had to be guaranteed that they would not be taken out of their area to do military service. This town council also assured the government that the residents had always cooperated in defense matters but that if the government wanted the population to form companies, the community would need monetary support.[56] This was no exaggerated request since the paraphernalia of the militia, such as uniforms, was expensive and weapons were scarce. Lampazos informed the government, for example, that there were almost no weapons in the hands of the militia force. They had had to sell them since the inhabitants of that town had suffered shortages and hunger. The members of the Civic Militia in the northeast could not act under the national agenda dictated by the center due to the lack of resources.[57]

One of the ways they tried to address the question of resources was by obtaining their own income through a system of exemption, according to which some townspeople paid to avoid doing the armed service. All those exempted by law and those who wished to be exempted had to pay a monthly tax. In the case of Nuevo León, the exemption tax ranged from one and a half to three reales, depending on the individual's economic capacity.[58] In Texas, it was higher: from

CHAPTER 4

two to ten pesos, an enormous figure, especially for the purchasing power of Texans who could barely pay two reales.[59] Nevertheless, the monthly tax for the Civic Militia became common and accepted in the northeastern towns. There were attempts to raise revenue in other ways, as in the case of Coahuila-Texas, where the state government allocated 1 percent of all tax revenue from commerce to the Civic Militia.[60] The availability of resources varied according to the place. While in Lampazos, the revenue records registered small amounts such as 2 to 16 pesos available, in San Antonio the Civic Militia came to have as much as 160 pesos in cash at its disposal.[61] In a territory with little cash in circulation, however, it was difficult to collect the exempt person's tax. Above all, there were times when the population was unable to pay the fee due to losses caused by Comanche and Apache raids.[62] This would repeat itself again and again throughout the region. In San Antonio, men over the age of fifty found it challenging to pay the fee, so the city council suspended the collection for them.[63] At other times, people who could no longer afford to pay the exemption fee returned to armed service activities in the militia, which involved both police work and defense against any possible military eventuality.[64] For the exemption, there was a whole variety of ailments and physical impediments suffered by people who, in theory, could be recruited. Examples abound: Juan de Maldonado, from San Antonio, was in no physical or economic condition to serve or pay for the exemption, so it was necessary to exempt him completely.[65] A similar case was that of Anastasio Mansolo, who asked not to serve because he was over fifty years old and ill.[66] There were also those who suffered accidents that prevented them from serving and chose to pay, such as Juan José Cisneros, a cavalryman in Lampazos's Civic Militia company.[67] The fact that people involved in the militia had to serve or finance a military force was widespread in the northern towns because it represented the prolongation of an old tradition into the republican era, so this new form of military service did not represent, in essence, something much different from what they had practiced.

The continuity of military traditions was most evident in how local officers acted. The constitutions of the northeastern states noted that officers in charge of local militia units were to be chosen and approved by the state legislature.[68] This form of selection showed how the political elite determined the appointment of military leaders. Officers were thus selected based on their influence and resources rather than based on a sense of patriotic duty, as it was primarily a political decision. This was the case of the Zuazua family in Lampazos. Juan de Zuazua, a Basque and resident of Lampazos since 1770, was the patriarch of the clan. During the War of Independence, he supported the royalist side, for which he was rewarded with the concession of the postal service administration. He was part of the local military forces as one of the leading figures and went so far as to refuse the oath of allegiance to the newly independent Mexican state and to insult the members of the town council in 1821. According to some witnesses, he was amassing weapons to lead a counterrevolution and was arrested and placed at the disposal of the authorities. Despite all this, in 1823 he reappeared as the ensign of Lampazos's Civic Militia. Without any voting procedure, the mayor, Mariano Ayala, commissioned Zuazua as an officer.[69] This case shows how the local elite used the new republican regulations as long as they were to their benefit, and when they were not, they gave preference to the traditional customs of military organization. The Zuazuas continued to use their influence to involve the family in the local military organization until the mid-nineteenth century. Juan de Zuazua died in 1824, but his son Francisco Zuazua continued the patriarch's tradition by becoming involved in local politics and military affairs.[70] Francisco was elected several times as president of the town council and elector, and he was also part of the Civic Militia as ensign and lieutenant in charge of formations and weapons practice.[71] His brother, Carlos Zuazua, was also part of the same militia.[72] The youngest member of this family, Juan Zuazua, would become an outstanding officer during the Mexican-American War (1846–1848) and the Reform War (1857–1860), commanding characters such as Ignacio Zaragoza. In short, the Zuazua family perfectly exemplifies the marriage of political rights and military participation during the nineteenth century.

A similar case was that of the Benavides clan in Laredo. Basilio Benavides (1800–1863) headed the family and was a direct descendant of Tomás Sánchez, the founder of Laredo. Like Juan de Zuazua in Lampazos, Basilio Benavides was postmaster during the War of Independence.[73] He apparently did not take part in the insurrection but later welcomed the change from monarchy to republic in Mexico.[74] He was part of the Civic Militia as a lieutenant in the Laredo company,[75] and he held the office of mayor on several occasions. Again, political and military leadership were intertwined. Basilio's nephews, Santos and Refugio Benavides, would follow in his footsteps.

The Navarros were another family clan that followed the same pattern but in San Antonio. This lineage originated with Angel Navarro (1748–1808), a Corsican who settled near Laredo in 1769 and moved to San Antonio in 1777. There he became a prosperous merchant and became mayor in 1790.[76] His son, José Ángel

CHAPTER 4

Navarro (1784–1836), would emerge as a prominent figure in San Antonio. In 1813, he debuted as a lieutenant in the local militia force; his brother, José Antonio Navarro (1795–1871), sympathized with the independence movement. Upon Arredondo's arrival in the region, José Antonio spent the conflict in exile in Louisiana, while José Ángel remained in San Antonio. After the war, the Navarro family's fortune improved notably.[77] José Ángel Navarro became deeply involved in the formation of the first National Militia unit and later in the Civic Militia; in both, he commanded the San Antonio units as lieutenant.[78] His brother, José Antonio Navarro, who was politically inclined, was elected deputy to the Coahuila-Texas legislature and later to the federal Congress in Mexico City.[79]

Another Bejareño clan that followed the same path was the Seguín family. In 1800, Erasmo Seguín (1782–1857) married the daughter of an officer of the Presidio de La Bahia. From 1807 to 1835, he was postmaster, just like Juan de Zuazua and Basilio Benavides. During the upheaval of independence, he leaned toward the royalist side. Later he was elected mayor of San Antonio and occupied other political positions. He was also deeply involved in the creation of the Civic Militia in San Antonio.[80] His son, Juan Nepomuceno Seguín, would become mayor of San Antonio in 1833, and in 1834 he was already the political chief of the Department of Bexar, where he participated in the local militia.[81] In this way, the Navarro and Seguín families repeated the same pattern of associating politics and militia activities common in the northeastern borderlands. Thus, as the Civic Militia became an instrument of the local elite, friction with the army became more acute.

PROBLEMS WITH THE REGULAR ARMY

Undoubtedly for the constituents of 1824, who represented the elites and notables of the states, the creation of the Civic Militia was a concrete way of safeguarding state's rights against the federation, which had inherited from the colony and the brief empire of Agustín I the bad reputation of always tending to centralization. It has been constantly said in all the literature of the time, and about the time, that the constituents wrote a constitution in such a way that the center would not govern; this is why some authors in the field of the history of law affirm that the federation of 1824 was not a federation but a confederacy, given the wide limits in favor of the autonomy of the states. On the other hand, there was the economic aspect: If it was not cheap to set up a militia instead of sending the blood quota to the army, it was still less onerous for the local economies since it kept economically active men in partial service and within their communities.

In 1824, the federal government agreed that Tamaulipas should provide 2,600 men for the regular army as well as the officers to command them. The Provincial Council opposed this measure, arguing that it would be costly and that the state did not have the resources to carry it out. More importantly, it would take labor away from agriculture and industry. To comply with the mandate, it was said, would also have the consequence of bringing many people under military jurisdiction, which would complicate the jurisdiction of the civil authorities in legal proceedings.[82] The government of Tamaulipas flatly refused to obey the order dictated from Mexico City and instead suggested gathering 2,600 men for the Civic Militia. After all, if national integrity were endangered, the Tamaulipas militia, like those of other states, could be mobilized to serve outside the state and under presidential command as long as it was authorized by the federal Congress.[83] These refusals and the fact that the militias were kept far from the reach of the regular army meant that, in practical terms, the militia became a safeguard and defense for the inhabitants of the states against being recruited by the regular army, where the life of the soldier was difficult.[84] To put it bluntly, the militia replaced the regular army, especially in the northeastern borderlands, which served the regional needs of security and order in an economical way without suffering the presence of a regular army, which was not only incompetent to fight "Indians" but was also a parasite because of its constant foraging when on a campaign.

The regular army of the federation, which was none other than Agustín de Iturbide's Ejercito Trigarante (Army of the Three Guarantees), thus lost its place among the borderlands populations and ceased to be the place where local elites could make a military career. After independence, the federal governments did not bother to consolidate the military presence in the northeast, contrary to what the colonial authorities had done. On the other hand, the regular army became an important protagonist in the country's political scenario, first of all because, being the same army that had consummated independence by abandoning its royalist attitude and reaching an agreement with Vicente Guerrero's insurgent forces, its officers and chiefs felt they were the sole guarantors of that independence. Officers of a certain importance and with ambitions were more interested in being close to the center of power, Mexico City, because from there, supposedly, the policies for the whole country were being forged. Additionally, the center of the country, the old and true New Spain, held a strategic position for any project that wanted to subdue the states, as long as, of course, the road to Veracruz and the dominion over this port were preserved. Several historians have pointed out that the Mexican army entered a period of attrition during the first decades of the nineteenth century due to the lack of resources to equip it. In addition, the continuous uprisings and internal revolts killed many of its best men and not a few officers thus began losing any semblance of military discipline, training, and strategy.[85] As a consequence, any officer with political pretensions preferred to be away from serving in the northeastern borderlands chasing smugglers and defending towns from elusive Lipan and Comanche attacks. Thus the emergence of the Civic Militia, along with the politicization of the regular army cadres, led the northeasterners to refuse service in the presidios' forces.

Another problem that plagued the regular army was the lack of resources due to the continuous nonpayment of the federal contingent, which was nothing more than the amount of money that the states had to pay annually to the national treasury. Even though the national government frequently reduced the amount owed to it, the debt accumulated over the years. Hence, by 1829, the states owed around five million pesos to the national government, approximately 10 percent of total revenues. The Mexican government had to resort to borrowing from abroad in order to meet its minimum operating needs. The fall of debt bonds, however, deprived the national authorities of continuing with this option.[86] On the other hand, it was impossible to collect resources where there simply were none; the northeastern economy was precarious, so the collection was insufficient.[87] Also, in the complicated context of nomadic Indigenous invasions and US expansionist ambitions, local militias were insufficient. Regular troops were needed from a national government that lacked the resources to deal with this problem effectively.

But despite all of the above, the army continued to reorganize its forces in this area. In 1825, for example, in Laredo, members of the former provincial militias organized during the War of Independence who wanted to continue their career in the regular army were given the option of joining the local presidio's force with the promise that their rank would be respected.[88] In 1826, 27 citizens of Laredo voluntarily enlisted in the presidio's company of Laredo.[89] A year later, there were 83 inhabitants serving in the same unit.[90] The law passed in 1826 established that that town should have a garrison of 150 men, and by 1834 it had a deficit of 63. So in less than a decade, the regular military service seemed to have lost its appeal to the population. This meant that most of the recruits for the presidio's troops came from other areas and even included criminals or those recruited by levy, troops who were unfamiliar with the peculiar conditions of the northeastern borderlands. The commander of Laredo complained about the situation, saying that the recruits would be useless if they did not come from the area: "they are the scum of the towns that send them, and they have no goods to defend nor families to love honestly in these borderlands." He added that "a painful experience has proven that since [the authorities] had wanted to replace the presidios' companies' casualties with convicts, their destruction was hastened, because such recruits only come to sow their demoralization in the presidios." He also mentioned that "It is a proven thing that to be a good soldier of a presidio's cavalry and to resist or wage war fruitfully against the savage nations that harry our borderlands, voluntary men are needed, of much personal courage, who know practically the way and the terrains with whom and where they have to fight, they must be agile to ride even on untamed horses ... robust, sober." Finally, the commander pointed out that such recruits could only be found in the "borderlands towns."[91] This communication reveals not only the decline of the regular armed forces in the region but also highlights a whole new discourse on how to defend the borderlands, which lay not in the what and how but with whom, an argument that would later emerge again as a result of the War of Reform (1857–1861).

The case of the Laredo garrison was not isolated from the regional military decline. As early as 1824, the San Antonio garrison had no resources to pay salaries or buy food for its troops. The garrison requested permission for some individuals to go out to work to support themselves and their families.[92] By 1830, the *bejareño* city council referred to the conditions of the garrison as "the useless situation of the troop,"[93] so the abhorrence the inhabitants felt toward the armed service in the regulars is not surprising. Lampazos's company had the same problems; its garrison should have numbered 125 men, but already in 1826, it had 70 vacancies. Its commander said there were no volunteers and requested that the missing places be filled with veterans from the extinct provincial companies. Like in Laredo, the commander of Lampazos was looking for men "based on the borderlands" who were accustomed to their hardships, with knowledge of the terrain, and who knew how to fight the Indians, with fortitude and the ability to ride on horseback.[94] This commander had problems with the local town hall in his efforts to fill the gaps in the troops; the local authorities argued that he had more men than reported, which was false.[95] To make matters worse, the town council asked to reduce the number of soldiers the army was requesting, saying that the place was short of men.[96] By the end of September, they were still 44 soldiers short, so the commander asked the mayors of the neighboring towns to send replacements.[97] One month later, the company was still incomplete.[98]

The population of San Miguel was ordered to contribute men to the army; it was the blood quota established in the constitution. The response to this request was not much different from those of Lampazos and Laredo. Right off the bat, three of the men sent by the town council were rejected for not "being useful for service." The commander demanded that potential recruits must pass a physical examination and have their condition verified before being incorporated into the unit; to meet the assigned quota, the commander suggested that elements of the Civic Militia be transferred to the regular army. But the townspeople, warned by word of mouth of what was happening, did not sit with their arms crossed to see what would happen in this dispute between the town council and the commander. The recruitable elements of San Miguel, men with the characteristics desired by the commander, had fled to avoid being enlisted.[99] The results of this antipathy to military service in the standing army went from bad to worse. Soon after, twenty-one prospects were sent for the draft, of whom seventeen were too short in stature and therefore unfit for service. Of the remaining four, one was a servant, which exempted him from service; another was lame; the third was unfit to ride a horse; and the fourth was crippled in both arms.[100] The cynical village authorities again sent more men with similar qualities. Of forty-three sent, twenty-two were in their sixties and the other twenty-one were "most wretched and useless for horseback fatigue."[101] Faced with what already seemed like a mockery, the army had no choice but to fine the town councils when they failed to send fit recruits.[102] Forced conscription was another measure to which the army resorted. María del Carmen Espinosa, a resident of San Miguel, denounced her son's forced enlistment when he was leaving mass. Due to her widowhood, María del Carmen asked for his exemption and suggested that he be replaced with "another one of the many that there are in this town, without the obligations that this one has and creditors to the military service because they are unemployed."[103] But whether the men were sent or forcibly recruited, the fact is that animosity against the army increased, as did desertions, which became commonplace. These actions provoked a strong reaction from the army: it threatened the inhabitants of the villages with conscription if they did not hand over the deserters.[104] As a result of this lack of sympathy from the population of the region and the evident neglect of the authorities in the center of the country, the northeastern army entered a period of decadence never seen before and was no longer in a position to defend and protect the area from the attacks of nomadic Indians.

REAL PREOCCUPATIONS OF THE NORTHEASTERN COMMUNITIES

As mentioned earlier, after Mexico became an independent nation, the new authorities lost interest in securing the northeastern borderlands from the growing Indigenous threat. This was practically an invitation to hostile groups to plunder the area. Iturbide's brief government established a peace treaty with the Lipans in 1822. In 1827, Gen. Anastasio Bustamante, commander of the eastern interior provinces, made another peace treaty with Comanches and Tancahuanos at San Antonio. In reality, this last peace treaty was never enforced because the military forces capable of doing so did not exist.[105] During the period from 1821 to 1835, there were constant attacks from different tribes on the northern borderlands. The communities of San Antonio, Laredo, Lampazos, and San Miguel gave punctual accounts of these incursions.[106] In Lampazos alone, a rancher reported the loss of 1,400 head of cattle, not including stolen horses.[107] The towns in the northeast viewed the peace treaties between the federal government and the Indigenous factions with suspicion and referred to them as "underhanded peace."[108] These four localities had to take drastic measures to deal with attacks, with residents traveling in groups of thirty or more armed men. The ranchers had to arm their cowboys and servants appropriately.[109]

An attempt was made to organize a self-defense effort using the structures of the colonial period. Projects and proposals abounded to attack the Indigenous hamlets, as had been done since the seventeenth century and with great effectiveness during the Bourbon period. The San Antonio city council justified such actions by calling them the product of "noble feelings of revenge."[110] The people living in the region made an effort to finance this type of campaign with donations and taxes. Those who had weapons were required to keep them ready regardless of

CHAPTER 4

whether or not they were affiliated with an armed institution.[111] Most of the punitive raids, which is their proper name, lacked resources and support from the federal authorities and almost never materialized.

In those years, the populations of the region had everything against them, given the bellicose nature of the Indigenous people. Very often the scale of the attacks destroyed the regular army units, the Civic Militia, and the population in general, which was summoned to defend itself. This happened especially when each group acted alone and on its own. The experience made it clear that these three defensive forces had to cooperate in spite of their local rivalries, given the hostile Indians' unique ways of fighting. Reports of various defense actions of the time constantly mention that the local forces called into action were composed of regular, civic, and resident soldiers.[112] Cooperation immediately extended to the financial field: the San Antonio city council, for example, lent money on several occasions to the regular garrisons of Laredo and San Antonio.[113] Such a willingness on the part of the town council to gather resources in money or in kind suggests the implementation of long-standing regional customs, according to which the local elite assumed their role in the community and were more than willing to finance and organize the local defense. Such a willingness derived from the colonization pattern followed in the region where the colonizer was at the same time defender. A native of Lampazos who headed this type of initiative, Andrés de Sobrevilla, a veteran of the Apache battles and the War of Independence, was a prominent rancher who had proudly retained the honorary title of auxiliary captain of the regular army; he had the rank but no troops under his command.[114] He was in charge of organizing the local defense by gathering what was left of the regular forces, those of the Civic Militia, and any man willing to contribute to or collaborate with the community defense.[115] At some point, he had to take charge of the Laredo forces since that garrison, close to Lampazos, had found itself isolated for not receiving news from the state authorities of Tamaulipas.[116] If we follow with certain care and detail the performance of Sobrevilla, it becomes evident that he acted more like a captain-entrepreneur of the sixteenth and seventeenth centuries than a military officer of the nineteenth century. The circumstantial factors make the warrior; traditions and necessity imposed on him the forms of action.

It was then that a feeling began to flourish that would soon become a conviction and that some decades later would lead to an express and conscious effort to base defense only on the region's own resources. Against the backdrop of the constant armed cooperation between the different towns, such as Lampazos and Laredo, the feeling took root that the federal government, and sometimes the state authorities themselves, were indifferent to the concerns of the towns' inhabitants.[117] Fed up with the indifference of the Tamaulipas state authorities, Laredo's town council went so far as to request a change of jurisdiction to Nuevo León.[118] But above all, the pitiful situation acted as a catalyst for a feeling of regional animosity against the federal government in Mexico City.

In short, with successes and setbacks, the independent nation that was born in 1821 changed the regional interaction. After the promulgation of the 1824 constitution, the new authorities tried to impose a series of measures from the country's capital to lay the foundations of a national identity. One of these was the instruction given to all the states for them, in turn, to proceed to establish civic committees of residents in all the towns to celebrate September 16. All in all, the only date of national festivity available at that time gave rise to rivers of ink consigned in speeches by the notables of the people that contributed, drop by drop, to the development of a republican ideology. Much remains to be studied about the impact of these civic committees, but from what is known, it is possible to affirm that they were the forge from which the national heroes emerged in their mythic stature. An example of this series of measures to encourage the establishment of a participatory and educated citizenry was the creation of patriotic societies. This type of citizen group had the function of providing help to individuals through the dissemination of scientific knowledge in order to improve agricultural production, mining, and national trade and industry. It was intended to eliminate begging, idleness, and bad upbringing and to lay the foundations of morality and public wealth. The core of such an organization should be made up of individuals of proven patriotism, and later more citizens could be incorporated.[119]

Another way to develop civic sentiment was the implementation of new forms of military organization. This policy would encourage civic zeal in the region, as well as regionalism, to the extent that the communities tended, as we have already pointed out, to adapt the civic-military novelties to the realities they lived and suffered on a daily basis. Just as the Bourbon regime had realized a generation before, now the inhabitants of the region were not willing to change their local traditions either. It is true that certain terms and symbols were changed, such as the strong religious burden that was replaced by a nationalist and republican approach. The traditional military-service infrastructure controlled by local elites remained in place; the close identification between political participation and military service is clear. It was a continuation of the same system used in the area since the first conquistadors arrived in the northeast in the sixteenth century. It has been a typical example of long-lasting institutional arrangements, which functioned in borderland zones where the authority of the central state was difficult to impose. Neither the Habsburgs nor the Bourbons succeeded in imposing their centralized models of military administration in northeastern Mexico. The much weaker Mexican government would also fail during the first half of the nineteenth century. Like the colonial authorities, the Mexican government refused to use the system of local armed organization, which, together with the expansion of Anglo-American settlers into the region and the powerful Comanche onslaught during the late 1830s, would eventually alienate the region from the national authorities.

CHAPTER 5

The Northeast in Flames

The decade of 1835–1845 became a point of no return in the history of the northeastern borderlands. The imposition of a centralist regime from Mexico City had severe consequences in this region. During this period, there was a major revolt in Texas that led to its separation from Mexico and another in the rest of the northeastern provinces called the Federalist Rebellion. At the same time, the largest wave of Indian attacks in the history of the borderlands began. This cataclysm would have a single feature: a permanent state of war. This section studies the impact of this decade on the local inhabitants and their traditions of warfare, which had been in use for several centuries. Identifying the context of the decade beginning with the return of a centralist regime in the Mexican government helps to understand the impact it had on Anglo-Saxon and Tejano* interests in the province of Texas and how it polarized the region against the central government. The effect of the Federalist Rebellion and the great Comanche invasions are also explored within the framework of the interests, reactions, and clashes within the local structures of armed organization of the residents of San Antonio, San Miguel, Lampazos, and Laredo.

---

* The term "Tejano" is used to name the population of Hispanic origin that had settled in Texas since the eighteenth century.

CHAPTER 5

THE RETURN OF CENTRALISM

After the first decade of Mexico organized as a federal republic, many important political and military changes took place starting in 1835. A year earlier, the administration of President Valentín Gómez Farías tried to reduce the size of the army, which gave rise to fierce opposition among the officers, who would end up staging a coup. In March, the congress of the new government approved a motion to modify the 1824 constitution to impose a centralist regime, and among the measures it imposed was the reduction of the Civic Militia in the states. In December, a new constitution known as Las Siete Leyes [The Seven Laws] was approved. It established that the states would be transformed into departments and that the president would appoint governors. The code intended to establish a sort of liberal centralism. Among the most important changes was the creation of a fourth power, called the conservative power, which could veto any of the decisions of the other powers (executive, legislative, and judicial). In addition, only men with property or capital could vote; the laws abolished the town councils established in 1808 and implemented other measures concerning the militias. These changes were met with much resistance in powerful federalism-oriented states such as Zacatecas. Due to its silver production, it was one of the wealthiest states, and it had the largest Civic Militia force. Zacatecas refused to comply with the laws and openly rebelled, so Santa Anna led the army to subdue it. Apparently, the militia forces dissolved, and there was no real military confrontation, so Santa Anna took the capital on May 10, 1835.[1] Things would be much more complicated in the northeast.

IMPLOSION OF THE NATION, EXPLOSION OF THE REGION

In October 1835, a revolt began in Texas that quickly escalated into a separatist movement led by Anglo-American settlers who had established themselves in the territory. The official presence of these settlers dates back to 1819, when Moses Austin (1761–1821), a New England merchant, sought to obtain land to establish a colony of three hundred American families in Spanish Texas. The local authorities, still colonial, were enthusiastic about the plan to bring settlers to the sparsely populated province, and they readily approved the project. Unfortunately, though, Moses died, and his son Stephen F. Austin (1793–1836) took up the project. On top of that, when Mexico became independent, the whole deal had to be renegotiated. Stephen Austin would travel to Mexico City in 1822, where he spent a year trying to get the go-ahead. Meanwhile, Iturbide's administration gradually became aware of the danger to national sovereignty posed by having a sparsely populated northern region. In February 1823, the Imperial Colonization Law was enacted, and Austin was its only beneficiary because, just a month later, Iturbide was overthrown and the law was annulled. In 1824, a new colonization law was unveiled that granted land, promised security, and granted tax exemption for four years to foreign settlers, but it had only one limitation: settlers could not have land within twenty leagues of the border with another country. The legal organization of colonization became an important issue for the Mexican government, which did not want to encourage an exodus from the center to the peripheries, but rather wanted to encourage the entry of foreigners and, with them, new agricultural techniques and capital to try to develop the vast unpopulated territories in the north of the nascent republic. By 1823, there were three thousand Anglo-Americans illegally settled in Texas, but at the same time the local authorities were reluctant to enforce the new law, fearing that in the future the newcomers would choose to secede from Mexico and become part of the United States.[2] In the meantime, Austin returned to Texas and, during 1825, established three hundred families. He would later fulfill three more contracts, settling nine hundred more families in Texas. Between 1825 and 1832, there were new contracts entered into with American businessmen that led to the settlement of nearly eight thousand families in the area.[3] Because of this, the Anglo-American population soon outnumbered the Mexican population in the area, altering the balance of power in the region.

In 1830, there were at least seven thousand Anglo-American settlers in Texas, but this number must have been much higher, while the Mexican population was barely three thousand. As is natural in such cases, the newcomers did not assimilate into the local culture and managed their affairs with complete independence from the Mexican authorities. In 1826, the Mexican government issued regulations to reduce the entry of this class of settlers, which contradicted the initial purposes of the national colonization policy. That same year, Hayden Edwards, another businessman, attempted to create the Republic of Freedonia in Texas but did not have the support of the majority of the Anglo settlers and was crushed by Mexican troops. In 1828, Gen. Manuel Mier y Terán traveled throughout Texas to analyze the situation in the province. He noted the influence of the new settlers

CHAPTER 5

and concluded that this segment of the population would not assimilate because they were the majority. A year later, Mier y Terán was named general commander of the eastern internal provinces, which included Coahuila-Texas, Tamaulipas, and Nuevo León. Convinced that the Anglo-American colonists already represented a severe danger, he requested reinforcements for the military garrisons in Texas, as well as the establishment of a greater commercial flow between these provinces and the rest of Mexico. This last purpose was unrealistic since the Tampico-Zacatecas axis blocked any attempt at serious and stable trade between the northeastern provinces and the country's center-south. On April 30, 1830, the Mexican authorities enacted a law prohibiting the immigration of settlers from the United States while encouraging immigration from Europe and other areas of Mexico. But a second, much more critical preventive measure was the prohibition of the entry of slaves into Mexican territory.[4]

No matter how many laws the federal government issued, the problem it faced was that it had no resources to enforce them. Mier y Terán realized that any attempt to do so would only provoke hostility from Anglo-American settlers in Texas, and such a measure would discourage entrepreneurs who were trying to run their businesses legitimately, such as Stephen F. Austin. But in any event, the national government was unable to prevent the illegal entry of more settlers. Historian David Weber has noted that in those years, Texas became a "haven for vagabonds and refugees."[5] The proposal to bring Mexican settlers to the borderlands failed miserably due to the governors' lack of interest in contributing by establishing quotas for aspiring settlers. The influx of Europeans also did not happen, and the expansion of the military presence proved unaffordable. Mexican government envoys in Texas became aware of the serious situation and urged the authorities in Mexico City to intervene. Any intervention, however, would have been met with resistance from the Coahuila authorities, who were more interested in doing business by selling large amounts of land to Anglo-American settlers than enforcing and safeguarding national sovereignty. On top of that, the interests of the northeastern borderlands were not on the agenda of the politicians in the nation's capital. In November 1833, the Senate repealed the Immigration Act of 1830. Four years later, a new observer, Gen. Juan Nepomuceno Almonte, was sent to Texas to investigate the local situation once more. Almonte basically came to the same conclusions his predecessor, Mier y Terán, had reached years earlier. By 1834, there were about 20,700 Anglo-Americans in Texas.[6]

Meanwhile, the Tejano population was trying to adapt to this complicated situation. Tejanos were never content to be political subordinates to Saltillo, the

Coahuila capital, much less to the nation's capital. There was an accurate perception that politicians in Saltillo and Mexico City were ignorant of the local traditions of Texas and unaware of its geographic peculiarities and needs. The economic vision of the Tejanos was radically opposed to the one imposed from the center of the country that was based on the monopoly system, which had been in force since colonial times. The Texan economic practice was centered on the plantation system dedicated to cotton with slave labor, which soon began to produce profits for the Anglo-Americans, whether through cotton production and trade or the slave trade. The expansion of cotton plantations in Texas benefited the Tejanos because they were directly involved in the allocation of land and made a profit. Therefore, they were against the prohibition of slavery, which affected their Anglo partners, so they disguised it as indentured servitude. While all this was going on in Texas during the 1830s, the political orbit of the country gravitated toward a centralist vision of national administration. The Tejanos opposed Bustamante's coup of 1830 because it favored the imposition of centralism and a unitary regime, and the two Texas delegates were expelled from the federal legislature. The town councils of Texas, including San Antonio and the Anglo colony of Austin, proclaimed that only they could determine the continuity of the deputies in the legislature. Little by little, the Tejano population was distancing itself from and opposing the policies of the Mexican government. They also opposed the colonization law of 1830. Prominent San Antonio residents met and wrote a brief complaining about this new colonization law because it affected the goodwill of businessmen like Stephen F. Austin. They emphasized that only the city council and the residents could make decisions on this matter since they were the only ones who knew the topography of the department.[7]

While the interests of the Mexican Tejanos were clearly opposed to the centralists, they also had to be careful to keep the balance of power with the American settlers. Initially, the Mexican population of Texas welcomed the settlers from the United States with open arms. As their numbers increased, however, the Anglo-Americans became increasingly inclined to promote only their own interests. Not only were there problems in the sale of land to American businessmen that was already owned by Tejanos, but the newcomers were also involved in land fraud, which at one point almost sparked an armed confrontation between Mexican Tejanos and Anglo-American Texans. Nevertheless, one thing united them: opposition to the return of centralism in 1835. In the beginning, Texans and Tejanos took a belligerent attitude but without seeking secession; they only wanted a return to federalism since it was the type of regime that best suited their

CHAPTER 5

tradition of making their own political decisions.[8] The radicalization of federalism in the region began with Mexico's return to centralism in the Siete Leyes of 1836, whose central purpose was laudable in addressing the issues of balance of powers, control of constitutionality, and definition of individual guarantees but which was abhorred by the federalists for establishing the unitary state.[9] The congress of the state of Coahuila-Texas, headed by Governor Andrés Viesca, opposed the new regime. The governor called a war council and gave his support to Zacatecas in the armed revolt. As happened elsewhere, there were clashes between the Civic Militia units and the regular garrisons. Soon the federalist opposition was reduced to the regions of Parras and Monclova in Coahuila. Viesca realized that he needed the support of Texas to continue the rebellion. He went so far as to request that the Civic Militia units of San Antonio join them, and the Tejanos decided to support the inhabitants of Coahuila despite their differences and even though since 1834, the elite of San Antonio had been holding meetings in which they seriously discussed the issue of Texas's independence. There were attempts to send the civic Bejaranos to help the rebellion in Monclova, but in the end they did not materialize due to the chaotic scenario. The temper of the Tejano population in San Antonio against the centralist administration was heating up more and more, to the point that a crowd threatened to assault the garrison of the regular army in San Antonio. At the last minute, it was called off because local leaders kept a cool head, thus avoiding a bloodbath.[10]

At first, the Anglo settlers did not support any faction in the centralist vs. federalist conflict. Some speculators supported Governor Viesca, seeking profit, but these were few and far between. Uncertainty over the issue of slavery in Texas was what really concerned the Anglo-Americans. Eventually, the slave owners realized that slavery was not on the agenda of either side in the conflict. Therefore, the idea of seeking separation from Mexico grew and took hold among the majority of American-born settlers. The Mexican authorities were not unaware of this delicate situation and tried to take preventive measures to avoid an uprising, such as confiscating the weapons previously given to the militias in the Anglo settlements. Thus, on September 27, 1835, a Mexican force of a hundred soldiers under the command of Lt. Francisco de Castañeda went to the Anglo-American town of González to confiscate an old cannon that had been assigned to this town to defend itself from Indian attacks. The population of González refused to hand over the artillery piece, and on October 2 a battle broke out between the colonists and the Mexican force. Thus, a revolt broke out and spread throughout Texas, and by the end of the month the Anglo settlers had already put San Antonio under siege.

At first, the revolt lacked a clear purpose; it seemed more like a visceral reaction against the measures imposed by the Mexican government, which the colonists perceived as authoritarian. At this point, the rebellion resembled a continuation of the series of federalist revolts in Zacatecas and Coahuila.[11]

In November, the autonomist mood in Texas was growing, as the colonists refused to recognize the authority of Coahuila's governor Viesca, in spite of his being a fervent federalist. The outbreak was rapidly becoming more radical as the moderate rebels who leaned toward federalism were losing ground to the more extreme ones who sought secession from Mexico. Meanwhile, the Anglo-American settlers called a council to discuss the course of action. On December 9, the last Mexican troops surrendered in San Antonio, and the revolt had reached a revolutionary dimension. Just as he had done in Zacatecas in 1835, General Santa Anna marched to Texas to suppress the rebellion in early 1836. The Anglo-Americans reacted by organizing a new convention that ended up declaring the independence of Texas on March 2. Four days later, Santa Anna took the Alamo fort in San Antonio, where he executed the entire rebel garrison. This action only managed to fuel the fire of the rebellion. At this point, the strength of the Mexican government seemed solid. It was on the offensive, marching in pursuit of the rebels, who, in contrast, were fearful of a frontal confrontation. The fate of the conflict, however, changed unexpectedly. On April 21, Santa Anna had the rebel forces cornered in San Jacinto, near the Gulf Coast. Surprisingly and against all common sense, in one of the most ridiculous actions in Mexican military history, General Santa Anna ordered his men to stop operations to rest. The rebel colonists took advantage of this and launched a surprise attack that managed to defeat Santa Anna's forces in less than fifteen minutes. This is how Texas consummated its independence and became a republic with its own authorities. Thus, the Mexican government lost any real authority over the territory, but the Mexican authorities, lacking a realistic and pragmatic vision but with a wounded national pride, would refuse to recognize Texas as an independent nation. For more than a decade, the northeastern territory would live in a permanent state of war between the two governments.[12]

One way or another, San Antonio's Hispanic population was involved in the conflict between centralists and federalists. Part of their interests coincided with those of their Anglo-American counterparts. Merchants, ranchers, and the political authorities were decidedly pro-federalist, so they initially used their military organization to oppose centralism. The Civic Militia, the only real local military structure, played a key role in this task. As mentioned before, in 1835, when the national government tried to depose the governor of Coahuila-Texas in

CHAPTER 5

Monclova, the Texan Civic Militia intervened decisively by gathering a hundred men and preparing them to march to Coahuila.[13] The town councils of Goliad, San Patricio, and San Antonio also carried out serious preparations to move to Coahuila. San Antonio supplied thirty-nine men with weapons and horses to defend the federalist cause.[14] Although, in the end, they did not mobilize because the organizer, Ángel Navarro, wanted to avoid a violent outcome with the regular troops, the threat remained, as well as the pro-federalist position of the population expressed in its militias.

When hostilities began in Mexico, some Tejanos joined the federalist rebellion, and they used the structures of the Civic Militia. Some of its prominent members, such as Juan N. Seguín and Salvador Flores, among others, joined the movement.[15] Although there were many grievances, real or imagined, that the Tejanos attributed to the unitary system imposed from central Mexico, the most heartfelt was the abolition of the militia system that the constitution of 1836 had brought about. Even Anglo-American towns had militia units, which was why the Austin colony protested the disappearance of the Civic Militia.[16] In fact, the gravitation of the centralizing measures, which tended to weaken the periphery, had little effect in Texas. This would become more than evident years later when former members of the Civic Militia organized another militia unit in 1839 to fight Comanches, using the same structure and people of supposedly disbanded units.[17] This obstinance in the face of the Comanche danger shows that at least in the case of Texas, the militia, more than a vehicle for nationalist affirmation, was an instrument for defense and survival, which accentuated the traditional behavioral patterns of the area in the process of colonization of unknown and dangerous lands. Once again, out of fear or ignorance, the national government remained on the sidelines of the path of social development in the area, which, at least in Texas, was already pointing toward independence.

This is even clearer in the intervention and leadership of local elites in the Texas conflict. Let us look at the case of Ángel Navarro, merchant, politician, and organizer of Tejano Civic Militia units. Navarro, an influential San Antonio figure, came from a family with a long history of political activity in the region. He personally supported the federalist movement and was involved in the organization of local forces. At the last moment, however, Navarro backed out of the rebellion and decided to support Texas remaining under Mexican sovereignty. Ángel Navarro probably acted in this way because he was concerned about the consequences of open warfare in the region, as he had witnessed the disastrous effects of the persecutions unleashed by Arredondo twenty years earlier. In addition, it is possible that his action was due to the fear that the Texan territory would become an independent state dominated by an Anglo-Saxon majority, which would undoubtedly push the Mexican population into the background.* Because of this, Ángel Navarro went so far as to gather a militia of twenty men in San Antonio to support his position against independence. He even launched a proclamation that read, "Fellow citizens: You are covered with scars: you inherit from your grandfathers the custom of war in defense of your properties in this frontier of lifelong raids of barbarians and enemies. This time, show your patriotism."[18] This should be understood as the pronouncement of someone trying to seek support for local interests rather than an expression of Mexican nationalism. Navarro drew on local power structures and military leadership to support his political position. A comparable situation, in which there was an appeal to the same structures but in this case to support the opposite position, was Juan N. Seguín's way of proceeding. Son of Erasmo Seguín, he also came from a family with military and regional political lineage. He had experience in public affairs, and in 1834 he acted as political chief of Bexar. He also had military experience since he had been ensign of San Antonio's Civic Militia in 1835 and had participated in important combat against hostile Indians.[19] Perhaps because he belonged to a younger generation than Navarro, Juan N. Seguín joined the separatist movement with the rank of captain in command of a Tejano militia; he participated militarily throughout the conflict.[20] Both Seguín and Navarro,

---

* The actions of the local elites of Hispanic origin with respect to Texas's independence in 1836 should be understood according to the local circumstances and interests of the moment and not to a clear political identification with the centralist, federalist, or secessionist sides. This is the case with Ángel Navarro's brother, José Antonio Navarro, who aligned himself with the Tejano rebel side. Antonio, as a delegate of Bexar, ended up voting for independence on March 2, 1836. He actually voted in favor because of the aggressive pressure from the other delegates, Anglo-Saxons who were fervently secessionist, and so as not to be left out of the political decisions. José Antonio Navarro was one of the three Mexicans who signed Texas's Declaration of Independence. David Montejano, *Anglos and Mexicans in the Making of Texas, 1836–1986* (University of Texas Press, 1987), 26, 39; Raúl A. Ramos, *Beyond the Alamo: Forging Mexican Ethnicity in San Antonio, 1821–1861* (University of North Carolina Press, 2008), 145–46; James E. Crisp, "José Antonio Navarro. The Problem of Tejano Powerlessness," in *Tejano Leadership in Mexican and Revolutionary Texas*, ed. Jesús F. de la Teja and Raúl A. Ramos (Texas A&M University Press, 2010), 146–68.

although supporting different causes, made use of the same political and military practices used in the region since the seventeenth century to defend local interests. The behavior of the Tejanos of San Antonio would not be an isolated case in the northeastern borderlands.

The northeastern population's rejection of the central government became the norm in the region. In 1838, a new rebellion began in northern Tamaulipas, called the Movimiento de las Villas del Norte (Northern Villages Movement). The uprising began as an extension of the federalist movement in Tampico, the most important port in the entire northeast. As in the case of Texas, the establishment of the unitary regime and the consequent return of centralism affected the functioning of the other northeastern states-departments due to the lack of support in the fight against the hostile Indians, the commercial preference granted to the departments of the center of the country, and the hostility toward the elites and local bureaucracies. In October 1838, in that Tamaulipas town, Lt. Col. Longinos Montegredo pronounced himself in favor of the liberalization of foreign trade and against centralism. On November 5, lawyer Antonio Canales took the same stance in the Guerrero village of the same state.[21] Canales, a native of Monterrey, had made his political career in Tamaulipas, where he served as deputy. He obviously formed part of the local militias and acquired ample experience in warfare against Apaches and Comanches, and he had since 1834 been opposed to the centralist efforts in the country's center. Antonio Zapata, a native of the town of Guerrero, was another of the local leaders who participated in the movement initiated by Canales. Like anyone who wanted to stand out, he had participated as a commander in the militias that fought against the Indians. During the Texas campaign, he served in the Mexican army as an ensign.[22] Canales and Zapata, as part of the local elite, spearheaded the northeasterners' sense of grievance toward the centralist government. Part of their success in spreading this rebellion came from the legitimacy they had derived from their prominent participation in the local defense against hostile Indian tribes, earning them the respect of the other settlers.

Tampico became the epicenter of the uprising because it had customs resources from the port's commercial traffic. Thanks to the relative isolation of the area, at first the movement had some success. They defeated the federal troops and obtained the support of other garrisons, such as that of Matamoros. In addition, the central government focused on recovering Tampico and neglected other areas. Hence, by February, the federalist forces had taken several towns in Nuevo León. In addition, on March 2, 1839, Monterrey's city council pronounced the re-establishment of the federalist order in Monterrey. The rebel troops advanced to Coahuila, established

THE NORTHEAST IN FLAMES

themselves in Monclova, and forced the governor of Coahuila to abandon Saltillo. In this way, the rebellion extended to the states of Nuevo León and Coahuila, uniting the entire Mexican northeast in rebellion against the central government. But the Mexican government did not take long to react to these actions, and it sent more troops. During the first half of 1839, the federalists had a triumph, and their military advance continued. But then they began to stumble. In June, government forces took Tampico, taking away the rebellion's customs resources. Zapata suffered a series of defeats in Nuevo León and Tamaulipas in August, and the revolt seemed to die out. The Coahuila towns that had spoken out were returning to the official course. In October, Zapata would be defeated again in Coahuila, and by then only the north of Tamaulipas remained on the warpath.[23]

One of the peculiarities of this rebellion is that it was focused on a borderland region involving newly independent Texas. Unlike the Mexican authorities in Mexico City, the rebel group led by Canales pragmatically recognized the independence of Texas without any qualms. So from the beginning, he engaged in communications with Texas's president Mirabeau B. Lamar, asking for help. The latter refused to do so through official channels but tried to obtain commercial advantages; he could not prevent the Tejano population from getting involved in the conflict on its own. Therefore, just when the federalist cause seemed lost, Canales received reinforcements from Texas. The leader of the past conflict, Seguín, assembled a force of volunteers to join the federalists. Zapata and Canales defeated a government force near Guerrero in October and took Mier on the Tamaulipas-Texas border. A month later, Canales attacked Nuevo León and in December attempted to take Matamoros. By then, volunteers from Texas began to desert the federalist side due to the lack of booty and the casualties suffered in the fighting. Despite this, on the 29th of that month, Canales tried to take Monterrey but was defeated by Gen. Mariano Arista. In Coahuila, they suffered another defeat on January 7, 1840. But despite the setbacks, the movement's radicalization was increasing, and the rebel leaders met on January 17 in Laredo. There they established a provisional government for the northeastern states. Some historians point out that—inspired by Texas's independence attempts—a separatist movement to create the so-called República de la Sierra Madre (Republic of the Sierra Madre) was conceived at that meeting, but the evidence does not point to a clear conclusion in this regard, as such a stirring seems to have been an invention of American journalists. In any case, the leader of the new order would be Jesús Cárdenas as president and Canales as commander. The previous Coahuila and Nuevo León governors, Francisco Vidaurri and Manuel María del Llano, signed the proclamation. They established

CHAPTER 5

their headquarters in Laredo and later moved them to Guerrero. Canales took the offensive and confronted Arista in Morelos, Coahuila, on March 24. After a hard battle, Canales lost and Zapata was captured and taken prisoner. Arista offered him a pardon if he abandoned the federalist cause, but he refused and was executed. Canales retreated to San Antonio, where he sought support from Texas. There he reorganized his forces and soon occupied Tamaulipas's capital, Ciudad Victoria, and on October 25 he launched himself onto Saltillo but failed. By the end of 1840, Arista had managed to control the situation militarily, but the threat of new subversive outbreaks remained latent, so he had to look for a political solution instead of a military one. In November, he signed a peace treaty with Canales, pursuant to which Canales assumed the position of military commander of the northern towns of Tamaulipas. Although the centralist forces won most of the battles, the fighting could have continued for a long time as the neighbors of the region were experts in guerrilla warfare. In any case, the same situation as that of Texas in 1836 was repeated in the rest of the northeast from 1838 through 1840. The Federalist Rebellion highlighted the dissatisfaction of the inhabitants and local elites with the policies of the central Mexican government.[24]

The impact of the federalist insurrection among the northeastern populations varied according to each one's circumstances. In various parts of Nuevo León and Tamaulipas, the federalists were accused of looting and extorting money from their inhabitants, which according to some sources, made the movement unpopular in some areas. There were many complaints about looting from all over northern Nuevo León. The town of San Miguel was among those affected.[25] There local authorities reported the capture of thieves who identified themselves as federalists.[26] This seems more like the opportunism of some individuals trying to take advantage of the prevailing instability and insecurity. On the other hand, the population of San Miguel did not seem to be particularly against the federalist cause, at least in some cases. For example, the governor of Nuevo León sent communications to that town about certain reports that some people from San Miguel had been "seduced" by the federalist cause.[27] The letter warned about the dissolution of the associations and threatened to arrest their members, which shows that the local residents maintained ties with the rebels. When Antonio Zapata passed through the town, he sent a letter to the "main residents" asking them for a loan of five hundred pesos to help his troops. Zapata emphasized that the money would be returned.[28] Rather than extortion, it was a request that showed that the local elite had ties with the insurrectionists and was interested in the success of the armed movement.

Lampazos was not totally hostile to the federalist cause. At some point, the townspeople stated that some federalist forces, without specifying which ones, had tried to impose an exorbitant tax on the town, but Antonio Canales reduced the request "to a moderate contribution."[29] This shows that the federalists were not only seeking resources but also, above all, the support of the population. The authorities of Lampazos pointed out that its inhabitants were not in a position to mount a defense against the federalists, should they arrive. They argued that "in this town there were many who adhered to the federalists."[30] In fact, there were several residents of Lampazos who actively participated in the rebellion.[31] The government tried to protect the town by stationing a section of the regular army since the local presidio's company was fighting the federalists elsewhere.[32] It was a futile act because the rebels had informants in Lampazos, and the rebels from Lampazos were on the lookout to return the moment the regulars left the plaza.[33] Moreover, the army garrison aroused the hatred of the population because they confiscated horses and mules and slaughtered cattle indiscriminately.[34] It was clear to the centralist authorities that in order to suppress the federalist movement, it was necessary to obtain the support, or at least the neutrality, of the locals. That was why those inhabitants of Lampazos involved in the rebellion received amnesty.[35] Arista was aware of this situation and requested the participation of the residents to act as informants in places inaccessible to the army.[36]

If Lampazos and San Miguel sympathized discreetly with the federalist movement, Laredo embraced it openly. On January 6, 1839, barely two months after Canales's pronouncement, the community of Laredo sided with the federalists. It began with the thirty-three men of the First Permanent Company quartered in Laredo, most of whom were natives of the community. This unit called the population to communicate their decision and the local authorities then immediately and unanimously supported them.[37] Thus, without any significant problem, the federalist forces had access to the army's arms depots in Laredo.[38] During the conflict, Laredo was taken by both sides several times; although it is not well-documented, it seems that several of its inhabitants actively participated in the war against the centralists. Laredo was the scene of several battles and became the administrative capital of the rebellion during the year 1840. The attitude of the people of Laredo was a radical case of armed resistance to the Mexican government's centralist policies. Although not all the towns went to the extreme of rising up in arms, it is unquestionable that they felt aggrieved by the Mexican government's attitude.

CHAPTER 5

Opposition to the dominant political system of the time was something that local elites in the northeast had in common, as was the case with Basilio Benavides, who belonged to the local elite descended from Laredo's founder. Benavides headed Laredo's political and military power during the first two decades of Mexican independence. He had stood in disagreement with the Mexican government's administrative policies regarding the border towns, particularly the policy of providing substitutes for the Mexican army and, at the same time, defending the area from Indian attacks. Benavides pointed out that during its multiple campaigns in the area, the army had subjected the population to a heavy burden of requisitions and taxes that had left the town in poverty, making life extremely difficult for the locals.[39] For these reasons, Basilio Benavides supported the federalist rebellion. His nephew, Santos Benavides, also followed in these footsteps and was related to the once powerful Ramón clan. Santos Benavides's father, José María Báez Benavides, had been an officer in the local military forces. Thus, Santos Benavides, like his uncle, came from an old borderlands lineage of military and political leadership. During the Federalist Rebellion, he participated in several battles at Zapata's side and commanded a force of between thirty and forty inhabitants of Laredo who were in charge of harassing the centralist troops.[40] He would eventually become an influential politician and a Confederate officer during the American Civil War. Thus the policies of centralism alienated not only the elites of the northeastern borderlands towns but also the old political-military leadership structures that played a prominent role in the federalist revolt.

The Vidaurri family is another case with the same pattern. Through a series of marriage alliances, this family was related to the Vázquez-Borrego family and had numerous family connections in the area of Monclova in Coahuila, Lampazos, in Nuevo León, and Laredo in Tamaulipas. This family consolidated its position in the northeastern borderlands during the eighteenth century, and one of its members, Francisco Vidaurri-Villaseñor, was governor of Coahuila-Texas in 1834 and opposed the centralist government. He later supported the Federalist Rebellion and was part of the provisional federalist government for the northeastern states in 1840. This federalist fervor undoubtedly influenced his nephew, Santiago Vidaurri Valdés. There is no lack of historians who maintain that Santiago participated directly in the federalist movement, together with his uncle, and was initiated in politics together with Manuel María de Llano, another figure who was involved in the revolt.[41] Following the pattern of behavior of the northeastern local elites, Santiago Vidaurri is also a product of this combination of politics and military affairs. His father had been a soldier in the Lampazos garrison during colonial times, and Santiago had participated in organizing the defense against the nomads in Lampazos and San Miguel.[42] Like the Benavides family, Vidaurri showed the dissatisfaction of the area's leaders with the central government. This tense situation of constant frustration of the prominent locals against the centralist political disaster would prevail for the next four decades.

From 1836 to 1846, the Mexican government, headed by centralist authorities, became obsessed with recovering Texas. Although there were no resources to achieve the objective, the idea was never completely discarded during those years. There is no worse cause for friction and conflict than the creation of a new border to the detriment of the neighbor, which is why new tensions were added to those derived from the severe problem of hostile Indian raids. Incursions abounded from both the Mexican side and the Republic of Texas side, and their sole purpose was to harass the other side. On March 5, 1840, Mexican army troops took the town of San Antonio by surprise, forcing the local militia to quickly abandon the place. The Mexican forces abandoned it four days later. Again, on September 11, a force of 1,200 Mexican soldiers under the command of Adrián Woll took the same town and left on September 20.[43] The Texas forces acted in the same way; it was not unusual for Anglo-American parties from that territory to arrive in San Miguel, Lampazos, or Laredo seeking to provoke armed encounters or just rob the towns. After Woll's action, however, the Texan forces wanted to take an action of great magnitude, to give a blow that would seem definitive. On December 8, 1842, a force of seven hundred Texan volunteers took Laredo and, shortly after that, Guerrero.[44] The Texans made the mistake of dividing their forces, and one of their detachments was defeated in Mier by Gen. Pedro Ampudia, who took 176 prisoners.[45] This latent state of undeclared war occupied the attention and scarce resources of the Mexican government, which meant that local requests and needs remained, as always, in the background. At the same time, the populations of the region were indifferent to the nationalist petitions for the retaking of Texas since they were facing a much more dangerous problem: a gigantic wave of Indigenous attacks.

CHAPTER 5

AVALANCHE OF INDIGENOUS RAIDS

IN THE NORTHEAST

In the three lustrum between 1830 and the beginning of the Mexican-American War in 1846, northern Mexico was ravaged by Indian attacks, especially by Comanches. There were several reasons for the increase in raids on Mexican territory. Among them, first of all, were the efforts of the U.S. government to make peace with the Comanches and other tribes. This policy aimed to spend fewer resources to obtain, in the long run, greater expansion into western North America. In 1834, a cavalry force under Col. Henry Dodge reached the Great Plains of what is now U.S. territory, where it negotiated a peace treaty with Comanches and their allies. This motivated other traditionally antagonistic groups, such as the Osages and Kiowas, to make peace with each other; negotiations repeated in 1835 and 1837. By making peace with the Americans, the various tribes had time available and idle human resources to make a living at the expense of the Mexican ranches, since tribute or booty was the means of subsistence for these preponderantly nomadic groups. Thus the peace agreements immediately provoked increased expeditions to northern Mexico. The leading group, Comanches, no longer had to watch out for their Anglo-American neighbors or other tribes, so it redeployed its forces on wide-ranging predatory expeditions in distant places.[46]

The loss of Texas was another important factor in the increase of these raids. It implied that the Mexican government had lost access to the Great Plains of North America, so the possibility of organizing large punitive expeditions against Comanches had vanished, and the northern territories immediately became a sanctuary for the hostile Indians after their predatory expeditions. In addition, San Antonio, the traditional base where diplomatic dealings between the government and the different tribes had been carried out since the eighteenth century, had been lost. At the same time, the fight against the Anglo-American settlers had become Mexico's military priority. The door was left open, and massive Comanche attacks began in the Rio Grande area, precisely around the towns of Laredo, Lampazos, and San Miguel.[47]

During the 1835–1836 biennium, the raids were catastrophic for the northeasterners, particularly in northern Tamaulipas. In that period, Laredo lost close to a thousand head of cattle, and the Comanches killed twenty-six people, which was a lot given the low population density of the area at the time. Over the next two years, Laredo would drastically reduce crop and livestock production.[48] The range of the attacks reached Nuevo León. In April 1836, the mayor of Lampazos reported the presence of Comanche war parties marauding near town, and a force of residents went out to fight them and recovered about two hundred animals. But even so, it became known that the Indigenous had been able to sneak away with large numbers of horses and mules after killing many, many goats.[49] The town of San Miguel also reported losses from looting by the same group that had raided the area around Lampazos.[50] The plundering expeditions continued during 1836, so San Miguel and Lampazos were forced to join forces to defend themselves, with some effectiveness. Nevertheless, given the magnitude of the attacking groups, it was impossible to prevent all the robberies and deaths that were multiplying throughout the borderland territory.[51]

After 1836, Comanches faced difficulties that hindered their predatory incursions into northeastern Mexico. The most important decision of the independent government of Texas was to fight them without quarter. By 1837, Texas had made peace with Lipan Apaches, establishing a powerful alliance against Comanches, their long-time enemies. At the same time, the Comanche allies, the Kiowas and Yamparikas, came into conflict with Cheyennes, Arapahos, and Sioux. In 1839, a smallpox epidemic decimated their rancherías, severely limiting their warrior capacity, and Comanches drastically reduced their incursions into northeastern Mexico.[52] In any case, this did not mean that the region was peaceful, because Comanches continued raiding in the north of Tamaulipas and Nuevo León in 1837. In February of that year, a Comanche party of 500 warriors combed the area, killing sixteen people and destroying 1,400 animals, including horses and cows.[53] These violent actions were performed with a viciousness that cannot be explained merely from an economic point of view. Comanches did not only attack villages in northern Mexico in search of booty; they also did so because practicing violence through warfare was an integral part of their culture, in which the death of the enemy and the destruction of their means of subsistence were a way of gaining honor in their culture. Therefore, the razing of crops and livestock that they could not take back to their rancherías was a protocol in the Comanche way of warfare.[54]

Ultimately, the Lipan peace with the Texas government was not beneficial to Mexico. While they were able to concentrate on the fight against Apaches, helping to reduce their incursions into Mexican soil, the peace also freed up Lipan

CHAPTER 5

resources so that the Lipans could begin their own incursions into the borderlands zone. By the end of 1837, they were already causing problems in the corridor from Lampazos to Laredo, and in October, 150 Lipans attacked Lampazos to steal horses. In December, a temporary camp of 300 Comanches was established on the Salado River, which caused great alarm in Lampazos and San Miguel, where they killed two men, took captives, and stole nearly a thousand horses and mules.[55] In only two years, the Indian attacks had increased in the northeast, and there were no signs that the situation was going to change. In fact, it started to get worse in 1839; in January of that year they caused eighty deaths in Nuevo León. San Miguel and Lampazos suffered substantial looting. It was then that the horror stories that were to characterize the Indigenous raids began: According to accounts of the time, they even killed babies by throwing them into the air and catching them with the tip of their spears.[56] In February, Lampazos authorities reported that a captive who managed to escape warned them that the Indians would attack at the next full moon to steal all the horses.[57] Three days later, the attacks took place.[58] This party later killed a muleteer and stole twenty-seven of his mules.[59] The attacks continued in March when two groups attacked the area of San Miguel and Lampazos.[60] During the rest of the year, the villagers remained on constant alert for the possibility of such raids.[61] They still did not realize that the Indigenous concentrated their attacks during the winter. For this reason, in October at least two more attacks took place.[62]

The year 1840 was the year of the highest rate of raids, mainly because Comanches and Kiowas had made peace again with Cheyennes and Arapahos. Beginning in September 1840, Comanches thus set their sights on the northern territory of Mexico and began raiding in large numbers in Tamaulipas, Nuevo León, Coahuila, Chihuahua, and Durango. They were able to gather more men and reach further into Mexican territory. In less than six months, Comanches launched seven major raids, with forces that at times numbered close to eight hundred warriors.[63] The intensity of the attacks grew so much that they even attacked relatively large towns such as Lampazos, which they usually avoided because they were armed with artillery. On October 3, a cowboy from a ranch in that town detected a party of Indians crossing the Salado River. The local judge of Lampazos tried to gather a force of residents to pursue them, but at that time most of the inhabitants were working in the fields, so it was impossible to get them together until the following morning. Once this force assembled, three hundred Comanches suddenly appeared at the entrance to Lampazos. Never in the history of that town had such a large force of Indians tried to attack it since, at that time, it had a population of more than two thousand people. To the good fortune of its inhabitants, the force of thirty neighbors assembled by the judge held off the attack in a gun battle that lasted more than an hour. After that time, the Comanches showed a white flag to agree to a truce. The justice of the peace of Lampazos in charge of the defense agreed to parley because he had not been able to get reinforcements and thus tried to gain time, as well as to verify the state of the captives the Indians had taken. The Comanches demanded to be able to enter the town and obtain piloncillo, tobacco, and dried meat, among other things. The judge gave them part of what they requested, but they still refused to free the captives. By this time, the negotiations had reached an impasse. In addition, more vecinos reinforced the defense force and managed to sneak in and load an old cannon with shrapnel. The shooting resumed, but the Comanches retreated, realizing that it would be too costly to try to take the town. Even so, the party killed eight people.[64] This situation was not an isolated case; something similar would happen in San Miguel days later.

The same Comanche party rode south to attack San Miguel on October 5. Two cowboys from that village reported the sighting of Indians. The local judge summoned the inhabitants by beating a drum at the moment that a dustup announced the arrival of Comanches. Meanwhile, ten men on horseback gathered the people working in the nearby fields to take refuge in the larger houses of the village. Half an hour later, the Comanches arrived at the town's farmlands and tried to enter from the east side. As in the case of Lampazos, an improvised advance guard of some twenty-five or thirty vecinos met them and managed to block their advance. The invading force circled around San Miguel and tried to enter the town from the south. Again, the residents prevented it, and a brief firefight ensued. The Comanche party retreated half a league and set up their camp while the residents gathered more forces and observed the camp from a watchtower. Around two o'clock in the afternoon, the Comanches approached with a white flag, asking for a parley. In the negotiations that followed, they asked for a "fat horse" to free a local captive woman named María Josefa Cruz. The neighbors offered three horses, which the Indians refused because they were not fat enough. The woman's brother-in-law, along with another man, went to the area where the Comanches had taken refuge with two horses to negotiate the woman's release. Once there, the Comanches killed both men and the woman, took the horses, and left the area. In total, they killed eleven people, took thirteen captives, and

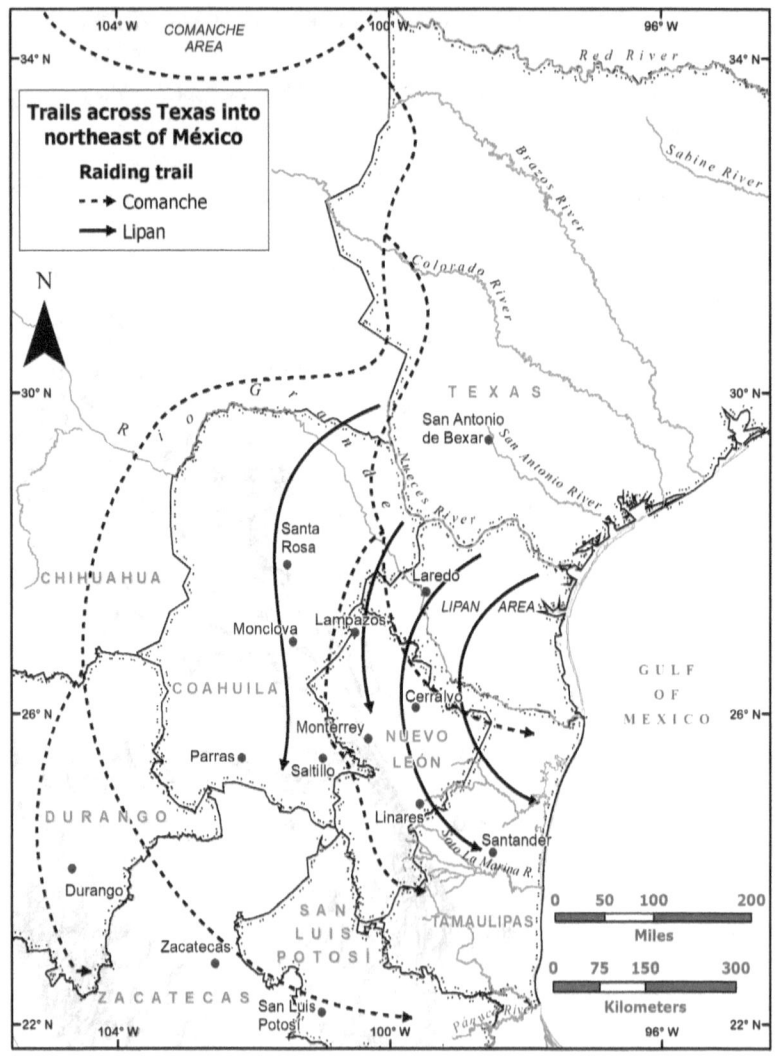

FIGURE 7. Comanche and Lipan attack routes during the 1840s. Gabriela Arreola Meneses.

destroyed the cultivated fields. In the reports rendered, it was calculated that the invading force was no less than four hundred warriors.[65]

The towns of Lampazos and San Miguel were not saved by luck but by their residents, who quickly organized the defense of these towns. They were not novices in the matter; they had always resorted to arms, and doing so was a long local tradition of self-defense and military organization. At the time of the attacks described above, the towns within the path of the Comanche raids were more exposed and vulnerable than ever, for they could not count on the protection of the Mexican government, which was busy subduing the federalist revolt. Consequently, Comanches moved at will farther and farther south of the Rio Grande, making the large-scale raids suffered by Lampazos and San Miguel common in most of the northeastern borderlands' communities. Not even large towns like Saltillo were safe.

Between December 1840 and January 1841, a large Comanche party ventured into the departments of Zacatecas and San Luis, causing much damage to populations that were not accustomed to facing this type of threat. They were forced to pass through Coahuila to return to their rancherías in the northern plains, so the populations of that department were under alert. A force of residents and troops, under the command of Gen. Isidro Reyes, was stationed at the Hacienda de Patos (today General Cepeda) with the intention to cut off the Comanches and confront them. The problem was that they did not calculate the flexibility with which these nomads could change their routes and plans of attack. So instead of taking the expected path, they decided to attack Saltillo, which was completely unprepared. On January 10, 1841, at six o'clock in the morning, the bells of Saltillo's temples rang out in alarm as a party of four hundred Comanches appeared at the southern entrance of the capital of Coahuila. As in the case of Lampazos and San Miguel, an improvised group of thirty-five residents formed for the defense, headed by the former centralist governor and magistrate José María Goríbar, and tried to contain them. The militia unit went out to the encounter and fell into an excess of confidence when the Indians pretended to retreat. In that instant, the Comanches counterattacked ferociously, massacring the residents' militia, including the former commander. Now without opposition, the Indians caused enormous damage in the outskirts of Saltillo. They took 25 captives, seized about 1,700 horses and mules, and killed more than 100 settlers and 1,100 head of livestock.[66]

While this was going on, the governor organized an armed defense of about 150 men between infantry and cavalry that succeeded in making the Comanches retreat when the former's artillery began to fire on them. They also managed to recover some captives and more than 500 animals. At that moment, Lt. Col. Juan José Elguezabal and Víctor Blanco arrived with a force of 164 residents coming from Monclova and Parras. With these reinforcements, the men from Coahuila left in pursuit of the nomads, who moved slowly due to the substantial booty that they were carrying. They reached them in the mountain range of the Boca del Tule. There, combat was unleashed that lasted about two hours and cost 18 wounded residents, but at least some captives and another 500 animals were recovered. The following day, the enemy retreated to the north, but not before taking revenge on the Palo Blanco ranch, where they burned the main house with its thirteen occupants inside.[67]

The tragedy suffered by the people of Saltillo clearly illustrates the scale and scope of the Comanche raids on the populations of the northeast. They had the demographic density, weaponry, and collective drive necessary to attack large populations; at that time, Saltillo was the largest and most important city in the northeast and had occupied that position since colonial times. During the decade from 1837 to 1847, Comanches raised forty war parties, of which there is some record, that penetrated northern Mexico, always using groups of more than a hundred warriors. Of all their campaigns, half were composed of four hundred or more men, and at least four included eight hundred to one thousand men.[68] During this period, the communities had to reorganize their defenses against the Indians, and they did so as best they could, drawing on old local experiences and traditions that had been in place since the seventeenth century.

This period of major incursions reinforced and expanded the old military structures that had existed in the area since the beginning of Spanish colonization. The use of these autonomous structures began to be more important from 1836 onwards, while the Mexican army was busy fighting the separatist movement in Texas. Therefore, no forces other than the local militias of Lampazos, San Miguel, and Laredo towns were available to combat the Comanche avalanche. These communities constituted the vertexes of a defensive triangle of the rest of the northeastern territory; this territorial defense had to be mounted by themselves and with their own resources. An official letter pointed out that "never have the borderlands towns by themselves and in isolation been able to resist and punish the barbarian tribes that harass them without close-by groups of residents coming to their favor, especially when the number of the enemies is greater than the force that each town can oppose them."[69] These towns had to support each other to contain the invasions, coordinated by the governor in the same way as they had done during the colonial period.[70] And so they did when, in 1836, a group of Comanches entered the jurisdiction of Lampazos, and San Miguel sent a group of fifteen mounted, properly armed men.[71] In Tamaulipas, Laredo sent fifty men to other towns in the Rio Grande area to cooperate in the local defense. There were attempts to set up an offensive and pursuit campaign, but it was never possible to do so, mainly due to the lack of resources.[72] In spite of all the vicissitudes, Laredo continued to carry out the regional defense and maintained communication with Lampazos and other towns to coordinate with one another.[73] Little by little, and almost without realizing it, a change in mentality was taking place among the northeasterners who were on the front line of the Apache and Comanche raids. Not only was the idea of the need to rely on one's own resources for defense becoming a reality, but it also acquired a regional dimension; the defense was not limited to one's own homestead, nor should it stop at the town's borders. This change of mentality would be fundamental for what would come later: the constitution of the National Guard in a way peculiar to the region after the war with the United States.

The particular character and organization of the local militias is an example of the use of traditional and local defense structures. The Civic Militia was never completely dismantled in these borderlands towns, so the institution the centralist government had tried to abolish remained in place, with or without permission from the country's political center. Thus when these towns were organizing the defense in 1838, they only eliminated the name "Milicia Cívica." Everything else remained the same; it was the same members and uses pretending to be a "new" military organization. Even the municipal authorities maintained the Civic Militia exemption tax collection as late as 1840.[74] It was one of the few ways to finance the defense against the Indians. These towns never abandoned their martial traditions and experience in this type of irregular warfare. This letter makes that point: "The troop [militias of residents] that was enlisted under the name of defenders, or auxiliaries, and formerly civics, is among the best and most suitable for this service ["Indian" wars]."[75]

In September 1840, the governor of Nuevo León created "a frontier force" of at least a hundred men for the defense of the department. The vecinos would pay a proportional tax according to their means to finance it. This company would be stationed in Lampazos and integrated by residents from that town, San Miguel, and other nearby towns. It was called Defensores de la Frontera (Defenders of the

CHAPTER 5

Frontier). In December, it was already tracking enemy parties.[76] In Tamaulipas, the authorities established a similar defense force. In December of that year, Laredo formed an analogous unit composed of volunteers that adopted the same name as the one in Nuevo León.[77] The captains of these companies also belonged to families that had always combined political power and military command. The commander of the Lampazos force was Santiago Vidaurri, and that of the Laredo force was Basilio Benavides.[78] This type of militia provoked animosity on the part of the regular army because, at least in the case of Nuevo León, its militias had the appearance of a self-financed alternative army. The centralist regime did not want to deal with military institutions composed of citizens again, as they considered them a threat for being out of their control, as had happened with the militias that had participated in the recent Federalist Rebellion. Due to pressure from Mexico City, the governor had to abolish the tax decree in February 1841.[79] Again, friction between the region and the nation prevented the organization of a coordinated defense. The inhabitants of the northeast wanted to have returned to them the defensive system implemented in colonial times, something to which the Mexican government would hardly agree. In turn, the latter was incapable of providing an effective defense of the territory with regular army units, which, in addition, left behind a trail of confiscations, robberies, and even unjustified murders every time they passed through these departments on the way to Texas. In fact, the northeasterners began to see the regular army as a worse threat than the Indigenous raids.

An article in the official newspaper of 1842 evidences this conflict of opinions. It points out that prior to 1813 the region had enjoyed relative stability, but the "independence movement [had come to unhinge] the admirable system of defense that the Spanish government had wisely founded to make the borderlands prosper."[80] The article goes on to expose how internal strife had squandered national resources and left the borderlands to their own devices. In short, the inhabitants of the northeastern frontier had seen their traditional defense system undermined after the consummation of independence in 1821. For this reason, at first, they repeatedly asked the central government for reinforcements to the old system based on presidios and vecinos-militiamen. The residents of Lampazos argued that in order to pacify the region, the government should populate the area with settler-soldiers, which was nothing more than an old colonial strategy.[81] The general of the small standing army stationed in the northeast at that time was Mariano Arista, who was fully aware of the justice that attended the claims of the borderlands' population. Unlike Santa Anna, he was not narrow-minded and realized that he had to cooperate with the area's inhabitants in order to defend the region. Since the 1830s, the borderlands' residents had insisted on organizing punitive campaigns against Lipans and Comanches.[82] Arista approved of this initiative and tried to arrange one that would coordinate all the northern territories. In the end, the plan fell apart due to a lack of resources and because, at that time, an uprising had begun in Tabasco that occupied the energy and attention of the Mexican government.[83] The northeast continued to be a secondary issue in the minds of the rulers in Mexico City, but Arista proposed to continue with the cooperation of the borderlands settlers by developing a new defensive plan in which the populations would be heavily involved.[84] Even though the Defensores de la Frontera force had been disbanded, the general authorized the creation of a similar detachment, called Milicia Auxiliar (Auxiliary Militia), which was again integrated by people from Lampazos and San Miguel, for being "more instructed in that kind of warfare [Indian wars]."[85] Arista also promoted the formation of local militias such as the Compañía de Defensores de Lampazos and the Compañía de Defensores de Laredo.[86] The general went so far as to authorize residents who participated militarily against the nomadic Natives to keep part of the spoils of war.[87] In short, Mariano Arista was acting in exactly the same way as the Bourbon administrators sixty years earlier and was making use of local defense traditions, which in spite of all the changes over time were still current after several centuries.

The first decades of Mexico as an independent nation did not abound with measures that would serve to integrate the northeastern territory into a national spirit, shall we say. On the contrary, almost everything that was done, particularly during the centralist years, ended up distancing it, consigning it to a second or third plane of importance. Tensions were accentuated, and pressure built up throughout the years from 1835 to 1845. The imposition of centralist policies, but above all the refusal to recognize local structures of political-military organization, alienated the region from the Mexican government. In an area where war constituted an important aspect of daily life, the central government's refusal to recognize local self-defense groups antagonized the inhabitants. The Mexican government reacted by trying to impose and use the policies of modern European states, but these could not simply be generalized to a region experiencing a true borderlands war with traditions rooted in medieval Spain. This war would grow even more dramatic with the Anglo-American expansion into North America and the

CHAPTER 5

unprecedented increase in Indigenous raids. The alienation of the local inhabitants from the Mexican state was undoubtedly one of the reasons for the weakening of Mexican military power in the northeastern borderlands. On the other hand, the local structures of combining political representation with military participation survived this period of uncertainty and were eventually strengthened. In different ways, the inhabitants of the northeast, together with their warlike traditions, would be incorporated into the centers of regional power: those located north of the Rio Grande were incorporated into the Confederacy during the American Civil War (1861–1865), and those on the south side by the powerful liberal leaderships during the Reform War (1857–1860) and the French Intervention (1862–1867). In fact, these structures survived into the periods of American Reconstruction (1865–1877) and the Restored Republic (1867–1876). Thus the borderlands military heritage and spirit of the Spanish Reconquista survived and flourished in the northeast until the end of the nineteenth century, proving to be not only a long-lasting phenomenon but also an example of how traditional structures can become modernizing. But this is another matter.

CONCLUSION

Outcome and Final Considerations

U.S. expansionism in the region changed the dynamics of northeastern communities in a variety of ways, depending on the particular circumstances of each settlement. The case of Texas deserves special attention because of the arrival of large numbers of Anglos who brought with them their own legal, religious, and racial traditions. This inevitably led to a variety of conflicts with the Hispanic population, especially since by 1836, the Anglos in Texas outnumbered the Mexicans by at least ten to one, according to conservative estimates. After Texas independence, the position of the local San Antonio elite of Hispanic origin was affected and displaced by the new political order led by the Anglo faction. At first, things seemed to follow the usual order: José Antonio Navarro and Juan N. Seguín served in the Texas legislature. Seguín came to participate in the army of the new republic in the defense of the territory against aggressions from Mexican military forces and against Comanche raids. They tried to use the long-established political and military leadership system they and their ancestors had practiced for generations. In addition, they acted as cultural intermediaries between the traditional population of Hispanic origin and the Anglo population.[1]

Seguín tried to defend his group from the political discrimination that Spanish speakers were beginning to face and tried to make the Texas political system more inclusive. But he witnessed how the original Tejanos were becoming suspect characters in the eyes of the new majority. They began to be discriminated against because of their skin color, religious traditions, language, and ignorance of the newly introduced legal forms, and they were accused of being loyal to the Mexican government, but above all, the Anglos coveted the productive lands owned by Tejanos. This factor and military tensions caused by Mexico's military hostility toward Texas widened the rift between the two groups. Seguín tried to argue for the participation of the Tejanos in his uprising against Mexico to show his loyalty to Texas. At the same time, he used the tradition of military involvement to give his Tejanos a strong political voice. All these strategies ended up failing, and Seguín went into exile in Mexico. He would be the last mayor of Hispanic origin in San Antonio for the rest of the nineteenth century, which shows how geopolitical and racial issues displaced his ethnic group.[2] Seguín would later say, "[I have become] a foreigner in my native land."[3] It meant the end of the traditional defense organization structures used in Texas since the seventeenth century. Another event also changed the way of life for the inhabitants of the northeastern frontier during the second half of the nineteenth century: the US-Mexico War (1846–1848).

During the 1840s, the US government made great efforts to realize its goal of extending US territory to the Pacific Ocean. New Mexico, California, and the newly independent republic of Texas were to become part of the United States as part of this vision. The government of that nation made offers to purchase California and New Mexico from the Mexican government, offers that were flatly rejected by the Mexican authorities, who also warned that they would consider the act of incorporating Texas into US territory a declaration of war. The threats, however, were of little avail, and Texas was admitted as another state of the American union in December 1845. In May 1846, hostilities began in the territorial strip between the Nueces and Rio Bravo rivers, initiating a conflict in which the Mexican army's chances of success were utterly nil. A little more than a year later, on September 16, 1847, the Stars and Stripes were raised on the Zocalo in Mexico City. Peace was signed on February 2, 1848, through the Treaty of Guadalupe Hidalgo, where Mexico ceded more than half its national territory to the United States.*

It was an unequal war that showed the Mexican army's and authorities' lack of preparation to face a conflict against a modern and industrialized nation. They faced an enemy army led by professional officers, West Point Military Academy graduates, including Ulysses S. Grant and Robert E. Lee, who had the advantage of better logistics and supply lines. It was not only Mexico's technological and financial backwardness or the low level of training of the Mexican army that prevented an adequate defense; internal divisions also contributed. It was useless for the Mexican government to revive the former Civic Militia, now called the National Guard. Moreover, at the same time as the armed conflict with the Americans, Mexico

---

* It included the present-day states of New Mexico, California, Arizona, Utah, and Colorado.

was facing Indigenous rebellions in Yucatan, the Sierra Gorda region, and Oaxaca. As if that were not enough, disputes among politicians and within the Mexican army were also the order of the day. Such was the case of Gen. Mariano Paredes Arrillaga, who was sent to San Luis Potosí with one of the best divisions of the Mexican army in late 1845, when war was imminent. But instead of protecting the country's north, he returned to Mexico City to overthrow President José Joaquín de Herrera. This type of action showed a country divided and incapable of mounting an effective opposition.[4]

Four significant battles took place in the northeast. The first two were Palo Alto and Resaca de la Palma on May 8 and 9, 1846. There the Mexican army was overwhelmed by U.S. artillery and the enemy's great maneuvering ability. The brave charges of the Mexican cavalry were useless and a waste of men. Later, the Battle of Monterrey took place from September 20 to 23, 1846. There the Mexican army inflicted heavy losses on the American invaders. Although there were severe tactical errors by the defending force and a lack of communication between the various Mexican units, there were enough men and supplies to continue resisting. After three days of combat, however, Gen. Pedro Ampudia inexplicably surrendered the city to the American army. Finally, the last great battle would be the Battle of Buena Vista, held on the outskirts of Saltillo on February 22 and 23, 1847. In this encounter, the Mexican forces were on the offensive and had the advantage for most of the combat. But the long journey of the Mexican troops from San Luis—nearly five hundred kilometers—had left the Mexican forces exhausted and with an inadequate supply train. Therefore, on February 23, Santa Anna, in command of these forces, was satisfied with the successes of the day before and withdrew the troops from the battlefield. It was a retreat that foreshadowed defeat. The people of the northeast witnessed firsthand the mistakes and problems of the central government in carrying out the region's defense. Santiago Vidaurri, a native of Lampazos, was the secretary of the government of Nuevo León during the war. His fellow countryman, Juan Zuazua, enlisted as a National Guard volunteer and participated in the battles at Monterrey and Buena Vista and later joined the guerrillas. Juan N. Seguín from Bejar, who had taken refuge in Mexico in 1842 fleeing Anglo persecution, fought in Buena Vista under the Mexican flag.[5] The aftermath of this conflict would profoundly affect the northeast.

After annexation by the United States in 1848, Laredo became part of Texas, and political control of the town remained in local hands. This was attributable to the fact that unlike San Antonio, Laredo did not have significant Anglo immigration,

CONCLUSION

which allowed the Benavides clan to maintain its status as a source of political and military leadership for several decades. Santos Benavides, for example, would play an essential role in the area's defense. Benavides was a prominent fighter in the armed conflicts against Lipan Apaches, protected the town from banditry, and chased escaped slaves from southern plantations. During the Civil War, he supported the Confederate side, as many Tejanos did. In this conflict, Benavides formed a cavalry company made up of Laredo citizens, where he rose to the rank of captain and successfully defended the area against Union raids and attacks. Despite his remarkable participation in the military actions of the war, Benavides and his men suffered discrimination in their pay, up to nine months in arrears. This was also reflected in the unfair conditions of enlistment imposed by the Anglo officers of the Confederacy, who wanted to force the Natives to serve longer than the Anglos and to equip them with lances instead of the Sharps rifles that they regularly used. The soldiers complained to Benavides, who conveyed their grievance to the governor of Texas. The authorities realized that if they did not address this situation, there would be no volunteers for Laredo's defense, so they brought the officers to heel. This illustrates how Benavides used his political and military authority effectively, just as his uncle Basilio had done a generation earlier. At the same time, it shows how the people of Laredo continued to use their armed participation to weigh their political decisions. During Reconstruction (1865–1877), Santos Benavides ceased to be a military leader but remained a political one, as well as a prominent merchant and rancher along with his brother Cristóbal. Santos Benavides served in the Texas legislature from 1879 to 1884; he would later use his political capital to support the public career of his son Juan V. Benavides.[6] The end of armed military conflicts in the area during that time, however, made it unnecessary to continue martial traditions. By the close of the nineteenth century, the old connection of political power and military service that had characterized Laredo since colonial times had disappeared.

In Mexico, the towns of San Miguel and Lampazos experienced a different political-military process. Santiago Vidaurri used the military structure of the border towns to lead a successful revolution against Santa Anna in 1855. Vidaurri would become the most powerful leader in the northeast for nearly a decade (1855–1864), largely due to his involvement in the local military. He formed a regional army under the name of the National Guard but organized along local lines, played a significant role in the Reform War, and was able to field six thousand men on the battlefield. Later, during the French Intervention, figures trained in this force would play a crucial role in the resistance against the invading force. Officers such as Ignacio Zaragoza, the Mexican general who led the battle of May 5, or Mariano Escobedo, the general who defeated Maximilian's forces in 1867, were products of this local military tradition. Even after this conflict, such a military force would remain powerful. New local leaders, such as Jerónimo Treviño and Francisco Naranjo, led them. When Porfirio Díaz plotted his Tuxtepec insurrection in 1876, he had to negotiate the support of Treviño and Naranjo; otherwise, Díaz's triumph would have been impossible. Porfirio Díaz was aware of the military capabilities of Nuevo León and was therefore cautious in how he dealt with the political forces in the region. Although he politically and militarily subjugated most of the national territory during the 1880s, it took him another decade to do so in Nuevo León.[7] By then, the borderlands had been pacified and the region was developing an important industrial sector, so the need for the local towns to maintain the local customs of military organization faded away.

The Treaty of Guadalupe Hidalgo would also have another impact at the regional level, as redrawing the US-Mexico border around the Río Bravo would significantly alter population dynamics in the northeast. Ironically, this arbitrary political redrawing did not divide but further integrated the region. Initially, this was in response to the commercial opportunities it brought, both legal and illegal. This new factor was already evident in the midst of the war between the United States and Mexico in 1846. In September 1846, the mayor of Lampazos complained that the vecinos of that town were "bad Mexicans ... without attending to the state of war that the nation has with the United States and without attending to their honor and decorum, are [...] trading and traveling to Texas."[8] This situation continued throughout the war, and Lampazos's inhabitants openly organized wagon trains to trade in Béjar instead of "contributing as Mexicans to the defense of the homeland."[9] In this way, the commercial dynamics strengthened regional interests over national ones. From 1848 onwards, trade networks between Texas and the northeastern Mexican states increased. The governor of Nuevo León and Coahuila, Santiago Vidaurri, was able to capitalize on this commercial boom and use the resources of the customs offices to consolidate his power. In addition, access to an arms market allowed him to build a powerful military force. Later, the American Civil War (1861–1865) would increase trade, as the southern states could not export their cotton production to Europe because their Unionist enemies blocked their ports. Therefore, this white gold was transported to the northeast and shipped mainly to England through the ports of Matamoros and Tampico.[10]

CONCLUSION

This type of exchange took place largely thanks to the networks between the Mexican populations on the southern and northern banks of the Rio Grande. They took advantage of their geographic location and their identity bonds as frontiersmen. Such cooperation was not limited to commercial exchange but was a largely military cooperation based on regional needs, independent of national directives from Mexico City, Washington, or Richmond. Mexicans in northeastern Mexico and southern Texas worked together to fight Native Americans, filibusters, and common enemies. Military forces from Laredo often crossed the Rio Bravo to pursue rivals with Vidaurri's full approval and without diplomatic repercussions. Likewise, the control of trade in the region denied their allies' rivals basic necessities such as weapons or grain. It is essential to mention the network of information they had on the movements of their rivals. Such was the case of Santos Benavides, who, as an officer in the Confederate army, had privileged information about the movements of the French army in Nuevo León and Tamaulipas, information that Benavides unashamedly provided to the Mexican guerrillas under the command of Mariano Escobedo. Occasionally, when military fortune did not favor them, they crossed to the opposite bank of the Rio Bravo, seeking refuge and protection in this support network woven along the border, which allowed them to regroup and return to the fight. These movements would be in both directions, north to south and south to north, since the arbitrary territorial division existed only to gain advantage. What mattered to these people and their communities was that they shared a culture and a tradition of military organization and cooperation.[11]

The old political-military leadership structure in all the villages studied formed a vital part of the local traditions. This tradition originated in the Hispanic Middle Ages within the particular context of a disputed frontier between Christians and Muslims. From that period, the tradition established that political privileges went to those individuals who, through their own resources, could colonize and establish military control in the new borderland territories. Thus the figures of "adelantados" and "caudillos" became an archetypal part of this pattern of territorial control. This pattern was successfully exported to other areas, from the Canary Islands to New Santander, where colonization and settlements were established in the mid-eighteenth century. The individuals who used this form of leadership were cut from the same cloth, from El Cid, through Hernán Cortés, Luis Carvajal y de la Cueva, to Alonso de León and José de Escandón; they all shared the same characteristics and approach to territorial expansion. They were warlords, businessmen, administrators, and politicians, all simultaneously, with the authorization

OUTCOME AND FINAL CONSIDERATIONS

of the Crown. In places where the authority of the state had no way of asserting itself, this type of leadership became an excellent tool for expansion. But when the Spanish Crown was strong enough to take the reins of new territories, this type of leadership became unnecessary and lost its privileges, as happened to Cortés years after the conquest of Mexico. Ironically, as this mechanism became obsolete in Europe and the large urban populations of the Americas, it experienced a renaissance on the northeastern frontier of New Spain from the seventeenth to the mid-nineteenth centuries. This form of colonization would lead to the emergence of a local elite firmly rooted in the region and whose influence rested on this medieval power structure. For two centuries, this elite would control the political and military structure of the area.

The political reconfiguration of the northeastern frontier was firmly anchored to this cultural heritage of the Castilian frontier of the Reconquest. Local leaders based their power on their ability to defend local populations and conduct military operations; they had to be able to provide and finance the means to mount military defense operations on the frontier. This power structure spread through family networks that arrived in the region during the seventeenth century, such as the Ramón, Benavides, and Urrutia families. Moreover, during some historical events, such as the War of Independence, some of these clans lost their influence and were replaced by other new ones that used the same operation. The social structure in which this "aristocracy" operated remained firmly rooted. This fact would lead to constant struggles with the authorities that sought to control the territory from the administrative capitals, as the Bourbons tried to do during the last period of Spanish hegemony in the area, or the different national authorities of the Mexican government throughout the nineteenth century. This externally imposed administrative approach would cause resentment among the local elites against the central administrations. The Bourbons would soon realize that without the cooperation of local authority figures, the defense of Spain's imperial interests on the frontier was doomed to failure. Therefore, the Bourbon authorities reluctantly had to use the original defense structures and coordinate with local forces. This is a continuation of the same order that arose since the Middle Ages, in which the state authority had no way to achieve complete control of any place. These were in full use in the eighteenth century on the Spanish frontier in North America. On the other hand, during the first half of the nineteenth century, the Mexican government never realized the importance of the collaboration of local authority figures and that it had to respect their traditional methods of defense if it wanted

CONCLUSION

to exert any kind of territorial control. The result was that these elites, in one case, supported separatist movements and, in another, were indifferent to the defense of the territory against the United States in its conflict with Mexico. Finally, those who failed in their autonomist rebellions would lead a revolutionary movement that would overthrow the national government. Until the national governments could control the territory politically and economically, following the decline of hostile Indigenous groups, improved communications, and the beginning of industrialization in the late nineteenth century, local elites continued to maintain control of the area using their military power structures.

The way the northeastern leaders exercised their authority was not the only vestige of the Spanish past on this frontier. These leaders drew their political backing from the towns' inhabitants; the way these settlers supported their leaders was also an adaptation of the Reconquest through their tradition of military service in a conflict-ridden territory. The Crown initially granted economic and social privileges to people who agreed to settle in areas dangerously close to Moorish possessions. This practice led to the emergence of a warrior sector of the population, dedicated to military action, whose members followed their leaders whenever they could obtain these privileges. This ethos of practicing war in exchange for privileges emerged at that time and would be replicated during the period of colonial expansion. Internalizing these martial values in popular culture fueled the Spanish conquistadors' fever for military glory in the sixteenth century. Much of the expansion in the northeast during the seventeenth and eighteenth centuries was founded on these attitudes and integrated into the same tradition of centuries of military expansion. That pattern would lead to the emergence of a way of understanding and obtaining the rights of citizens/vecinos through the service of arms. It became an inclusive system that allowed for the integration of frontier society and an opportunity to climb social hierarchies. In the northeast, some Indigenous communities even became integrated with the Hispanic populations when they shared the same sense of defense duty. Over time, changes in politics, administration, and development influenced the region. Such a process affected local categorizations of individual military service, but, at the same time, the core of these values remained the same throughout the centuries. Not only were the locals prepared for military service, but war itself represented a way of life on which their traditions were based. The people of the northeast were willing to serve in arms and understood this act as an inherent part of their local identity, just as their ancestors had done centuries before.

OUTCOME AND FINAL CONSIDERATIONS

One of the bases of this attitude toward war was that it represented not only a hope for social advancement but also a way to generate material gain; this was one of the first tools that Iberian monarchs used to motivate individuals to colonize places that were risky frontier zones. The first and most significant incentive to settle was the opportunity to plunder and obtain booty. High-ranking prisoners could be forced to pay a ransom, but for most, there was no choice but to remain captive. This way of acquiring slaves became a widespread way of making war profits. Slave hunting was extensively practiced in colonizing the Americas through legal formulas adapted and refined over the centuries. Encomienda and congrega were inspired by Castilian traditions or requerimiento, which used theological arguments about just war and Christianity and became ritualized tools for profiting from war practices. Over time, the authorities eliminated such practices from Spain and the economically important areas of the Spanish viceroyalties in the Americas. Ironically, they would become one of the pillars of colonizing settlements in northeastern New Spain. Spanish colonizers widely practiced them and repeated this pattern of territorial expansion until the mid-eighteenth century.

As in the case of political leadership and categories of social inclusion, the tradition of practicing war as an economic activity was transforming. The Bourbons succeeded in eliminating Indigenous slavery, at least on a large scale, in the northeast. Settlers in the area, however, continued to profit from their military activity in other ways. The tradition of participating in war parties to attack Indigenous villages in exchange for loot, such as horses, continued during the Bourbon period and also under Mexican authorities. Outside authorities had to accept these customs to get the northeastern settlements to cooperate with them. The same would happen with the attempts to make institutional changes from the outside. Such was the case with the implementation of the Civic Militia, whose system of quotas and payments mirrored contemporary European institutions, whose origins were very different from medieval conceptions of organized defense. Instead of "modernizing" local defense structures, the frontier populations used the Civic Militia to perpetuate their control over military finances. By controlling them, they obtained their own resources and financed military actions. In this way, the economic organization for war continued to function.

The same military traditions were applied on a symbolic level. During the colonial period, the use of symbols and rituals to reinforce the martial ethos had a clearly medieval origin. The use of religious representations, such as the cult of the figure of the apostle Saint James, armed processions for defensive purposes during

CONCLUSION

Holy Week, or the military reviews, known as alardes, was a cultural heritage that continued through generations. Although discontinued as a military practice in Spain, these traditions retained this function in the northeastern frontiers. They provided the ideological superstructure that supported the culture of military service on the frontier. They served a pragmatic and necessary purpose, as this was the only way a society could successfully settle and colonize the contested northern landscape. These structures proved their adaptability over time. The Bourbons, whose paradigm was to obtain an efficient administration of resources, had to accept the usefulness of these symbols. Instead of eliminating them, they promoted them so that throughout the colonial period, the use of religious symbols as a way of encouraging military participation remained in force.

The nature of the symbols was changing, and the inhabitants of the northeast omitted those with a religious character to frame them in the ideology of a republican nation-state. The Civic Militia was thus intended to be a tool to foster a sense of patriotism and national identity; it was a civic institution. The symbols now functioned around things like the national flag, periodic assemblies to indoctrinate loyalty to the nation, military reviews to verify military training and internalization of military values, and the introduction of various holidays to commemorate recent historical events like Independence Day. These changes represented a change only in the appearance of the ideological superstructure; it had the same function of helping the settlers to survive in an area full of armed threats. The symbolic transformation was only of form but not of substance, and it did not change the social conformation of the region. The military reviews made during the Mexican period to commemorate dates were essentially a continuation of the ancient boasts made during the seventeenth and eighteenth centuries to celebrate Saint James. The cultural infrastructure was left intact despite the apparent imposition of changes due to historical processes. The inhabitants of the northeastern frontier adapted the symbols that supported their way of life to the political particularities of the moment. It was not a change but an evolution of their defense system.

The continuity and reproduction of a military organization of Iberian-medieval origin on the northeastern borderlands continued to function until the end of the nineteenth century. This did not mean that this area lived in an era of ignorance and stagnation in terms of the use of technologies. This work shows the versatility of the eminently medieval cultural structures that allowed the establishment and

OUTCOME AND FINAL CONSIDERATIONS

survival of populations in frontier regions. Their inhabitants successfully used these structures and their implications for political leadership to resist external impositions that sought to limit their autonomy. Contrary to what some traditional historiography portrays, the population of this region was not a passive entity amid geopolitical conflicts of different empires and nations, nor was it passive in the face of waves of hostile incursions by nomadic Natives. The local people broadly defined the historical events that occurred in this area, such as the US-Mexico War. This interpretation also serves as a model for analyzing the Spanish process in other frontier regions of the Americas. Figures such as José Gervasio Artigas in Uruguay, José Manuel de Rosas in Argentina, or Álvaro Obregón and Francisco Villa in northwestern Mexico were part of the same historical process as people such as Juan N. Seguín, Santos Benavides, or Santiago Vidaurri. It is no coincidence that the rise of caudillos during the nineteenth century in Latin America plagued the region until nation-states could impose themselves. Values and cultural systems are hard to destroy.

NOTES

INTRODUCTION

1. In 1834, a surprised American traveler in northern Mexico described how some muleteers prepared for an Indigenous attack by using weaponry such as the *adarga*. John Joseph Linn, *Reminiscences of Fifty Years in Texas* (D. & J. Sadlier & Company, 1935), 33.
2. Brian DeLay, *War of a Thousand Deserts: Indian Raids and the U.S.-Mexican War* (New Haven, CT: Yale University Press, 2008); Sean F. McEnroe, *From Colony to Nationhood in Mexico: Laying the Foundations, 1560–1840* (Cambridge University Press, 2012); Luis Medina Peña, *Los bárbaros del Norte. Guardia nacional y política en Nuevo León, siglo XIX* (Fondo de Cultura Económica, 2012).
3. Jorge Cañizares-Esguerra, *Puritan Conquistadors. Iberianizing the Atlantic, 1550–1700* (Stanford University Press, 2006); Daniel K. Richter, *Before the Revolution. America's Ancient Past* (Belknap Press of Harvard University Press, 2011).
4. David J. Weber, *The Spanish Frontier in North America* (New Haven, CT: Yale University Press, 1992), 11–13; Miguel A. Ladero Quesada, *La formación medieval de España* (Alianza Editorial, 2014), 174–75; Thomas Devaney, *Enemies in the Plaza. Urban Spectacle and the End of Spanish Frontier Culture, 1460–1492* (University of Pennsylvania Press, 2015), 9–14.

CHAPTER 1

1. Joseph Pérez, *Historia de España* (Crítica, 2000), 37–41.
2. Pérez, *Historia de España*, 42–43; Angus MacKay, *Spain in the Middle Ages: From Frontier to Empire, 1000–1500* (Macmillan, 1977), 40–41.
3. Pérez, *Historia de España*, 43.
4. James F. Powers, *A Society Organized for War: The Iberian Municipal Militias in the Central Middle Ages, 1000–1284* (University of California Press, 1988), 184–85.
5. Pérez, *Historia de España*, 47; MacKay, *Spain in the Middle Ages*, 2–3.

6. Pérez, *Historia de España*, 2003, 40–42.
7. Bernard F. Reilly, *Cristianos y Musulmanes, 1031–1157. Historia de España, VI* (Crítica, 1992); Simona Artusi, "El Esplendor Islámico en Europa: La España Musulmana y Mozárabe," in *La Edad Media. 1. Bárbaros, cristianos y musulmanes*, coord. Umberto Eco (Fondo de Cultura Económica, 2015), 767–74.
8. Pérez, *Historia de España*, 47–55.
9. Pérez, *Historia de España*, 47–55; Adeline Rucquoi, *La Historia Medieval de la Península Ibérica* (El Colegio de Michoacán, 2000), 231–36.
10. Pérez, *Historia de España*, 2003, 44–45; MacKay, *Spain in the Middle Ages*, 18–19.
11. Powers, *A Society Organized for War*, 17.
12. Powers, *A Society Organized for War*, 23.
13. Powers, *A Society Organized for War*, 23.
14. Francisco García Fitz, "Una Frontera Caliente: La Guerra en las Fronteras Castellano-Musulmanas (siglos XI–XIII)," in *Identidad y Representación de La Frontera En La España Medieval, Siglos XI–XIV: Seminario Celebrado En La Casa de Velázquez y La Universidad Autónoma de Madrid, 14–15 de Diciembre 1998*, Colección de La Casa de Velázquez vol. 75 (Casa de Velázquez: Universidad Autónoma de Madrid, 2001), 166.
15. Powers, *A Society Organized for War*, 21, 29, 66.
16. Powers, *A Society Organized for War*, 208.
17. Margarita Torres Sevilla, "La España del Norte (Siglos VIII a XI)," in Miguel A. Ladero and Martín Almagro Gorbea, *Historia Militar de España* (Ediciones del Laberinto S. L, 2010), 110–40; Miguel Ángel Ladero Quesada, "Baja Edad Media 1250–1504," in Miguel A. Ladero and Martín Almagro Gorbea, *Historia Militar de España* (Ediciones del Laberinto S. L, 2010), 242; García Fitz, "Una Frontera Caliente," 167–68.
18. Francisco García Fitz, "La Reconquista y la Formación de la España Medieval (de mediados del siglo XI a mediados del siglo XIII)" in Miguel A. Ladero and Martín Almagro Gorbea, *Historia Militar de España* (Ediciones del Laberinto S. L, 2010), 141–215, 223.
19. Juan Carlos Ruiz Guadalajara, "…A Su Costa E Minsion … El Papel de los Particulares en la Conquista, Pacificación y Conservación de la Nueva España," in *Las Milicias Del Rey de España: Sociedad, Política e Identidad en las Monarquías Ibéricas* (Fondo de Cultura Económica, 2009); Ladero Quesada, "Baja Edad Media 1250–1504," 220.
20. *Las Siete Partidas del rey don Alfonso el Sabio, cotejadas con varios códices antiguos por la Real Academia de la Historia: Partida segunda y tercera* (En la Imprenta Real, 1807), 238.
21. *Las Siete Partidas del rey*, 238–39.
22. *Las Siete Partidas del rey*, 77.
23. *Las Siete Partidas del rey*, 77.

24. Carlos de Ayala Martínez, "Las órdenes militares castellano-leonesas y la acción de frontera en el siglo XIII," in *Identidad y Representación de La Frontera En La España Medieval, Siglos XI–XIV* (Casa de Velázquez: Universidad Autónoma de Madrid, 2001), 155.
25. José María Ortuño Sánchez-Pedreño, *El adelantado de la Corona de Castilla* (EDITUM, 1997), 34.
26. Ladero Quesada, "Baja Edad Media, 1250–1504," 299–325; Pérez, *Historia de España*, 2003, 75–93.
27. Ladero Quesada, "Baja Edad Media, 1250–1504," 299–325; Pérez, *Historia de España*, 2003, 75–93.
28. Manuel García Fernández, "Violencia y sociedad feudal. Reflexiones desde la Frontera del Islam Peninsular (Siglos XIII-XV)," in *La Violencia En La Historia: Análisis Del Pasado y Perspectiva Sobre El Mundo Actual*, Collectanea 165 (Universidad de Huelva, 2012), 31–32.
29. García Fernández, "Violencia y sociedad feudal," 31–32.
30. García Fernández, "Violencia y Sociedad Feudal," 34–36; Ladero Quesada, "Baja Edad Media, 1250–1504," 290–291.
31. García Fernández, "Violencia y Sociedad Feudal," 36–37; Ladero Quesada, "Baja Edad Media, 1250–1504," 332.
32. Ladero Quesada, "Baja Edad Media, 1250–1504," 328.
33. García Fernández, "Violencia y Sociedad Feudal," 37–39.
34. Pérez, *Historia de España*, 2003, 128–31; Ladero Quesada, "Baja Edad Media," 299–325.
35. Joseph Pérez, *Carlos V, emperador de dos mundos* (Ediciones B, 1998), 13–31.
36. Pérez, *Historia de España*, 2003, 145–48.
37. Powers, *A Society Organized for War*, 208–9.
38. Christian Duverger, *Crónica de La Eternidad: ¿Quién escribió la Historia Verdadera de la Conquista de la Nueva España?* (México: Taurus, 2012), 49.
39. John Huxtable Elliott, *Imperial Spain, 1469–1716* (Penguin, 1970), 57–58; Ladero Quesada, "Baja Edad Media 1250–1504," 352–53.
40. Felipe Fernández-Armesto, *The Canary Islands after the Conquest: The Making of a Colonial Society in the Early Sixteenth Century* (Oxford University Press, 1982), 132, 200.
41. Fernández-Armesto, *The Canary Islands*, 38–39, 48–49, 54, 132, 146–50.
42. Fernández-Armesto, *The Canary Islands*, 38–39, 48–49, 54, 132, 146–50.
43. Rafael Gutiérrez Cruz, *Los Presidios Españoles Del Norte de Africa en tiempo de los Reyes Católicos* (Ciudad Autónoma de Melilla, Consejería de Cultura, Educación, Juventud y Deporte, Servicio de Publicaciones, 1997); Andrew C. Hess, *The Forgotten Frontier: A History of the Sixteenth Century Ibero-African Frontier* (University of Chicago Press, 1978); Elliott, *Imperial Spain, 1469–1716*, 52–55.

44. Christon I. Archer, *World History of Warfare* (University of Nebraska Press, 2002), 237–40; Ladero Quesada, "Baja Edad Media, 1250–1504" 356–62.
45. Geoffrey Parker, *The Army of Flanders and the Spanish Road, 1567–1659; the Logistics of Spanish Victory and Defeat in the Low Countries' Wars* (Cambridge University Press, 1972), 33.
46. MacKay, *Spain in the Middle Ages*, 210–11; Powers, *A Society Organized for War*, 213.
47. Luis Weckmann, *La Herencia Medieval Del Brasil* (Fondo de Cultura Económica, 1993), 18; Luis Weckmann, *La Herencia Medieval de México* (El Colegio de México, Fondo de Cultura Económica, 1994), 27.
48. Jérôme Baschet, *La Civilización Feudal: Europa Del Año Mil a La Colonización de América* (Fondo de Cultura Económica, 2009), 29.
49. Weckmann, *La Herencia Medieval de México*; Weckmann, *La Herencia Medieval Del Brasil*, 19; MacKay, *Spain in the Middle Ages*, 211–12; Powers, *A Society Organized for War*, 213. Baschet, *La Civilización Feudal*, 24, 29; Guillermo Céspedes del Castillo, *América Hispánica, 1492–1898* (Marcial Pons Historia, 2009); Pérez, *Historia de España*, 2003, 45; Matthew Restall and Felipe Fernandez-Armesto, *The Conquistadors: A Very Short Introduction* (Oxford University Press, 2012), 21; Jacques Lafaye, *Los conquistadores* (Fondo de Cultura Económica, 1999), 13–19; Elliott, *Imperial Spain, 1469–1716*, 31–32; Silvio A. Zavala, *Las Instituciones Jurídicas en la Conquista de América* (Editorial Porrúa, 2006); Amy G. Remensnyder, *La Conquistadora: The Virgin Mary at War and Peace in the Old and New Worlds* (Oxford University Press, 2014).
50. Castillo, *América Hispánica*, 59–62.
51. Castillo, *América Hispánica*, 67–68.
52. Weckmann, *La Herencia Medieval de México*, 95; Castillo, *América Hispánica*, 67–68.
53. Castillo, *América Hispánica*, 74–75.
54. Restall and Fernández-Armesto, *The Conquistadors*, 26–27.
55. Archer, *World History of Warfare*, 240.
56. Lafaye, *Los conquistadores*, 56–59.
57. Lafaye, *Los conquistadores*, 45.
58. Restall and Fernández-Armesto, *The Conquistadors*, 57.
59. Restall and Fernández-Armesto, *The Conquistadors*, 58.
60. Charles Gibson, *Tlaxcala in the Sixteenth Century* (New Haven, CT: Yale University Press, 1952), 21–27; Laura E. Matthew and Michael R. Oudijk, *Indian Conquistadors: Indigenous Allies in the Conquest of Mesoamerica* (University of Oklahoma Press, 2007).
61. Gibson, *Tlaxcala in the Sixteenth Century*, 164.
62. Weckmann, *La Herencia Medieval de México*, 144–45.
63. Weckmann, *La Herencia Medieval de México*, 29.

64. Castillo, *América Hispánica*, 86–92; Robert Himmerich y Valencia, *The Encomenderos of New Spain, 1521–1555* (University of Texas Press, 1991).
65. Philip Wayne Powell, *Soldiers, Indians, & Silver; the Northward Advance of New Spain, 1550–1600* (University of California Press, 1952), 47.
66. Powell, *Soldiers, Indians, & Silver*, 43.
67. Carlos Lázaro Avila, *Las Fronteras de América y los "Flandes Indianos"* (Consejo Superior de Investigaciones Científicas, Centro de Estudios Históricos, Departamento de Historia de América, 1997), 59–60.
68. Powell, *Soldiers, Indians, & Silver*, 52–53.
69. Avila, *Las Fronteras de América*, 60.
70. Avila, *Las Fronteras de América*, 60–64; Powell, *Soldiers, Indians, & Silver*, 32–54.
71. Powell, *Soldiers, Indians, & Silver*, 58, 68.
72. Powell, *Soldiers, Indians, & Silver*, 119; Philip Wayne Powell, *Mexico's Miguel Caldera: The Taming of America's First Frontier, 1548–1597* (University of Arizona Press, 1977), 28.
73. Powell, *Mexico's Miguel Caldera*, 34.
74. Powell, *Soldiers, Indians, & Silver*, 129.
75. Powell, *Soldiers, Indians, & Silver*, 64, 100; Avila, *Las Fronteras de América*, 58.
76. Powell, *Soldiers, Indians, & Silver*, 73–101.
77. Powell, *Soldiers, Indians, & Silver*, 115–19.
78. Powell, *Soldiers, Indians, & Silver*, 120.
79. Powell, *Soldiers, Indians, & Silver*, 123.
80. Powell, *Soldiers, Indians, & Silver*, 132.
81. Powell, *Soldiers, Indians, & Silver*, 129.
82. Powell, *Soldiers, Indians, & Silver*, 124–25.
83. Powell, *Soldiers, Indians, & Silver*, 151–57.
84. Charles Gibson, *Tlaxcala in the Sixteenth Century*, 183; Powell, *Soldiers, Indians, & Silver*, 193.
85. Charles Gibson, *Tlaxcala in the Sixteenth Century*, 184–89; Powell, *Soldiers, Indians, & Silver*, 194–99, 216.
86. Powell, *Soldiers, Indians, & Silver*, 187.
87. Powell, *Soldiers, Indians, & Silver*, 206–7.

NOTES TO PAGES 36–44

CHAPTER 2

1. Peter Gerhard, *The North Frontier of New Spain* (University of Oklahoma Press, 1993), 344–56.

2. Sean F. McEnroe, *From Colony to Nationhood in Mexico: Laying the Foundations, 1560–1840* (Cambridge University Press, 2012), 42–43, 75; David B. Adams, "At the Lion's Mouth: San Miguel de Aguayo in the Defense of Nuevo León, 1686–1820," *Colonial Latin American Historical Review* 9, no. 3 (2000): 324–46.

3. 1745–1751. File about the foundation of the Villa of Lampazos, Archivo General de la Nación (AGN), civil, vol. 194, file 1, fol. 1–198. January 23, 1745. Document about the uprising of Natives from the Punta de Lampazos, Archivo Municipal de Monterrey (AMM), civil, vol. 74, file 2, fol. 53.

4. 1745–1751. File about the foundation of the Villa of Lampazos, Archivo General de la Nación (AGN), civil, vol. 194, file 1, fol. 1–198.

5. Gerhard, *The North Frontier of New Spain*, 335–41.

6. Gerhard, *The North Frontier of New Spain*, 358–67.

7. 1753–1753. Document that grants Tomas Sánchez the authorization to found Laredo, AGN, Tierras, vol. 3519, file 7, fol. 1–6.

8. October 23, 1777. Document that informs the viceroy of an attack in the Tlaxcalan settlement of San Miguel de Aguayo, AMM, Correspondencia, vol. 118. file 87, fol. 0.

9. Eugenio del Hoyo, *Historia del Nuevo Reino de León* [History of Nuevo León] *(1577–1723)* (Fondo Editorial Nuevo León, 2005), 102–35; Valentina Garza-Martínez, "Poblamiento y Colonización en el Noreste Novohispano Siglos XVI–XVII" (PhD diss., Colegio de México, 2002), 50–90.

10. Garza-Martínez, Poblamiento y Colonización, 131–87; *Los Gobernantes de Nuevo León: Historia* [The Rulers of Nuevo León: History] *(1579–1989)* (México, D.F: J.R. Fortson y Cia, 1990), 41.

11. Hoyo, *Historia del Nuevo Reino de León (1577–1723)*, 188–425; Garza-Martínez, Poblamiento y Colonización, 188–298.

12. Donald E. Chipman, "De Leon, Alonso," in *Handbook of Texas Online*, Texas State Historical Association, accessed April 21, 2024, https://www.tshaonline.org/handbook/entries/de-leon-alonso; Israel Cavazos Garza, *Diccionario Biográfico de Nuevo León*, 1st ed. (Monterrey, México: Universidad Autónoma de Nuevo León, 1984), 262–65. Alonso de León et al., *Historia de Nuevo León: con noticias sobre Coahuila, Tamaulipas, Texas y Nuevo México* (Fondo Editorial Nuevo León, 2005).

13. Grant D. Jones, *Maya Resistance to Spanish Rule: Time and History on a Colonial Frontier*, 1st ed. (University of New Mexico Press, 1989), 130, 269; Grant D. Jones, *The Conquest of the Last Maya Kingdom* (Stanford University Press, 1998), 295, 338.

14. Jones, *Maya Resistance to Spanish Rule*, 272.

15. One of his ancestors was Pedro de Ursúa, a conquistador who subjugated Indigenous groups, founded the towns of Pamplona and Ocaña in Nueva Granada (present-day Colombia), served as military governor, crushed a rebellion by black slaves in Panama, and finally was murdered by Spanish bandits in Peru in 1560. Jones, *The Conquest of the Last Maya Kingdom*, 114.

16. Jones, *The Conquest of the Last Maya Kingdom*, 417, 455, 519.

17. María Elena Galaviz de Capdevielle, "Descripción y pacificación de la Sierra Gorda," *Estudios de Historia Novohispana* 4, no. 4 (1971); Patricia Osante, *Orígenes Del Nuevo Santander (1748–1772)* (Universidad Nacional Autónoma de México; Universidad Autónoma de Tamaulipas, 1997), 77.

18. Herbert Eugene Bolton, *Texas in the Middle Eighteenth Century: Studies in Spanish Colonial History and Administration* (University of California Press, 1915), 289–91.

19. Osante, *Orígenes Del Nuevo Santander (1748–1772)*, 104.

20. September 3, 1746. Report by José de Escándon about the exploration of the Seno Mexicano, Archivo General de Indias (AGI) [These are transcripts from the AGI located at UT.] Audiencia de Guadalajara, Dunn Transcripts, Briscoe Center for American History, University of Texas Austin, 2Q148. fol. 89, 112–33.

21. August 27, 1746. Files about the pacification and settling of the borderlands of the New Kingdom of León, Archivo General de Indias (AGI), Audiencia de Guadalajara. Dunn Transcripts. Briscoe Center for American History, University of Texas Austin, 2Q148. fol. 89, 44–45.

22. Bolton, *Texas in the Middle Eighteenth Century*, 292.

23. Osante, *Orígenes Del Nuevo Santander (1748–1772)*, 123.

24. Osante, *Orígenes Del Nuevo Santander (1748–1772)*, 117.

25. Silvio A. Zavala, *Las Instituciones Jurídicas en la Conquista de América* [The Legal Instititutions in the Conquest of America] (Editorial Porrúa, 2006), 94–95, 129.

26. August 27, 1746. Files about the pacification and settling of the borderlands of the New Kingdom of León, Archivo General de Indias (AGI), Audiencia de Guadalajara, Dunn Transcripts, Briscoe Center for American History, University of Texas Austin, 2Q148. fol. 89, 48.

27. Osante, *Orígenes Del Nuevo Santander (1748–1772)*, 118.

28. José Alfredo Rangel Silva, *Capitanes a Guerra, Linajes de Frontera: Ascenso Y Consolidación de Las Élites En El Oriente de San Luis, 1617–1823* (El Colegio de México, 2008), 16; McEnroe, *From Colony to Nationhood in Mexico*, 144.
29. 1753–1753. Document that grants Tomas Sánchez the authority to found Laredo, AGN, Tierras, vol. 3519, file 7, fol. 1–6.
30. 1753–1753. Document that grants Tomas Sánchez the authority to found Laredo, AGN, Tierras, vol. 3519, file 7, fol. 1–6.
31. 1753–1753. Document that grants Tomas Sánchez the authority to found Laredo, AGN, Tierras, vol. 3519, file 7, fol. 1–6.
32. 1753–1753. Document that grants Tomas Sánchez the authority to found Laredo, AGN, Tierras, vol. 3519, file 7, fol. 1–6.
33. May 10, 1704. File about the representation of Diego Ramón, AGI, Audiencia de Guadalajara, Dunn Transcripts, Briscoe Center for American History, University of Texas Austin, 2Q136, fol. 20, 30–32.
34. Robert S. Weddle, "Ramón, Diego," *Handbook of Texas Online*, Texas State Historical Association, accessed April 27, 2024, https://www.tshaonline.org/handbook/entries/ramon-diego. Updated August 4, 2020.
35. Donald E. Chipman, "Ramón, Domingo," *Handbook of Texas Online*, Texas State Historical Association, accessed April 27, 2024, https://www.tshaonline.org/handbook/entries/ramon-domingo. Updated August 4, 2020.
36. February 23, 1716. Expedition to Texas in 1717, AGI, Audiencia de Guadalajara, Dunn Transcripts, Briscoe Center for American History, University of Texas Austin, 2Q146, fol. 80, 150–52.
37. Weddle, "Ramón, Diego," *Handbook of Texas Online*.
38. Eligio Edelmiro Hernández, *Secuestro y venta de los bienes de Don Juan Ignacio Ramón, héroe de la independencia* (Universidad Autónoma de Nuevo León, 2010), 15–33.
39. October 20, 1762. Services of the Captain Thorivio de Urrutia, AGI, Audiencia de Guadalajara, Dunn Transcripts, Briscoe Center for American History, University of Texas Austin, 2Q148, fol. 92, 183–85.
40. February 8, 1763. Request by Luis Antonio Menchaca for the post of captain of the San Antonio presidio, AGI, Audiencia de Guadalajara, Dunn Transcripts, Briscoe Center for American History, University of Texas Austin, 2Q148, fol. 92, 190.
41. This will be discussed in chapter 4.
42. Hoyo, *Historia del Nuevo Reino de León (1577–1723)*, 315.
43. June 6, 1643. Requirements made to the encomenderos, AMM, actas de Cabildo, vol. 001, fol. 0.

44. January 11, 1697. Caudillo Diego De Ayala, AMM, protocolos, vol. 6, fol. 49, no. 28.
45. June 6, 1643. Requirements made to the encomenderos, AMM, actas de Cabildo, vol. 001, fol. 0.
46. November 25, 1662. Review of encomenderos, AMM, civil, vol. 10, file 7, fol. 1. March 25, 1663. Review of encomenderos, AMM, civil, vol. 10, file 6.
47. March 25, 1663. Review of encomenderos, AMM, civil, vol. 10, file 6.
48. Tamar Herzog, *Defining Nations: Immigrants and Citizens in Early Modern Spain and Spanish America* (New Haven, CT: Yale University Press, 2003), 6, 18.
49. Herzog, *Defining Nations*, 25–28, 42.
50. Herzog, *Defining Nations*, 43–63.
51. March 25, 1663. Review of encomenderos, AMM, civil, vol. 10, file 6.
52. Hoyo, *Historia del Nuevo Reino de León (1577–1723)*, 263, 301.
53. 1768. Military census of the New Kingdom of León, AMM, civil, vol. 98, file 1.
54. 1768. Military census of the New Kingdom of León, AMM, civil, vol. 98, file 1. These women appear in the township of Cerralvo.
55. April 3, 1767. Resolutions about the San Antonio presidio by the Marquis de Rubí, Archivo General de Indias (AGI), Audiencia de Guadalajara, Dunn Transcripts, Briscoe Center for American History, University of Texas Austin, 2Q140. October 12. Military review of the vecinos in Lampazos, Archivo General del Estado de Nuevo León (AGENL), Fondo Colonial Correspondencia de Alcaldes Primeros, Lampazos, box 4.
56. 1765. Claim of the vecinos of Lampazos against the Mayor Domingo de Abasolo, AMM, miscelánea, vol. 1B, file 4.
57. 1765. Claim of the vecinos of Lampazos against the Mayor Domingo de Abasolo, AMM, miscelánea, vol. 1B, file 4.
58. 1765. Claim of the vecinos of Lampazos against the Mayor Domingo de Abasolo, AMM, miscelánea, vol. 1B, file 4.
59. July 25, 1751. File about the foundation of Lampazos, AGN, civil, vol. 194, file 1. fol. 100–101.
60. Around 1753. Military review of the vecinos in Lampazos, AGENL, Fondo Colonial, Correspondencia de Alcaldes Primeros, Lampazos, box 1.
61. July 25, 1754. Military review of the vecinos in Lampazos, Archivo Municipal de Lampazos (AML), box 1.
62. Adams, "At the Lion's Mouth: San Miguel de Aguayo in the Defense of Nuevo León, 1686–1820," 331–35.
63. McEnroe, *From Colony to Nationhood in Mexico: Laying the Foundations*.
64. January 23, 1745. Revolt of the Natives in the Mission of Lampazos, AMM, civil, vol. 74.

65. 1765. Claim of the vecinos of Lampazos against the Mayor Domingo de Abasolo, AMM, miscelánea, vol. 1B, file 4, 1745–1751. File about the foundation of the Villa of Lampazos, Archivo General de la Nación (AGN), Civil, vol. 194, file 1, fol. 1–198, AGN, civil, vol. 194, file 1, fol. 1–198.

66. Around 1753. Military review of the vecinos in Lampazos, AGENL, Fondo Colonial, Correspondencia de Alcaldes Primeros, Lampazos, box 1. July 25, 1754. Military review of the vecinos in Lampazos, AML, box 1. July 25, 1755. Military review of the vecinos in Lampazos, AML, box 1. July 25, 1756. Military review of the vecinos in Lampazos, AML, box 1. July 25, 1757. Military review of the vecinos in Lampazos, AML, box 1. July 25, 1758. Military review of the vecinos in Lampazos, AML, box 1.

67. Around 1753. Military review of the vecinos in Lampazos, AGENL, Fondo Colonial, Correspondencia de Alcaldes Primeros, Lampazos, box 1. 1765. Claim of the vecinos of Lampazos against the Mayor Domingo de Abasolo, AMM, miscelánea, vol. 1B, file 4.

68. April 17, 1790. Trinity University, microfilm, Mexican Collection, microfilm 733, AML, vol. 4, 1790–1799, file 13, 1790–1793; Héctor Jaime Treviño Villarreal, "Lampazos: Entre Catujanes y la Iguana [Lampazos: Between Catujanes and the Iguana] (1698–1810)," in *Apuntes para la historia de Lampazos de Naranjo*, vol. 1 (Universidad Autónoma de Nuevo León), 113–14.

69. November 28, 1730. Testimonies about the creation of councils and mayors. Presidio de San Antonio, AGN, Provincias Internas (P.I.), vol. 32, part 2, file 11, fol. 289.

70. March 12, 1736. Report of Manuel Sandoval, governor of Texas, P.I. vol. 32, part 2, file 14, fol. 330–32.

71. June 1741. Benito Fernández de Santa Ana, *Letters and Memorials of the Father Presidente Fray Benito Fernández de Santa Ana, 1736–1754: Documents on the Missions of Texas from the Archives of the College of Querétaro*, Documentary Series / Old Spanish Missions Historical Research Library at Our Lady of the Lake University, no. 6 (San Antonio, TX: Old Spanish Missions Historical Research Library at Our Lady of the Lake University, 1981), 36–37.

72. January 24, 1736. Report of the archbishop Juan Antonio de Bizarron about the situation in San Fernando, AGN, P.I., vol. 32, part 2, file 14, fol. 323–30.

73. February 3, 1733. Report of the San Antonio presidio by the governor of Texas, Antonio de Bustillo y Zevallos, AGN, P.I., vol. 32, part 2, file 15, fol. 395–96.

74. February 3, 1733. Report of the San Antonio presidio by the governor of Texas, Antonio de Bustillo y Zevallos, AGN, P.I., vol. 32, part 2, file 15, fol. 395–96.

75. There is a growing number of specialized books on the subject of Indigenous slavery: Eugenio del Hoyo, *Esclavitud y Encomiendas de Indios en el Nuevo Reino de León, Siglos*

XVI Y XVII (AGENL, 1985); Andrés Montemayor Hernández, *La congrega: Nuevo Reino de León : siglos XVI–XVII* (AGENL, 1990); James Brooks, *Captives & Cousins: Slavery, Kinship, and Community in the Southwest Borderlands* (University of North Carolina Press, 2002); Andrés Reséndez, *The Other Slavery: The Uncovered Story of Indian Enslavement in America* (Houghton Mifflin Harcourt, 2016).

76. Hoyo, *Historia del Nuevo Reino de León (1577–1723)*, 102–35, 166–67, 315; Garza-Martínez, "Poblamiento y Colonización," 50–90.

77. Maria Elena Santoscoy, "El Agua Organiza el Espacio," in *Coahuila: Historia Breve*, ed. Martha Rodríguez, Maria Eugenia Santoscoy, and Laura Elena Gutierrez (Fondo De Cultura Económica, 2011), 30–34; Garza-Martínez, "Poblamiento y Colonización," 50–51.

78. Hoyo, *Historia del Nuevo Reino de León (1577–1723)*, 398–400.

79. Hoyo, *Historia del Nuevo Reino de León (1577–1723)*, 442.

80. Hoyo, *Historia del Nuevo Reino de León (1577–1723)*, 316–17.

81. McEnroe, *From Colony to Nationhood in Mexico*, 62.

82. McEnroe, *From Colony to Nationhood in Mexico*, 69; Hoyo, *Historia del Nuevo Reino de León (1577–1723)*, 439–41. February 18, 1715. Natives of Nuevo León, AGI, Audiencia de Guadalajara, Dunn Transcripts, Briscoe Center for American History, University of Texas Austin, 2Q136. fol. 20, 77–82.

83. January 21, 1715. Files about the pacification and populating of the frontiers of the New Kingdom of León, AGI, Audiencia de Guadalajara, Dunn Transcripts, Briscoe Center for American History, University of Texas Austin, 2Q148. fol. 89, 28–29.

84. Hoyo, *Historia del Nuevo Reino de León (1577–1723)*, 317.

85. Alonso de León, Juan Bautista Chapa, and Fernando Sánchez de Zamora, *Historia de Nuevo León con noticias sobre Coahuila, Tamaulipas, Texas y Nuevo México* (Fondo Editorial Nuevo León, 2005) 39. Translation mine.

86. Hoyo, *Historia del Nuevo Reino de León (1577–1723)*, 321.

87. Hoyo, *Historia del Nuevo Reino de León (1577–1723)*, 447.

88. Hoyo, *Historia del Nuevo Reino de León (1577–1723)*, 447–49; McEnroe, *From Colony to Nationhood in Mexico*, 63. January 21, 1715. Files about the pacification and populating of the frontiers of the New Kingdom of León, AGI, Audiencia de Guadalajara, Dunn Transcripts, Briscoe Center for American History, University of Texas Austin, 2Q148, fol. 89, 28–29.

89. Hoyo, *Historia del Nuevo Reino de León (1577–1723)*, 493–99; McEnroe, *From Colony to Nationhood in Mexico*, 64–83. August 14, 1718. Files about the pacification and populating of the frontiers of the New Kingdom of León, AGI, Audiencia de Guadalajara, Dunn Transcripts, Briscoe Center for American History, University of Texas Austin, 2Q148,

fol. 89, 29–30. February 18, 1715. Natives of Nuevo León, AGI, Audiencia de Guadalajara, Dunn Transcripts, Briscoe Center for American History, University of Texas Austin, 2Q136, fol. 20, 77–82.

90. Hoyo, *Historia del Nuevo Reino de León (1577–1723)*, 499–500.

91. December 31, 1730. Report that Nicolás de Villalobos was never a protector of "Indians," AGI, Audiencia de Guadalajara, Dunn Transcripts, Briscoe Center for American History, University of Texas Austin, 2Q147, fol. 82, 32–33.

92. July 26, 1738. Files about the pacification and populating of the frontiers of the New Kingdom of León, AGI, Audiencia de Guadalajara, Dunn Transcripts, Briscoe Center for American History, University of Texas Austin, 2Q148, fol. 89, 33–34.

93. Galaviz de Capdevielle, "Descripción y Pacificación de la Sierra Gorda," 25.

94. September 23, 1772. Complaint against the vecinos of Nuevo Santander selling Natives as slaves, AGN, Historia, vol. 84, E-9.

95. December 1, 1731. Acts of the provisions given to the governor of the province of Texas to pacify the Apaches and their allies, AGN, P.I., vol. 32, part 2, E-15, fol. 337–43.

96. December 23, 1732. Acts of the provisions given to the governor of the province of Texas to pacify the Apaches and their allies, AGN, P.I., vol. 32, part 2, E-15, fol. 413. December 25, 1732. Acts of the provisions given to the governor of the province of Texas to pacify the Apaches and their allies, AGN, P.I., vol. 32, part 2, E-15, fol. 414–16. December 25, 1732. Acts of the provisions given to the governor of the province of Texas to pacify the Apaches and their allies, AGN, P.I., vol. 32, part 2, E-15, fol. 417. July 3, 1733. Acts of the provisions given to the governor of the province of Texas to pacify the Apaches and their allies. AGN, P.I., vol. 32, part 2, E-15, fol. 418.

97. December 23, 1732. Acts of the provisions given to the governor of the province of Texas to pacify the Apaches and their allies, AGN, P.I., vol. 32, part 2, E-15, fol. 413. December 25, 1732. Acts of the provisions given to the governor of the province of Texas to pacify the Apaches and their allies, AGN, P.I., vol. 32, part 2, E-15, fol. 414–16. December 25, 1732. Acts of the provisions given to the governor of the province of Texas to pacify the Apaches and their allies, AGN, P.I., vol. 32, part 2, E-15, fol. 417. July 3, 1733. Acts of the provisions given to the governor of the province of Texas to pacify the Apaches and their allies, AGN, P.I., vol. 32, part 2, E-15, fol. 418.

98. November 26, 1729. New regulations for the presidios. Regulations that all the governors of the provinces and the presidio captains must practice during the campaigns against the Natives. AGI, Audiencia de Guadalajara, Dunn Transcripts, Briscoe Center for American History, University of Texas Austin, 2Q146, fol. 81, 182. The commodifying language reflects the original Spanish.

99. February 23, 1750. Santa Ana, *Letters and Memorials of the Father Presidente Fray Benito Fernández de Santa Ana*, 168.

100. February 23, 1750. Santa Ana, *Letters and Memorials of the Father Presidente Fray Benito Fernández de Santa Ana*, 168.

101. February 23, 1750. Santa Ana, *Letters and Memorials of the Father Presidente Fray Benito Fernández de Santa Ana*, 168.

102. Patricia Seed, *Ceremonies of Possession in Europe's Conquest of the New World, 1492–1640* (Cambridge University Press, 1995), 69–99.

103. León, *Historia de Nuevo León*, 167–70.

104. León, *Historia de Nuevo León*, 175.

105. León, *Historia de Nuevo León*, 175.

106. León, *Historia de Nuevo León*, 175–80.

107. León, *Historia de Nuevo León*, 180–85.

108. April 6, 1714. Files about the pacification and populating of the frontiers of the New Kingdom of León, Archivo General de Indias (AGI), Audiencia de Guadalajara, Dunn Transcripts, Briscoe Center for American History, University of Texas Austin, 2Q148, fol. 89, 28–30.

109. 1732. Files about the pacification and populating of the frontiers of the New Kingdom of León, Archivo General de Indias (AGI), Audiencia de Guadalajara, Dunn Transcripts, Briscoe Center for American History, University of Texas Austin, 2Q148, fol. 89, 34–35.

110. June 6, 1643. Requirements made to the encomenderos, AMM, actas de Cabildo, vol. 001, fol. 0.

111. Pérez, *Historia de España*, 41–42.

112. Weckmann, *La Herencia Medieval de México*.

113. Weber, *The Spanish Frontier in North America*, 20.

114. June 13, 1776. About the military review of July 25, Archivo Municipal de Bustamante (AMB), Section: Cosas Consistoriales, box 1, fol. 1.

115. July 3, 1778. About the military review of July 2, AMB, Section: Cosas Consistoriales, box 1, fol. 3.

116. July 20, 1720. About the military review of July 25, Trinity University, microfilm, Mexican Collection, Rollo 921, AMB, vol. 1, 1695–1799, 1734. July 25, 1751. File about the foundation of the Villa of Lampazos, AGN, Civil, vol. 194, file 1, fol. 100–101. Around 1753. Military review of the vecinos in Lampazos, AGENL, Fondo Colonial, Correspondencia de Alcaldes Primeros, Lampazos, box 1, July 25, 1754. Military review of the vecinos in Lampazos, AML, box 1. July 25, 1755. Military review of the vecinos in Lampazos, AML,

box 1. July 25, 1756. Military review of the vecinos in Lampazos. AML, box 1. July 25, 1757. Military review of the vecinos in Lampazos, AML, box 1. July 25, 1758. Military review of the vecinos in Lampazos, AML, box 1. June 13, 1776. About the military reviews of July 25, AMB, Sección: Cosas Consistoriales, box 1, fol. 1. July 3, 1778. About the military reviews of July 25. AMB, Sección: Cosas Consistoriales, box 1, fol. 3.

117. March 27, 1746. About the defense during the Holy Week services in San Miguel de Aguayo, Trinity University, microfilm, Mexican Collection, rollo 921, AMB, vol. 1, 1695–1799, 1714. March 26, 1747. About the defense during the Holy Week services in San Miguel de Aguayo, Trinity University, microfilm, Mexican Collection, rollo 921, AMB, vol. 1, 1695–1799, 1714.

118. April 10, 1718. About the defense during the Holy Week services in San Miguel de Aguayo, Trinity University, microfilm, Mexican Collection, rollo 921, AMB, vol. 1, 1695–1799, 1714. April 5, 1719. About the defense during the Holy Week services in San Miguel de Aguayo, Trinity University, microfilm, Mexican Collection, rollo 921, AMB, vol. 1, 1695–1799, 1714. Translation mine.

119. March 11, 1716. Defense during the Holy Week services in San Miguel de Aguayo, Trinity University, microfilm, Mexican Collection, microfilm 921, AMB, vol. 1, 1695–1799, 1714.

120. March 26, 1714. About the defense during the Holy Week services in San Miguel de Aguayo, Trinity University, microfilm, Mexican Collection, microfilm 921, AMB, vol. 1, 1695–1799, 1714. March 11, 1716. About the defense during the Holy Week services in San Miguel de Aguayo, Trinity University, microfilm, Mexican Collection, microfilm 921, AMB, vol. 1, 1695–1799, 1714. April 10, 1718. About the defense during the religious Holy Week services in San Miguel de Aguayo, Trinity University, microfilm, Mexican Collection, microfilm 921, AMB, vol. 1, 1695–1799, 1714. April 5, 1719. About the defense during the religious Holy Week services in San Miguel de Aguayo, Trinity University, microfilm. Mexican Collection, microfilm 921, AMB, vol. 1, 1695–1799, 1714.

121. September 30, 1784. Report by Domingo Cabello about the Lipan Apaches, governor of Texas, AGN, P.I., vol. 64, file 2, fol. 69.

122. April 15, 1773. Texas reports by Ripperda, governor of Texas, AGN, P.I., vol. 20, file 7, fol. 238–41.

123. April 15, 1773. Texas reports by Ripperda, governor of Texas, AGN, P.I., vol. 20, file 7, fol. 238–41.

CHAPTER 3

1. John Lynch, *Bourbon Spain, 1700–1808*, History of Spain (Blackwell, 1989), 60.
2. Allan J. Kuethe and Kenneth J. Andrien, *The Spanish Atlantic World in the Eighteenth Century: War and the Bourbon Reforms, 1713–1796* (Cambridge University Press, 2014), 68–97.
3. Kuethe and Andrien, *The Spanish Atlantic World in the Eighteenth Century*, 98–130.
4. Kuethe and Andrien, *The Spanish Atlantic World in the Eighteenth Century*, 133–66.
5. Michael Howard, *War in European History* (Oxford University Press, 2001), 63–66.
6. Howard, *War in European History*, 69–70.
7. Francisco Andújar Castillo, *El sonido del dinero: monarquía, ejército y venalidad en la España del siglo XVIII* (Marcial Pons Historia, 2004).
8. Lynch, *Bourbon Spain, 1700–1808*, 123–26.
9. Lynch, *Bourbon Spain, 1700–1808*, 123–26.
10. Francisco Andújar Castillo, *Ejércitos y militares en la Europa moderna* (Síntesis, 1999), 63.
11. Andújar Castillo, *Ejércitos y militares en la Europa moderna*, 65.
12. Andújar Castillo, *Ejércitos y militares en la Europa moderna*, 65.
13. Andújar Castillo, *Ejércitos y militares en la Europa moderna*, 62.
14. Lynch, *Bourbon Spain, 1700–1808*, 306–10.
15. Lynch, *Bourbon Spain, 1700–1808*, 310.
16. Andújar Castillo, *El sonido del dinero*.
17. Lynch, *Bourbon Spain, 1700–1808*, 311–12.
18. Juan Marchena Fernández, *Ejército y Milicias En El Mundo Colonial Americano* [Army and Militias in the American Colonial World] (Editorial MAPFRE, 1992), 136.
19. Kuethe and Andrien, *The Spanish Atlantic World in the Eighteenth Century*, 239–41.
20. Christon I. Archer, *The Army in Bourbon Mexico, 1760–1810* (University of New Mexico Press, 1977), 10–12.
21. Allan J. Kuethe, Juan Marchena Fernández, and Lyle N. McAlister, *Soldados Del Rey: El Ejército Borbónico en América Colonial en Vísperas de la Independencia* (Castelló de la Plana: Universitat Jaume I, 2005), 120–21.
22. Marchena Fernández, *Ejército y Milicias en el Mundo Colonial Americano*, 147–48.
23. Lyle N. McAlister, *The "Fuero Militar" in New Spain, 1764–1800* (University of Florida Press, 1957).
24. Christon I. Archer, "Military," in *Cities & Society in Colonial Latin America*, ed. Louisa Schell Hoberman and Susan Migden Socolow (University of New Mexico Press, 1986), 204–5, 219.

25. Archer, *The Army in Bourbon Mexico, 1760–1810.*
26. Archer, "Military," 216.
27. Marchena Fernández, *Ejército y Milicias En El Mundo Colonial Americano*, 108.
28. Josefina Zoraida Vázquez, "Reflexiones Sobre el Ejército y la Fundación del Estado Mexicano," in *Fuerzas Militares en Iberoamérica: Siglos XVIII Y XIX*, ed. Juan Ortiz Escamilla (El Colegio de México; Colegio de Michoacán; Universidad Veracruzana, 2005), 224.
29. Archer, "Military," 216–17.
30. Archer, "Military," 204–5, 219.
31. Archer, "Military," 205.
32. Archer, *The Army in Bourbon Mexico, 1760–1810.*
33. Archer, "Military."
34. Archer, *The Army in Bourbon Mexico, 1760–1810.*
35. Archer, "Military."
36. Manuel Lucena Giraldo, "El Reformismo de Frontera," in *El Reformismo Borbónico: Una Visión Interdisciplinar*, ed. Agustín Guimerá Ravina (Alianza Editorial, 1996), 265–75.
37. Retta Murphy, "The Journey of Pedro de Rivera, 1724–1728," *Southwestern Quarterly* 41, no. 2 (Oct. 1937): 125–41.
38. Murphy, "The Journey of Pedro de Rivera, 1724–1728."
39. Thomas H. Naylor and Charles W. Polzer, eds., *Pedro de Rivera and the Military Regulations for Northern New Spain, 1724–1729: A Documentary History of His Frontier Inspection and the Reglamento de 1729* (University of Arizona Press, 1988), 101–2, 136–38.
40. Naylor, and Polzer, *Pedro de Rivera and the Military Regulations for Northern New Spain, 1724–1729*, 47–66, 138–39, 191–200.
41. Naylor, and Polzer, *Pedro de Rivera and the Military Regulations for Northern New Spain, 1724–1729*, 290–333.
42. Naylor, and Polzer, *Pedro de Rivera and the Military Regulations for Northern New Spain, 1724–1729*, 16; David J. Weber, *The Spanish Frontier in North America* (New Haven, CT: Yale Universty Press), 214.
43. Jeffrey D. Carlisle, "Apache Indians," *Handbook of Texas Online*, Texas State Historical Association, accessed April 29, 2024, https://www.tshaonline.org/handbook/entries/apache-indians. Updated September 29, 2020.
44. Carlisle, "Apache Indians"; Thomas A. Britten, *The Lipan Apaches. People of Wind and Lightning* (University of New Mexico Press, 2009). April 17, 1790. Trinity University, microfilm, Mexican Collection, film 733, AML, vol. 4, 1790–1799, exp. 13, 1790–1793; Héctor Jaime Treviño Villarreal, "Lampazos: entre Catujanes y la Iguana (1698–1810),"

in *Apuntes para la historia de Lampazos de Naranjo, Nuevo León*, vol. 1 (Universidad Autónoma de Nuevo León, 2003), 113–14.

45. Carol A. Lipscomb, "Comanche Indians," *Handbook of Texas Online*, Texas State Historical Association, accessed April 29, 2024, https://www.tshaonline.org/handbook/entries/comanche-indians. Updated October 9, 2020. Pekka Hämäläinen, *The Comanche Empire* (New Haven, CT: Yale University Press, 2008).

46. Lipscomb, "Comanche Indians"; Hämäläinen, *The Comanche Empire*.

47. Lipscomb, "Comanche Indians"; Hämäläinen, *The Comanche Empire*.

48. David J. Weber, *Bárbaros: Spaniards and Their Savages in the Age of Enlightenment* (New Haven, CT: Yale University Press, 2005), 138–77; Instrucciones del Virrey Bernardo de Gálvez para la defensa de las Provincias Internas del Norte, 1786, *Boletín del Archivo General de la Nación* [Gazette of the General Archive of the Nation]. 1937, First Series, vol. VIII, no. 4, October-December, 491–540.

49. Weber, *Bárbaros: Spaniards and Their Savages in the Age of Enlightenment*, 138–77; Instrucciones del Virrey Bernardo de Gálvez para la defensa de las Provincias Internas del Norte, 1786.

50. Weber, *The Spanish Frontier in North America*, 204–15.

51. Luis Navarro García, *Don José de Gálvez y la Comandancia General de las Provincias Internas del Norte de Nueva España* [Don José de Gálvez and the General Command of the Interior Provinces of the North of New Spain] (Consejo Superior de Investigaciones Científicas, 1964), 216–17.

52. Weber, *The Spanish Frontier in North America*, 217–19.

53. Navarro García, *Don José de Gálvez*, 220.

54. Weber, *The Spanish Frontier in North America*, 219–20.

55. Navarro García, *Don José de Gálvez*, 198; Hugo O'Conor, *The Defenses of Northern New Spain: Hugo O'Conor's Report to Teodoro de Croix, July 22, 1777* (Southern Methodist University Press, 1994); Weber, *The Spanish Frontier in North America*, 220–26.

56. Navarro García, *Don José de Gálvez*, 209–41.

57. Weber, *The Spanish Frontier in North America*, 222.

58. Navarro García, *Don José de Gálvez*, 281–84; Weber, *The Spanish Frontier in North America*, 225–27.

59. Kuethe and Andrien, *The Spanish Atlantic World in the Eighteenth Century*, 290.

60. Navarro García, *Don José de Gálvez*, 275–79; Weber, *The Spanish Frontier in North America*, 224–25.

61. Archer, *The Army in Bourbon Mexico, 1760–1810*.

62. 1768. Military Census of the New Kingdom of León, AMM, civil, vol. 98, file 1.

63. March 3, 1768. Cerralvo. Military Census of the New Kingdom of León, AMM, civil, vol. 98, file 1.
64. February 26, 1768. San Miguel de Aguayo. Military Census of the New Kingdom of León, AMM, civil, vol. 98, file 1.
65. March 25, 1769. Boca de Leones, Instructions for the military census, AMM.
66. 1770–1773. Texas, AGN, P.I. vol. 100, exp. 1, fol. 1–404.
67. May 5, 1775. Files About the Creation of a Garrison in New Santander to Protect Laredo, AGN, P.I. vol. 114, Hackett Transcripts, Briscoe Center for American History, University of Texas Austin, 2Q207, fol. 495, III.
68. May 4, 1772. Monterrey, AGN P.I. vol. 108, exp. 2, fol. 113–14.
69. August 3, 1774. Defense Plans for the New Kingdom of León, AGN, P.I. vol. 108. May 5, 1775. Files about the Creation of a Garrison in New Santander to Protect Laredo, AGN, P.I. vol. 114, Hackett Transcripts, Briscoe Center for American History, University of Texas Austin, 2Q207, fol. 495, III.
70. October 12, 1776. Instructions of the Comandante Inspector to the Governors of the Interior Provinces, AGN, P.I. vol. 108, fol. 285.
71. January 1, 1776. Document on the Apache Attacks Due to O'Conor's Campaign, AMM, Correspondencia, vol. 120, exp. 3. September 27, 1777. Report of Indigenous Attacks in the New Kingdom of León and Coahuila, AMM. Correspondencia, vol. 118.
72. November 16, 1774. The Governor of the New Kingdom of León Gives a Report on a Defense Plan, AGN, P.I. vol. 108, fol. 220–21. April 12, 1775. Report on Defensive Measures, AMM, Correspondencia, vol. 118. April 20, 1775. Meeting with the Main Vecinos of the New Kingdom of León, AMM, Correspondencia, vol. 118, exp. 52. June 15, 1778. Instructions for Defense with the Vecinos of the New Kingdom of León, AMB, box 1, fol. 3. November 21, 1778. Instructions of the Use of Sentries, AMB, box 1, fol. 3.
73. June 16, 1776. Report on the Indigenous Attack on San Miguel de Aguayo, AGN, P.I. vol. 108, fol. 276–77.
74. September 11, 1776. Congratulations to the Vecinos of the New Kingdom of León Who Repelled an Attack in August, AMM, Correspondencia, vol. 120, exp. 3.
75. November 21, 1778. Instructions for the use of sentries, AMB, box 1, fol. 3.
76. Archer, *The Army in Bourbon Mexico, 1760–1810*.
77. October 4, 1778. Meeting to Coordinate the Defense of the Interior Provinces, AGN, P.I. vol. 62, file 2, fol. 72–86.
78. October 4, 1778. Meeting to Coordinate the Defense of the Interior Provinces, AGN, P.I. vol. 62, file 2, fol. 72–86.

79. July 7, 1770. Details about the "Indian" Wars in San Antonio, Directed to the Governor of Texas, AGN, P.I. vol. 100, file 1, fol. 29–35.
80. October 14, 1770. Report of the Governor of Texas, AGN, P.I. vol. 100, exp. 1, fol. 53–54.
81. April 16, 1783. Government of Nuevo Santander about the Lipan and Comanche Attacks in that Province, AGN, P.I. vol. 64, file 1, fol. 6–8.
82. March 24, 1775. Meeting about the Defense Plans, AGN, P.I. vol. 108, fol. 242. October 23, 1776. Defense Measures in the New Kingdom of León, AGN, P.I. vol. 108, fol. 297–98.
83. August 3, 1774. Communication of the Governor of the New Kingdom of León with the Viceroy about the Defense Plans, AGN, P.I. vol. 108, fol. 200–201.
84. November 16, 1774. The Governor of the New Kingdom of León Gives a Report on the Defense Plan, AGN, P.I. vol. 108, fol. 220–21.
85. January 18, 1775. Informs about Planning a Defense Meeting, AGN, P.I. vol. 108, fol. 237.
86. March 24, 1775. Defense Meeting, AGN, P.I. vol. 108, fol. 242.
87. April 20, 1775. Meeting with the Main Vecinos of the New Kingdom of León, AMM, Correspondencia, vol. 108, exp. 52. October 18, 1775. Report of the Defense Meeting, AGN, P.I. vol. 108, fol. 257.
88. April 20, 1775. Meeting with the Main Vecinos of the New Kingdom of León, AMM, Correspondencia, vol. 108, exp. 52. October 18, 1775. Report of the Defense Meeting, AGN, P.I. vol. 108, fol. 257.
89. June 18, 1776. Communication of the Governor with the Viceroy, AGN, P.I. vol. 108, fol. 272–73.
90. May 8, 1776. Communication with the Viceregal Authorities, AGN, P.I. vol. 108, fol. 295.
91. October 23, 1776. Defense Measures in the New Kingdom of León, AGN, P.I. vol. 108, fol. 297–98.
92. November 21, 1778. Instructions Regarding the Use of Sentries, AMB, box 1, fol. 3.
93. June 13, 1776. About the Military Parade of the Twenty-fifth of July, AMB, Cosas Consistoriales, box 1, fol. 1. June 13, 1776. About the Military Parade of the Twenty-fifth of July, AMM, Correspondencia, box 120, file 3. July 3, 1778. About the Military Parade of the Twenty-fifth of July, AMB, Cosas Consistoriales, box 1, file 3.
94. April 20, 1775. Meeting With the Main Vecinos of the New Kingdom of León, AMM, Correspondencia, vol. 118, file 52.
95. April 20, 1775. Meeting With the Main Vecinos of the New Kingdom of León, AMM. Correspondencia, vol. 118, file 52.
96. August 3, 1774. Governor of the New Kingdom of León Requesting Armament, AGN, P.I. vol. 108, fol. 200–201.
97. August 31, 1774. Supply of Gunpowder for the Local Militias, AGN, P.I. vol. 108, fol. 206. July 6, 1782. Report on the Defense Measures Taken in the New Kingdom of León, AGN, P.I. vol. 144, exp. 4, fol. 48–54.

98. April 16, 1783. Report of Lipan and Comanche attacks in Nuevo Santander, AGN, P.I. vol. 64, exp. 1, fol. 6–8. October 4, 1786. Record of hostilities in Nuevo Santander during 1781–1783, AGN, P.I. vol. 64, exp. 6, fol. 315–23.

99. June 20, 1783. The Governor of Nuevo Santander Requests from the Viceroy Muskets and Pistols for the Militias, AGN, P.I. vol. 64-2, file 3, fol. 152–56. October 4, 1786. File on Hostilities in Nuevo Santander During 1781–1783, AGN, P.I. vol. 64, exp. 6, fol. 315–23.

100. June 22, 1783. Proposition of the Governor of Nuevo Santander to Pay the Militiamen for their Service, AGN, P.I. vol. 64, exp. 1, fol. 13. October 4, 1786. File on Hostilities in Nuevo Santander During 1781–1783, AGN, P.I. vol. 64, file 6, fol. 315–23.

101. August 29, 1783. Authorization to Gather Wild Horses, AGN, P.I. vol. 64, exp. 1, fol. 26–27.

102. March 15, 1783. Review of the Lampazos Garrison, AGN, P.I. vol. 144, file 8, fol. 127–34. April 12, 1783. About the Crown Paying the Salaries of the Lampazos Garrison, AGN, P.I. vol. 144, file 8, fol. 127–34. May 21, 1784, Report on the Military Changes in the New Kingdom of León, AGN, P.I. vol. 26, file 12, fol. 287–301.

103. December 2, 1782. Defense Measures in Nuevo Santander, AGN, P.I. vol. 64, file 1, fol. 1–2. February 9, 1783. AGN. P.I. vol. 144, file 8, fol. 127–34. October 4, 1786. Letter of the Governor of Nuevo Santander, Juan Miguel de Zozaya, AGN, P.I. vol. 64, file 6, fol. 300–328.

104. María Esther Domínguez, *San Antonio, Tejas, En La Época Colonial (1718–1821)* (Ediciones de Cultura Hispánica: Instituto de Cooperación Iberoamericana, 1989), 128.

105. February 13, 1756. Instructions to the Governors about How to Administer the Presidios, AGN, P.I., vol. 25, exp. 2, fol. 44–51.

106. September 19, 1787. Letter of Juan de Ugalde. AGN, P.I. vol. 64, file 6, fol. 300–328. Translation mine.

107. February 13, 1756. Instructions to the Governors about How to Administer the Presidios, AGN, P.I., vol. 25, file 2, fol. 44–51.

108. Domínguez, *San Antonio, Tejas, En La Época Colonial (1718–1821)*, 115.

109. Alexander von Humboldt, *Ensayo Político sobre el Reino de La Nueva España* (México: Editorial Porrúa, 1966), 557–58.

110. *Diccionario Porrúa de Historia Biografía Y Geografía de México* (México: Editorial Porrúa, 1976), 332; Archer, *The Army in Bourbon Mexico, 1760–1810*, 202–3; José Alfredo Rangel Silva, *Capitanes a Guerra, Linajes de Frontera: Ascenso Y Consolidación de Las Élites En El Oriente de San Luis, 1617–1823* (El Colegio de México, 2008), 225–33.

111. July 25, 1795. Report on the Provinces of the New Kingdom of León and New Santander by Félix María Calleja, AGI, Dunn Transcripts, Briscoe Center for American History, University of Texas Austin, 2Q154, fol. 126.

112. July 25, 1795. Report on the Provinces of the New Kingdom of León and New Santander by Félix María Calleja, AGI, Dunn Transcripts, Briscoe Center for American History, University of Texas Austin, 2Q154, fol. 126, 222.

113. July 25, 1795. Report on the Provinces of the New Kingdom of León and New Santander by Félix María Calleja, AGI, Dunn Transcripts, Briscoe Center for American History, University of Texas Austin, 2Q154, fol. 126, 245.

114. April 6, 1795. Trial Against Juan Ignacio Ramón, AGN, P.I. vol. 203, file 3, fol. 56.

115. February 10, 1795. Review of the Lampazos Company by Calleja, AGN, P.I. vol. 203, file 10, fol. 195.

116. March 13, 1795. Review of the Lampazos Company by Calleja, AGN, P.I. vol. 203, file 16, fol. 289.

117. March 13, 1795. Review of the Lampazos Company by Calleja, AGN, P.I. vol. 203, file 16, fol. 289.

118. March 13, 1795. Review of the Lampazos company by Calleja, AGN, P.I. vol. 203, file 16, fol. 295–96.

119. March 13, 1795. Review of the Lampazos Company by Calleja, AGN, P.I. vol. 203, file 16, fol. 295–96.

120. March 13, 1795. Review of the Lampazos Company by Calleja, AGN, P.I. vol. 203, file 16, fol. 295–96.

121. Archer, *The Army in Bourbon Mexico, 1760–1810*, 192.

122. March 13, 1795. Review of the Lampazos Company by Calleja, AGN, P.I. vol. 203, file 16, fol. 289.

123. Archer, *The Army in Bourbon Mexico, 1760–1810*, 84–86.

124. Raúl A. Ramos, *Beyond the Alamo: Forging Mexican Ethnicity in San Antonio, 1821–1861* (University of North Carolina Press, 2008), 23. April 20, 1810. Report by Manuel Ramos Arizpe, AGN, P.I. vol. 201. Briscoe Center for American History, University of Texas Austin, 2Q215, file 528, 104.

125. Isidro Vizcaya Canales, *En los albores de la independencia las Provincias Internas de Oriente durante la insurrección de don Miguel Hidalgo y Costilla, 1810–1811* (Fondo Editorial Nuevo León, 2005), 56–61.

126. April 20, 1810. Report by Manuel Ramos Arizpe, AGN, P.I. vol. 201, Briscoe Center for American History, University of Texas Austin, 2Q215, fol. 528, 105. 1807. Measures Taken to Help the Families of the Auxiliary Soldiers Serving in Texas, AGN, P.I. vol. 201, Briscoe Center for American History, University of Texas Austin, 2Q215, fol. 528, 14–58. October 27, 1807. Report on the Wives of the Militiamen of the New Kingdom of León who Are Serving in Texas, AGN, P.I. vol. 200, file 3, fol. 87–93.

127. August 4, 1810. Felix Calleja's Report on the Payment of the Militiamen, AGN, P.I. vol. 201, Briscoe Center for American History, University of Texas Austin, 2Q215, file 528, 60.

128. May 23, 1809. Meeting in San Antonio about the Defense Plan, AGN, P.I. vol. 200, file 1, fol. 14–17.

129. Vizcaya Canales, *En los albores de la independencia las Provincias Internas de Oriente durante la insurrección de don Miguel Hidalgo y Costilla, 1810–1811*, 56–61; Catherine Andrews and Jesús Hernández, "La Lucha por la supervivencia: El impacto de la Insurgencia en el Nuevo Santander, 1810–1821," in *La Independencia En El Septentrión de La Nueva España: Provincias Internas e Intendencias Norteñas*, ed. Ana Carolina Ibarra (Universidad Nacional Autónoma de México, 2010), 35–78.

130. Vizcaya Canales, *En los albores de la independencia las Provincias Internas de Oriente durante la insurrección de don Miguel Hidalgo y Costilla, 1810–1811*, 56–61.

131. Martín González de la Vara, "La Lucha por la Independencia en Texas" [The Fight for Independence in Texas], in *La Independencia En El Septentrión de La Nueva España: Provincias Internas e Intendencias Norteñas*, ed. Ana Carolina Ibarra (Universidad Nacional Autónoma de México, 2010), 79–85.

132. Vizcaya Canales, *En los albores de la independencia las Provincias Internas de Oriente durante la insurrección de don Miguel Hidalgo y Costilla, 1810–1811*, 56–61.

133. González de la Vara, "La Lucha por la Independencia en Texas," 84–92.

134. September 13, 1813. Arredondo's Report on the Battle of Medina, AGN, Operaciones de Guerra, Arredondo, vol. IV. Briscoe Center for American History, University of Texas Austin, 2Q194, fol. 423; Donald E. Chipman and Harriet Denise Joseph, *Spanish Texas 1519–1821* (University of Texas Press, 2010), 251; Bradley Folsom, *Arredondo: Last Spanish Ruler of Texas and Northeastern New Spain* (University of Oklahoma Press, 2017), 81–94.

135. Vito Alessio Robles, *Coahuila y Texas. Desde la Consumación de la Independencia hasta el Tratado de Paz de Guadalupe Hidalgo*, vol. I (Porrúa, 1979), 73–74.

136. May 20, 1820. Joaquin de Arredondo's Military File, Archivo Histórico de la Secretaria de Defensa (AHSEDENA), XI/III/3–103, 98.

137. Luis Jauregui, "Las Tareas y Tribulaciones de Joaquín de Arredondo en las Provincias Internas de Oriente, 1811–1815," in *La Independencia En El Septentrión de La Nueva España: Provincias Internas e Intendencias Norteñas*, ed. Ana Carolina Ibarra (Universidad Nacional Autónoma de México, 2010), 271–302.

138. Brian Hamnett, "Santiago Vidaurri, Northern Mexico, and Regional Identities, 1855–1864," *Tzintzun Revista de Estudios Históricos*, vol. 30 (1999), 85–119.

139. Eligio Edelmiro Hernández, *Secuestro y Venta de Los Bienes de Don Juan Ignacio Ramón* (Universidad Autónoma de Nuevo León, 2010).

140. July 22, 1819. List of People who Have Grocery Stores, Lampazos, box 3, Correspondencia de Alcaldes Primeros, Lampazos, 1817–1819, Fondo Colonial, AGENL.
141. Jesús Jesús Ávila. "Lampazos: Entre la Insurrección y el Desafío Continuo." In *Apuntes para la historia de Lampazos de Naranjo, Nuevo León*, vol. 1. (UANL: Patronato de Lampazos. 2003), 198.
142. Vizcaya Canales, *En los albores de la independencia las Provincias Internas de Oriente durante la insurrección de don Miguel Hidalgo y Costilla, 1810–1811*, 287; Israel Cavazos Garza, *Diccionario Biográfico de Nuevo León* (Universidad Autónoma de Nuevo León, 1984), 453.
143. This is what Eric Van Young describes in his study that focuses on areas of central Mexico. Eric Van Young, *The Other Rebellion: Popular Violence, Ideology, and the Mexican Struggle for Independence, 1810–1821* (Stanford University Press, 2001).
144. Vizcaya Canales, *En los albores de la independencia las Provincias Internas de Oriente durante la insurrección de don Miguel Hidalgo y Costilla, 1810–1811*, 112.
145. Gilberto Miguel Hinojosa, *A Borderlands Town in Transition: Laredo, 1755–1870* (Texas A&M University Press, 1983), 26.
146. Vizcaya Canales, *En los albores de la independencia las Provincias Internas de Oriente durante la insurrección de don Miguel Hidalgo y Costilla, 1810–1811*, 278–79.
147. 1812. Report on the Creation of the Urban Patriot Companies in San Miguel de Aguayo, Trinity University, microfilm, Mexican Collection, AMB, spool 923, vol. 3 (1806–1823); Hinojosa, *A Borderlands Town in Transition*, 28.
148. April 11, 1815. Order to Create an Urban Sapper force in San Miguel de Aguayo, Trinity University, microfilm, Mexican Collection, AMB, spool 923, vol. 3 (1806–1823).
149. This way of proceeding—using the militias of Indigenous origin in noncombat auxiliary work—was the common denominator throughout the viceroyalty during the independence period. In the central regions of New Spain, this represented a kind of social and political ascent for the Indigenous classes, where they obtained political privileges. In the northern regions, however, the forces of Tlaxcalan origin already had these social distinctions. Using them as second-line troops sounded more like demotion than anything else. Juan Ortiz Escamilla, *Guerra y Gobierno. Los pueblos y la independencia de México, 1808–1825* (El Colegio de México; Instituto de Investigaciones Dr. José María Luis Mora, 2014), 133–37.
150. March 29, 1815. Individual Records for the Urban Sapper Force in San Miguel de Aguayo (we counted fifty-eight individual records), Trinity University, microfilm, Mexican Collection, AMB, spool 923, vol. 3 (1806–1823).
151. March 29, 1815. Individual Records for the Urban Sapper Force in San Miguel de Aguayo, Trinity University, microfilm, Mexican Collection, AMB, spool 923, vol. 3 (1806–1823).

152. October 12, 1819. About Nobody Presenting Themselves in the General Assembly, Lampazos, AGENL, Fondo Colonial, Correspondencia de Alcaldes Primeros, Lampazos, box 4, 1817–1819. October 29, 1819. Military Dispositions in Lampazos by Arrendondo, AGENL, Fondo Colonial, Correspondencia de Alcaldes Primeros, Lampazos, box 4, 1817–1819.

153. March 3, 1820. File on the Capture of the Deserter Soldier, José Cándido Sánchez, AGENL, Fondo Militares, 1819–1820, box 5.

154. April 4, 1818. File where the Situation in San Antonio Is Described, Records of the City of San Antonio 1815–1835, Spanish Minute Book One, Briscoe Center for American History, University of Texas Austin, 2Q245, fol. 39.

155. June 19, 1815. Meeting with San Antonio's Vecinos to Assist the Troops, Records of the City of San Antonio 1815–1835, Spanish Minute Book One, Briscoe Center for American History, University of Texas Austin, 2Q245, fol. 5. June 22, 1815. Meeting with San Antonio's Vecinos to Assist the Troops, Records of the City of San Antonio 1815–1835, Spanish Minute Book One, Briscoe Center for American History, University of Texas Austin, 2Q245, fol. 5.

156. February 1, 1816. Meeting Where the Degree of Exhaustion of San Antonio's Population due to the Support of the Troops Is Reported, Records of the City of San Antonio 1815–1835, Spanish Minute Book One, Briscoe Center for American History, University of Texas Austin, 2Q245, fol. 11.

157. January 16, 1817. Soldiers Sacrificing Cattle, Records of the City of San Antonio 1815–1835, Spanish Minute Book One, Briscoe Center for American History, University of Texas Austin, 2Q245, fol. 22. April 2, 1818. Troops Confiscating Seed. Suggestion to Use Troops as Day Laborers, Records of the City of San Antonio 1815–1835, Spanish Minute Book One, Briscoe Center for American History, University of Texas Austin, 2Q245, fol. 34–35.

158. April 4, 1818. File describing the situation in San Antonio, Records of the City of San Antonio 1815–1835, Spanish Minute Book One, Briscoe Center for American History, University of Texas Austin, 2Q245, fol. 41.

159. May 21, 1819. Report of Attacks by Natives in Lampazos, AGENL, Fondo Colonial, Correspondencia de Alcaldes Primeros, Lampazos, box 4, 1817–1819. April 4, 1818. File Describing the Situation in San Antonio, Records of the City of San Antonio 1815–1835, Spanish Minute Book One, Briscoe Center for American History, University of Texas Austin, 2Q245, fol. 39. June 19, 1815. Meeting with the Neighbors of San Antonio to Assist the Troops, Records of the City of San Antonio 1815–1835, Spanish Minute Book One, Briscoe Center for American History, University of Texas Austin, 2Q245, fol. 5.

160. April 4, 1818. File describing the situation in San Antonio, Records of the City of San Antonio 1815–1835, Spanish Minute Book One, Briscoe Center for American History, University of Texas Austin, 2Q245, fol. 41.

161. October 5, 1818. Situation in Lampazos Due to Attacks by Indigenous groups, AGENL, Fondo Colonial, Correspondencia de Alcaldes Primeros, Lampazos, box 4, 1817–1819. October 30, 1818. Situation in Lampazos Due to Indigenous Attacks, AGENL, Fondo Colonial, Correspondencia de Alcaldes Primeros, Lampazos, box 4, 1817–1819. April 4, 1818. File Describing the Situation in San Antonio, Records of the City of San Antonio 1815–1835, Spanish Minute Book One, Briscoe Center for American History, University of Texas Austin, 2Q245, fol. 39.

162. January 16, 1817. Soldiers Sacrificing Cattle, Records of the City of San Antonio 1815–1835, Spanish Minute Book One, Briscoe Center for American History, University of Texas Austin, 2Q245, fol. 22. September 8, 1819. Suggestion to Create a Volunteer Force of Loyalists to Fight the Natives Records of the City of San Antonio 1815–1835, Spanish Minute Book One, Briscoe Center for American History, University of Texas Austin, 2Q245, fol. 62. November 17, 1819. Neighborhood Assembly After Mass to Organize a 50-Man Posse, AGENL, Fondo Colonial, Correspondencia de Alcaldes Primeros, Lampazos, box 4, 1817–1819.

CHAPTER 4

1. Alfredo Ávila, *En nombre de la nación. La formación del gobierno representativo en México* (Taurus: Centro de Investigación y Docencia Económica, 2002); Alfredo Ávila and Pedro Pérez Herrero, eds., *Las experiencias de 1808 en Iberoamérica* (Alcalá de Henares: Universidad de Alcalá / Universidad Nacional Autónoma de México, 2008); François-Xavier Guerra, *Modernidad e independencias. Ensayos sobre las revoluciones hispánicas* (Fondo de Cultura Económica / Fundación MAPRE-Tavera, 1992); Nettie Lee Benson, *The Provincial Council in Mexico: Harbinger of Provincial Autonomy, Independence, and Federalism* (University of Texas Press, 1992); Jaime E. Rodríguez O., *The Independence of Spanish America* (Cambridge University Press, 1998); Jaime E. Rodríguez O., *Nosotros somos ahora los verdaderos españoles. La transición de la Nueva España de un reino de la Monarquía a la República Federal Mexicana, 1808–1824*, 2 vols. (El Colegio de Michoacán: Instituto Mora, 2009); Peter Guardino, ed., *La independencia de México y el proceso autonomista novohispano, 1808–1824* (Universidad Nacional Autónoma de México/ Instituto Mora, 2001).

2. Lee Benson, *The Provincial Council in Mexico*.
3. Alfredo Ávila and Luis Jáuregui, "La Disolucion de la Monarquía Hispánica y el Proceso de Independencia," in *Nueva Historia General de México* [New Mexican General History] (Colegio de México, 2010), 369–96; Jan Bazant, *A Concise History of Mexico from Hidalgo to Cárdenas, 1805–1940* (Cambridge University Press, 1977), 5–29.
4. José Antonio Serrano Ortega and Josefina Zoraida Vázquez, "El Nuevo Orden, 1821–1848," in *Nueva Historia General de México*, ed. Erik Velásquez (El Colegio de México, 2010), 397–403; Bazant, *A Concise History of Mexico from Hidalgo to Cárdenas, 1805–1940*, 30–38.
5. Serrano Ortega and Vázquez, "El Nuevo Orden," 405–16.
6. Serrano Ortega and Vázquez, "El Nuevo Orden," 417–21.
7. Gunther E. Rothenberg, *The Napoleonic Wars* (Smithsonian Books; Harper Collins, 2006), 20–23.
8. Rothenberg, *The Napoleonic Wars*, 20–23.
9. Michael Howard, *Clausewitz: A Very Short Introduction* (Oxford University Press, 2002); Christon I. Archer, *World History of Warfare* (University of Nebraska Press, 2002), 392–409; Rothenberg, *The Napoleonic Wars*, 26–47; Jeremy Black, *Warfare in the Eighteenth Century* (Collins/Smithsonian, 2006), 198–207.
10. Richard English, *Modern War: A Very Short Introduction* (Oxford University Press, 2013), 11–13; Michael Howard, *War in European History* (Oxford University Press, 2001), 87.
11. English, *Modern War*, 13; Howard, *War in European History*, 94–115.
12. Roberto Luis Blanco Valdés, *Rey, Cortes y Fuerza Armada en los orígenes de la España Liberal, 1808–1823* (Madrid: Institució Valenciana d'Estudis i Investigació; Siglo Veintiuno Editores, 1988).
13. Manuel Chust and José Antonio Serrano Ortega, "Milicia y Revolución Liberal en España y México" [Militia and Liberal Revolution in Spain], in *Las Armas de La Nación: Independencia y Ciudadanía en Hispanoamérica (1750–1850)*, ed. Manuel Chust Calero and Juan Marchena Fernández (Madrid Iberoamericana: Vervuert, 2007), 81–110.
14. Rodrigo Moreno Gutiérrez, "Las Fuerzas Armadas en el Proceso de Consumación de Independencia: Nueva España, 1820–1821" (PhD diss., Universidad Nacional Autónoma de México, 2014), 69–71.
15. Moreno Gutiérrez, "Las Fuerzas Armadas en el Proceso de Consumación de Independencia," 72–80.
16. Moreno Gutiérrez, "Las Fuerzas Armadas en el Proceso de Consumación de Independencia," 72–80.
17. Moreno Gutiérrez, "Las Fuerzas Armada en el Proceso de Consumación de Independencia," 81–104; Juan Ortiz Escamilla, *Guerra y Gobierno. Los pueblos y la independencia de México, 1808–1825* (El Colegio de México; Instituto de Investigaciones Dr. José María Luis Mora, 2014), 302–3.

18. October 9, 1820. Arredondo Orders the Formation of the National Militia in San Antonio, Bexar Papers, microfilm, reel 65, August 1820–December 1820, frame 0390. November 13, 1820. Receipt of Two Royal Ordinances Concerning the Establishment and Organization of the National Militia, Bexar Papers, microfilm, reel 65, August 1820–December 1820, frame 0775.
19. December 19, 1820. Units of the National Infantry Militia in Texas, AGENL, Militares, box 9. December 19, 1820. Units of the National Infantry Militia in Texas, Bexar Papers, microfilm, reel 66, December 1820–March 1821, frame 0103.
20. December 29, 1820. Sending the Companies' Lists of the Infantry National Militia of Texas Chosen by the Town Council, Bexar Papers, microfilm, reel 66, December 1820–March 1821, frame 0149.
21. June 11, 1821. San Antonio's Town Council Asks How to Proceed in Relation to the Provincial Militias, Bexar Papers, microfilm, reel 67, March 1821–July 1821, frame 0791.
22. December 27, 1820. Sending the Companies' Lists of the Infantry National Militia of Texas, Bexar Papers, microfilm, reel 66, December 1820–March 1821, frame 0130.
23. February 26, 1821. Regarding the Provincial Council's Decision, Bexar Papers, microfilm, reel 66, December 1820–March 1821, frame 0783.
24. August 19, 1821. Organization of the National Militia in Tlaxcala (San Miguel de Aguayo) and Lampazos, AMB, Correspondencia del Estado, box 3, fol. 34.
25. August 19, 1821. Organization of the National Militia in Tlaxcala (San Miguel de Aguayo) and Lampazos, AMB, Correspondencia del Estado, box 3, fol. 34.
26. October 15, 1821. Organization of the National Militia in Tlaxcala (San Miguel de Aguayo), AMB, Correspondencia del Estado, box 3, fol. 34. July 8, 1821, Agustín de Iturbide's Regulations for the National Militia, Bexar Papers, microfilm, reel 67, March 1821–July 1821, frame 0949.
27. August 19, 1821. Organization of the National Militia in Tlaxcala (San Miguel de Aguayo) and Lampazos, AMB, Correspondencia del Estado, box 3, fol. 34.
28. August 19, 1821. Organization of the National Militia in Tlaxcala (San Miguel de Aguayo) and Lampazos, AMB, Correspondencia del Estado, box 3, fol. 34. October 24, 1821. Regulations for the National Militia, Bexar Papers, microfilm, reel 68, August 1821–November 1821, frame 0768.
29. August 19, 1821. Organization of the National Militia in Tlaxcala (San Miguel de Aguayo) and Lampazos, AMB, Correspondencia del Estado, box 3, fol. 34. October 24, 1821. Regulations for the National Militia, Bexar Papers, microfilm, reel 68, August 1821–November 1821, frame 0768.
30. December 30, 1821. Election of Don Bartolomé Cruz as Second Lieutenant of the National Militia Company of San Miguel de Aguayo, AMB, Correspondencia del Estado, box 3, fol. 34. December 30, 1821. Election of Don Luciano Flores as Sergeant

of the National Militia Company of San Miguel de Aguayo, AMB, Correspondencia del Estado, box 3, fol. 34. December 30, 1821. Election of Don Jacinto de Luna as Corporal of the National Militia Company of San Miguel de Aguayo, AMB, Correspondencia del Estado, box 3, fol. 34. December 30, 1821. Election of Don Luciano Flores as Corporal of the National Militia Company of San Miguel de Aguayo, AMB, Correspondencia del Estado, box 3, fol. 34.

31. July 10, 1821. Promise of Compliance With the Town Council's Request to Unite the Militia with the Local National Militia, Bexar Papers, microfilm, reel 67, May 1821–July 1821, frame 0958. October 27, 1821. Instructions to Disband the Cavalry Militia Company of Texas, Bexar Papers, microfilm, reel 68, August 1821–November 1821, frame 0768.

32. August 19, 1821. Organization of the National Militia in Tlaxcala (San Miguel de Aguayo) and Lampazos, AMB, Correspondencia del Estado, box 3, fol. 34.

33. March 2, 1822. Decree Ordering Not to Incorporate the Deserters into the National Militia, AMB, Correspondencia del Estado, box 3, fol. 34.

34. January 19, 1822. State of the Force of the National Militia in Lampazos, AGENL, Alcaldes Primeros Lampazos, box 6.

35. Alicia Hernández Chávez, *La tradición republicana del buen gobierno* (Fondo de Cultura Económica; Colegio de México, 1993), 17–45; Manuel Chust, "La Nación en Armas. La Milicia Cívica en México, 1821–1835," in *Revolución, Independencia y Las Nuevas Naciones de América*, ed. Jaime E. Rodríguez O. (Fundación MAPFRE TAVERA, 2005), 279–83; Chust and Serrano Ortega, "Milicia y Revolución Liberal en España y México," 93–95. There were exceptions to service for those who had been ordained *in sacris*, sailors, those with physical disabilities, and simple day laborers. Congress defined a day laborer as one who did not receive an income for each day he did not work.

36. Decree of August 3, 1822. Regulations of the Civic Militia, in Manuel Dublán and José María Lozano, *Legislación Mexicana ó Colección Completa de las disposiciones legislativas expedidas desde la Independencia de la República*, vol. II (Calle de Cordobanes número 8; Imprenta del Comercio a cargo de Dublán y Lozano, 1876), 619–26; Chust, "La Nación en Armas," 279–82; Chust and Serrano Ortega, "Milicia y Revolución Liberal en España y México," 93–95; Pedro Santoni "The Failure of Mobilization: The Civic Militia of Mexico in 1846," *Mexican Studies/Estudios Mexicanos* 12, no. 2 (Summer 1996): 169–94.

37. Chust and Serrano Ortega, "Milicia y Revolución Liberal en España y México," 93–105; Manuel Chust Calero, "Milicia, milicias y milicianos: nacionales y cívicos en la formación del Estado-nación mexicano, 1812–1835," in *Fuerzas Militares en Iberoamérica: Siglos XVIII Y XIX*, ed. Juan Ortiz Escamilla (El Colegio de México; Colegio de Michoacán; Universidad Veracruzana, 2005), 179–97. December 29, 1827. General Regulations of the Civic Militia (http://bibliohistorico.juridicas.unam.mx/libros/6/2881/32.pdf), accessed January 6, 2015.

38. Decree of August 3, 1822. Regulations of the Civic Militia, in Dublán and Lozano, *Legislación Mexicana ó Colección Completa de las disposiciones legislativas expedidas desde la Independencia de la República*, vol. II (Calle de Cordobanes número 8; Imprenta del Comercio a cargo de Dublán y Lozano, 1876), 619–26. December 29, 1827. General Regulations of the Civic Militia; Chust and Serrano Ortega, "Milicia y Revolución Liberal en España y México", 93–105; José Antonio Serrano Ortega, "Los Estados Armados: Milicias Cívicas y Sistema Federal en México (1824–1835)," in *La Guerra y la Paz. Tradiciones y Contradicciones*, vol. II, ed. Alberto Carrillo Cázares (El Colegio de Michoacán, 2002), 445–56.

39. Chust and Serrano Ortega, "Milicia y Revolución Liberal en España y México," 93–105; Pedro Santoni, "A Fear of the People: The Civic Militia of Mexico in 1845," *Hispanic American Historical Review* 68, no. 2 (May 1988): 269–88.

40. *Constitución Política del Estado Libre y Soberano de Nuevo León sancionada en 5 de Marzo de*, Monterrey, Imprenta de Don Mariano Ontiveros; *Constitución Política del Estado Libre de las Tamaulipas sancionada por su Congreso Constituyente en 6 de Mayo de 1825* 1825 (Ciudad Victoria. Imprenta del Congreso del Estado a cargo del C. Contreras); *Constitución Política del Estado Libre de Coahuila y Tejas, sancionada por su Congreso Constituyente en 11 de Marzo de 1827*, México: 1827 (Imprenta a cargo de Mariano Arevalo. Calle de Cadena num. 2).

41. December 15, 1823. Decree of the Diputación Provincial, Laredo Papers, microfilm, reel IV.

42. December 4, 1823. Civic Militia Regulations, Laredo Papers, microfilm, reel IV.

43. 1823. Extraordinary Meeting to Read the Civic Militia's Regulations, Bexar Papers, microfilm, reel 70, January 1822–March 1822, frame 1052.

44. 1823. Extraordinary Meeting to Read the Civic Militia's Regulations, Bexar Papers, microfilm, reel 70, January 1822–March 1822, frame 1052. December 15, 1823. List of the National Militia of Lampazos, AGENL, Alcaldes Primeros Lampazos, box 6. June 6, 1824. List of the Laredo Civic Company, Laredo Papers, microfilm, census reel. November 2, 1823. List of the Civic Militia Company in San Miguel, Trinity University, microfilm, Mexican Collection, reel 924, AMB, vol. 5, 1824–1826. 1822. Civic Militia Regulations in the Laredo Archives, Laredo Papers, microfilm, reel IV.

45. June 21, 1823. Instructions from Brigadier Felipe de la Garza, Commander of the Eastern Interior Provinces, Trinity University, microfilm, Mexican Collection, reel 924, AMB, vol. 4, 1821.

46. November 8, 1824. Measures with Respect to the Civic Militia's Officers, AMB, Correspondencia del Estado, box 4.

47. May 20, 1824. Minutes of the Town Council of San Antonio of May 12, 1824, Bexar Papers, microfilm, reel 77, May 1824–September 1824, frame 0127.
48. May 20, 1824. Minutes of the Town Council of San Antonio of May 15, 1824, Bexar Papers, microfilm, roll 77, May 1824–September 1824, frame 0127.
49. May 20, 1824. Response of the City Council of San Antonio to the Provincial Council of May 15, 1824, Bexar Papers, microfilm, reel 77, May 1824–September 1824, frame 0127.
50. May 20, 1824. Report on the Protests of Some Members of the Civic Militia, Bexar Papers, microfilm, reel 77, May 1824–September 1824, frame 0118.
51. May 20, 1824. The Help of Soldiers of the Regular Army Is Requested to Contain an Insubordination of the Civic Militia, Bexar Papers, microfilm, reel 77, May 1824–September 1824, frame 0123. May 21, 1824. Informing on the Discharge of Two Companies of the Civic Militia, Bexar Papers, microfilm, reel 77, May 1824–September 1824, frame 0136.
52. May 29, 1824. The Provincial Council Sends Copies of the Ordinances of the Civic Militia, Bexar Papers, microfilm, reel 77, May 1824–September 1824, frame 0179.
53. December 15, 1823. Letter that Explains That the Civic Militia Is Mainly Comprised of Day Workers, AGENL, Alcaldes Primeros Lampazos, box 6. October 26, 1824. Lampazos's Town Council Requests Modifying the Civic Militia Regulations, AGENL, Alcaldes Primeros Lampazos, box 6.
54. October 26, 1824. Lampazos City Council Requests Modification of the Civic Militia Regulations, AGENL, Alcaldes Primeros Lampazos, box 6.
55. October 20, 1829. Request concerning the Training Exercises of the Civic Militia, AMB, Correspondencia del Estado, box 9, fol. 5.
56. November 2, 1822. State of the Civic Militia in San Miguel, Trinity University, microfilm, Mexican Collection, reel 924, AMB, vol. 5, 1824–1826.
57. December 15, 1824. List of the Lampazos Civic Militia, AGENL, Alcaldes Primeros Lampazos, box 6.
58. Reglamento de la Milicia Cívica del Estado de Nuevo León, April 24, 1828, in *Colección de leyes, decretos y circulares: expedidos por el gobierno del estado, desde el 10 de agosto 1824 hasta . . .* (Tipografía del gobierno, 1882).
59. *Reglamento para la Milicia Civica del Estado de Coahuila y Texas*, Monclova 1834, Imprenta del gobierno dirigida por el ciudadano Sisto Gonzalez. April 22, 1830. Exemption Fee Payments in San Antonio, Minutes of the City of San Antonio 1830–1835, Spanish Minute Book Two, Briscoe Center for American History, University of Texas Austin, 2Q245, fol. 11–12.
60. *Reglamento para la Milicia Civica del Estado de Coahuila y Texas*.

61. January 5, 1832. Account Statements of the San Antonio Civic Militia, Minutes of the City of San Antonio 1830–1835, Spanish Minute Book Two, Briscoe Center for American History, University of Texas Austin, 2Q245, fol. 77. February 22, 1833. Account Statements of the San Antonio Civic Militia, Minutes of the City of San Antonio 1830–1835, Spanish Minute Book Two, Briscoe Center for American History, University of Texas Austin, 2Q245, fol. 112.
62. December 16, 1826. Lack of Funds for the Lampazos Civic Militia, Trinity University, microfilm, Mexican Collection, reel 176, AML, vol. 2, 1825–1827.
63. February 4, 1830. Actions Regarding Payment of Civic Militia Exemptions in San Antonio, Minutes of the City of San Antonio 1830–1835, Spanish Minute Book Two, Briscoe Center for American History, University of Texas Austin, 2Q245, fol. 5.
64. February 17, 1831. José María Hernández's Request to Enter the Civic Militia, Minutes of the City of San Antonio 1830–1835, Spanish Minute Book Two, Briscoe Center for American History, University of Texas Austin, 2Q245, fol. 47.
65. February 24, 1831. Regular Meeting of the San Antonio's Town Council, Minutes of the City of San Antonio 1830–1835, Spanish Minute Book Two, Briscoe Center for American History, University of Texas Austin, 2Q245, fol. 48.
66. June 5, 1834. Regular Session of the San Antonio City Council, Minutes of the City of San Antonio 1830–1835, Spanish Minute Book Two, Briscoe Center for American History, University of Texas Austin, 2Q245, fol, 147.
67. August 9, 1832. Juan José Cisneros's Request to the Town Council of Lampazos, Trinity University, microfilm, Mexican Collection, reel 738, AML, vol. 11, 1832–1833.
68. Reglamento de la Milicia Cívica del Estado de Nuevo León, April 24, 1828. *Reglamento para la Milicia Cívica del Estado de Coahuila y Texas*.
69. December 15, 1823. Complaints Against Lampazos' Mayor, AGENL, Alcaldes Primeros Lampazos, box 6. December 25, 1823. Complaints Against Lampazos' Mayor Mariano Ayala, AGENL, Alcaldes Primeros Lampazos 1821–1824, Fondo Colonial, box 5.
70. April 28, 1824. Juan Zuazua's Testament, Trinity University, microfilm, Mexican Collection, reel 736, AML.
71. July 15, 1829. Formation of the Local Civic Militia of Lampazos, Trinity University, microfilm, Mexican Collection, reel 177, AML, vol. 3, 1828–1829. August 13, 1829. List of the Persons of the Civic Militia to Train Under the Command of Francisco Zuazua, Trinity University, microfilm, Mexican Collection, reel 177, AML, vol. 3, 1828–1829. October 4, 1830. Francisco Zuazua Chosen as Lieutenant, Trinity University, microfilm, Mexican Collection, reel 177, AML, vol. 4, 1830–1831. December 15, 1831. Election of the Town Council's President, Trinity University, microfilm, Mexican Collection, reel 178, AML, vol. 4, 1830–1831. March

1, 1832. Lampazos Civic Militia Company List, Trinity University, microfilm, Mexican Collection, reel 738, AML, vol. II, 1832–1833. December 1, 1833. Election of Electors, Trinity University, microfilm, Mexican Collection, reel 178, AML, vol. 5, 1832–1834.

72. June 30, 1833. Civic Militia List, Trinity University, microfilm, Mexican Collection, reel 739, AML, vol. II, 1832–1833.

73. Teresa Palomo Acosta, "Benavides, Basilio," in *Handbook of Texas Online*, Texas State Historical Association, accessed May 1, 2024, https://www.tshaonline.org/handbook/entries/benavides-basilio.

74. March 23, 1823. Signatures of the People of Laredo Welcoming the New Republican System, Laredo Papers, microfilm, reel IV.

75. June 6, 1824. Civic Company of Laredo, Laredo Papers, microfilm, census reel.

76. Camilla Campbell, "Navarro, Angel," in *Handbook of Texas Online*, Texas State Historical Association, accessed May 1, 2024, https://www.tshaonline.org/handbook/entries/navarro-angel.

77. Camilla Campbell, "Navarro, José Angel [The Elder]," in *Handbook of Texas Online*, Texas State Historical Association, accessed May 1, 2024, https://www.tshaonline.org/handbook/entries/navarro-jose-angel-the-elder.

78. May 16, 1835. Navarro to the Commander, in John Holmes Jenkins, *The Papers of the Texas Revolution, 1835–1836* (Presidial Press, 1973), 1:110–11. December 19, 1820. Units of the National Infantry Militia in Texas, AGENL, Militares, box 9. December 19, 1820. Units of the National Infantry Militia in Texas, Bexar Papers, microfilm, reel 66, December 1820–March 1821, frame 0103. December 29, 1820. Sending the Companies' Lists of the Infantry National Militia of Texas Chosen by the Town Council, Bexar Papers, microfilm, reel 66, December 1820–March 1821, frame 0149. December 27, 1820. Sending the Companies' Lists of the Infantry National Militia of Texas, Bexar Papers, microfilm, reel 66, December 1820–March 1821, frame 0130. June 11, 1821. San Antonio's Town Council Asks How to Proceed in Relation to the Provincial Militias, Bexar Papers, microfilm, reel 67, March 1821–July 1821, frame 0791.

79. Stanley Siegel, "Navarro, José Antonio," in *Handbook of Texas Online*, Texas State Historical Association, accessed May 1, 2024, https://www.tshaonline.org/handbook/entries/navarro-jose-antonio.

80. Jesús "Frank" de la Teja, "Seguin, Juan Jose Maria Erasmo de Jesus," in *Handbook of Texas Online*, Texas State Historical Association, accessed May 1, 2024, https://www.tshaonline.org/handbook/entries/seguin-juan-jose-maria-erasmo-de-jesus. December 27, 1820, Review of a National Militia Unit of San Antonio signed by Erasmo Seguín, AGENL, Militares, box 9.

81. Jesús "Frank" de la Teja, "Seguin, Juan Nepomuceno," in *Handbook of Texas Online*, Texas State Historical Association, accessed May 1, 2024, https://www.tshaonline.org/handbook/entries/seguin-juan-nepomuceno.

82. February 6, 1824. The State of Tamaulipas Refuses to Form the Officers Corp, Laredo Papers, microfilm, reel V. February 17, 1824. Obstacles to Forming the Tamaulipas Officers Corp, Laredo Papers, microfilm, reel V. March 16, 1824. Proposal by the State of Tamaulipas to Use the Civic Militia Instead of the Line Troops, Laredo Papers, microfilm, reel V.

83. February 6, 1824. The State of Tamaulipas Refuses to Form the Officers Corp, Laredo Papers, microfilm, reel V. March 16, 1824. Proposal by the State of Tamaulipas to Use the Civic Militia Instead of the Line Troops, Laredo Papers, microfilm, reel V.

84. November 8, 1824. Document Mentioning that the Civic Militia's Officers Are Exempt from Serving in the Regular Army. AMB, Correspondencia del Estado, box 4.

85. Günter Kahle, *El ejército y la formación del Estado en los comienzos de la independencia de México* (Fondo de Cultura Económica, 1997); Josefina Zoraida Vázquez, "Reflexiones Sobre el Ejército y la Fundación del Estado Mexicano," in *Fuerzas Militares en Iberoamérica: Siglos XVIII Y XIX*, ed. Juan Ortiz Escamilla (El Colegio de México; Colegio de Michoacán; Universidad Veracruzana, 2005), 219–32; Serrano Ortega and Vázquez, "El Nuevo Orden," 397–403.

86. José Antonio Serrano Ortega, "Epílogo. La República Federal desde los Estados, 1824–1835," in *Práctica y fracaso del primer federalismo mexicano (1824–1835)*, ed. Josefina Zoraida Vázquez and José Antonio Serrano Ortega (El Colegio de México, 2012), 595–609.

87. Luis Jáuregui, "El Primer Federalismo en Nuevo León: Prácticas, Dificultades y Fracasos, 1825–1835," in *Práctica y fracaso del primer federalismo mexicano (1824–1835)*, ed. Josefina Zoraida Vázquez and José Antonio Serrano Ortega (El Colegio de México, 2012), 385–415.

88. August 22, 1825. Dispositions for the Previous Provincial Militias in Laredo, Laredo Papers, microfilm, reel V.

89. September 1, 1826. List of the Volunteers Enrolled in the Company of Laredo's Presidio, Laredo Papers, microfilm, reel V.

90. March 3, 1827. List of Laredo Residents Serving in the Presidio's Company, Laredo Papers, microfilm, census reel.

91. May 9, 1834. Comandante de la guarnición de Laredo explicando el tipo de tropas que necesita para la compañía presidial [Commander of the Laredo Garrison Explaining the Kind of Troops that He Needs for the Presidio's Company], Laredo Papers, microfilm, reel VII. Translation mine.

92. May 21, 1824. Estado de la guarnición de San Antonio [State of San Antonio's Garrison], Bexar Papers, microfilm, reel 77, May 1824–September 1824, frame 0136.
93. February 18, 1830. Sesión regular del cabildo de San Antonio [Regular Meeting of San Antonio's Town Council], Minutes of the City of San Antonio 1830–1835, Spanish Minute Book Two, Briscoe Center for American History, University of Texas Austin, 2Q245, fol. 6. Translation mine.
94. June 19, 1826. Commander of Lampazos's Garrison Requests More Troops, Trinity University, microfilm, Mexican Collection, reel 176, AML, vol. 2, 1825–1827.
95. May 11, 1826. Lampazos's Commander Complaints about the Inaccurate Reports on His Troops, Trinity University, microfilm, Mexican Collection, roll 176, AML, vol. 2, 1825–1827.
96. July 11, 1826. Lampazos Town Council's Request, Trinity University, microfilm, Mexican Collection, reel 736, AML, file 32, 1826.
97. September 28, 1826. Requesting Men for Lampazos's Garrison, Trinity University, microfilm, Mexican Collection, reel 176, AML, vol. 2, 1825–1827.
98. October 31, 1826. Lampazos's Garrison Was Not Completed, Trinity University, microfilm, Mexican Collection, reel 176, AML, vol. 2, 1825–1827.
99. October 18, 1826. The Military Commander Informs of the Required Qualities of the Recruits, Trinity University, microfilm, Mexican Collection, reel 926, AMB, vol. 5, 1826.
100. November 21, 1826. Hombres rechazados por la guarnición de Lampazos [Men Rejected by Lampazos's Garrison], Trinity University, microfilm, Mexican Collection, reel 926, AMB, vol. 5, 1826.
101. November 23, 1826. Hombres inútiles para el servicio [Men Unfit for Service], Trinity University, microfilm, Mexican Collection, reel 926, AMB, vol. 5, 1826. Translation mine.
102. 1829. Multas de 100 pesos para aquellos que no enviaran reclutas para la compañía de Lampazos [One-Hundred Pesos Fine for Those Who Did Not Send Recruits for Lampazos's Company], AMB, Correspondencia del Estado, box 9, fol. 35.
103. July 1, 1833. Denuncia de María del Carmen Espinoza sobre el reclutamiento forzado de su hijo [María del Carmen Espinoza's Complaint about Her Son's Forced Recruitment], Trinity University, microfilm, Mexican Collection, reel 931, AMB, vol. 8, 1833. Translation mine.
104. 1835. Disposiciones sobre el retorno de desertores [Dispositions for the Return of Deserters], Trinity University, microfilm, Mexican Collection, reel 933, AMB, vol. 9, 1835.
105. Isidro Vizcaya Canales, *Tierra de Guerra Viva: Incursiones de Indios y otros Conflictos en El Noreste de México Durante El Siglo XIX, 1821–1885* (Academia de Investigaciones, 2001), 23–52.

NOTES TO PAGES 137–138

106. May 11, 1825. Laredo's Garrison Faces Comanches, Laredo Papers, microfilm, reel V. August 24, 1830. Attack by 260 Comanches in Laredo, Laredo Papers, microfilm, reel VI. April 20, 1833. Party Organized in Laredo to Fend Off Comanche Attacks, Laredo Papers, microfilm, reel VII. November 25, 1826. Cautionary Measures for the Population, Trinity University, microfilm, Mexican Collection, reel 926, AMB, vol. 5, 1826. February 18, 1830. Difficult Situation in San Antonio Due to Indigenous Depredations, Minutes of the City of San Antonio 1830–1835, Spanish Minute Book Two, Briscoe Center for American History, University of Texas Austin, 2Q245, fol. 6. March 1, 1822. Comanche Attacks in Lampazos, Trinity University, microfilm, Mexican Collection, reel 175, AML, vol. 1, 1819–1824. September 5, 1831. Preparations against the Comanche Attacks in Lampazos, Trinity University, microfilm, Mexican Collection, reel 178, AML, vol. 4, 1830–1831.

107. March 14, 1826. Andres de Sobrevilla Reports Animal Losses in Lampazos, Trinity University, microfilm, Mexican Collection, reel 176, AML, vol. 2, 1825–1827.

108. November 16, 1830. Measures against the Indigenous Attacks in Laredo, Laredo Papers, microfilm, reel VIII.

109. October 18, 1826. Measures against the Indigenous Attacks, Trinity University, microfilm, Mexican Collection, reel 176, AML, vol. 2, 1825–1827. November 2, 1826. About Arming servants, Trinity University, microfilm. Mexican Collection, reel 176, AML, vol. 2, 1825–1827.

110. February 12, 1832. Plans for a General Campaign against the Comanches, Minutes of the City of San Antonio 1830–1835, Spanish Minute Book Two, Briscoe Center for American History, University of Texas Austin, 2Q245, fol. 81. February 17, 1833. Campaign Project against the "Indians" who Harass Texas, Nuevo León, and Tamaulipas, Minutes of the City of San Antonio 1830–1835, Spanish Minute Book Two, Briscoe Center for American History, University of Texas Austin, 2Q245, fol. 100. August 8, 1825. Proposal to Carry Out a Campaign with 800 Men, Laredo Papers, microfilm, reel V.

111. August 25, 1831. Measures Due to the War against the Comanches, Minutes of the City of San Antonio 1830–1835, Spanish Minute Book Two, Briscoe Center for American History, University of Texas Austin, 2Q245, fol. 57.

112. May 16, 1826. Troops and Organized Residents to Fight the Natives, Trinity University, microfilm, Mexican Collection, reel 176, AML, vol. 2, 1825–1827. September 27, 1832. Force of Troops and Civic Force to Pursue Comanches, Trinity University, microfilm, Mexican Collection, roll 739, AML, vol. 11, 1832–1833. January 13, 1833. Party of Soldiers and Residents, Trinity University, microfilm, Mexican Collection, reel 739, AML, vol. 11, 1832–1833. September 30, 1832. Force of Civic Militia and Regular Troops in Laredo, Laredo Papers, microfilm, reel VII. April 7, 1834. United Force of Civic Militiamen and Troops to Fight Comanches, Laredo Papers, microfilm, reel VII.

NOTES TO PAGES 138–139

113. October 3, 1830. The Commanders of the Companies of San Antonio and Laredo Request a Loan of 500 Pesos, Minutes of the City of San Antonio 1830–1835, Spanish Minute Book Two, Briscoe Center for American History, University of Texas Austin, 2Q245, fol. 31. October 21, 1830, Loan of 500 Pesos Approved, Minutes of the City of San Antonio 1830–1835, Spanish Minute Book Two, Briscoe Center for American History, University of Texas Austin, 2Q245, fol. 33. January 2, 1834. 500 Pesos Loaned to Laredo's Company, Minutes of the City of San Antonio 1830–1835, Spanish Minute Book Two, Briscoe Center for American History, University of Texas Austin, 2Q245, fol. 135.

114. Vizcaya Canales, *Tierra de Guerra Viva*, 70–71.

115. March 14, 1826. Andrés de Sobrevilla Reports Losses of Animals in Lampazos, Trinity University, microfilm. Mexican Collection, reel 176, AML, vol. 2, 1825–1827. September 27, 1832. Troop and Civics Force to Pursue Comanches, Trinity University, microfilm, Mexican Collection, reel 739, AML, vol. 11, 1832–1833. January 7, 1833. State of Lampazos's Defense, Trinity University, microfilm, Mexican Collection, reel 739, AML, vol. 11, 1832–1833.

116. September 3, 1832. José Andrés de Sobrevilla Acting as Laredo's Commander, Laredo Papers, microfilm, reel VII.

117. October 17, 1833. Laredo Reports Indigenous Attacks in Lampazos, Trinity University, microfilm, Mexican Collection, reel 739, AML, vol. 11, 1832–1833.

118. Gilberto Miguel Hinojosa, *A Borderlands Town in Transition: Laredo, 1755–1870* (Texas A&M University Press, 1983), 44.

119. In the Official Gazette of the state of Nuevo León, there are constant mentions regarding the regulation and organization of patriotic societies. February 26, 1827. Meeting of the Local Congress Regarding the Establishment of Patriotic Societies, in *Gazeta Constitucional del Estado de Nuevo León*, Thursday, March 8, 1827, no. 32, Periódico Oficial, AGENL. March 1, 1827. Session of the Local Congress on the Approval of Articles of Patriotic Societies, in *Gazeta Constitucional del Estado de Nuevo León*, Thursday, March 15, 1827, no. 33, Periódico Oficial, AGENL. March 8, 1827. Decree Number 128 on the Establishment and Formation of Patriotic Societies, in *Gazeta Constitucional del Estado de Nuevo León*, Thursday, July 12, 1827, no. 50, Periódico Oficial, AGENL. March 8, 1827. Decree No. 128 on the Officers and Duties of Patriotic Societies, in *Gazeta Constitucional del Estado de Nuevo León*, Thursday, July 19, 1827, no. 51, Periódico Oficial, AGENL. March 8, 1827. Decree Number 128 on the Sessions, Resolutions and Powers of Patriotic Societies, in *Gazeta Constitucional del Estado de Nuevo León*, Thursday, July 26, 1827, no. 52, Periódico Oficial, AGENL.

CHAPTER 5

1. Jan Bazant, "From Independence to the Liberal Republic, 1821–1867," in *Mexico Since Independence*, ed. Leslie Bethell (Cambridge University Press, 1991); José Antonio Serrano Ortega and Josefina Zoraida Vázquez, "El Nuevo Orden, 1821–1848," in *Nueva Historia General de México*, ed. Erik Velásquez (El Colegio de México, 2010), 423–25.
2. David J. Weber, *The Mexican Frontier, 1821–1846: The American Southwest under Mexico* (University of New Mexico Press, 1982), 158–65.
3. Weber, *The Mexican Frontier, 1821–1846*, 158–65.
4. Weber, *The Mexican Frontier, 1821–1846*, 158–65.
5. Weber, *The Mexican Frontier, 1821–1846*, 171–77.
6. Weber, *The Mexican Frontier, 1821–1846*, 171–77.
7. Andrés Tijerina, "Under the Mexican Flag," in *Tejano Journey, 1770–1850*, ed. Gerald Eugene Poyo (University of Texas Press, 1996), 33–43.
8. Tijerina, "Under the Mexican Flag," 44–47.
9. Luis Medina Peña, *Invención del sistema político mexicano. Forma de gobierno y gobernabilidad en México en el siglo XIX* (Fondo de Cultura Económica, 2007), 87–108.
10. Andrés Reséndez, *Changing National Identities at the Frontier: Texas and New Mexico, 1800–1850* (Cambridge University Press, 2005), 154–60.
11. Will Fowler, *Santa Anna of Mexico* (University of Nebraska Press, 2007); Reséndez, *Changing National Identities at the Frontier*, 161–70.
12. Fowler, *Santa Anna of Mexico*; Reséndez, *Changing National Identities at the Frontier*, 161–70.
13. Reséndez, *Changing National Identities at the Frontier*, 159.
14. April 26, 1835. Town Council of San Patricio to Ángel Navarro, Receipt of the Decree Concerning the Use of the Civic Militia, Bexar Papers, microfilm, reel 164, February 1835–May 1835, frame 0850. May 30, 1835. Ángel Navarro Informs on the Civic Militia Marching Toward Monclova, Bexar Papers, microfilm, reel 164, February 1835–May 1835, frame 0976. May 15, 1835. List of the Militia Members of Bexar Marching Toward Monclova, Bexar Papers, microfilm, reel 165, May 1835–July 1835, frame 0143.
15. December 6, 1836. List of Seguín's Company. February 10, 1858, "Seguín's Company at the Siege of Bexar," in *A Revolution Remembered: The Memoirs and Selected Correspondence of Juan N. Seguín*, ed. Jesús F. de La Teja (Texas State Historical Association, 2002), 147–51, 182–83.
16. June 22, 1835. "1835 Acta del pronunciamiento del estado libre de Coahuila y Texas [Act of the Declaration of the Free State of Coahuila and Texas]," http://www.memoria politicademexico.org/Textos/2ImpDictadura/1835PEC.html, accessed January 10, 2015.

17. September 28, 1860. Seguín's Company for the 1839 Campaign, in Teja, *A Revolution Remembered*, 184–86.
18. October 14, 1835. Letter of Ángel Navarro, in John Holmes Jenkins, *The Papers of the Texas Revolution 1835–1836* (Presidial Press, 1973), 128–29; Raúl A. Ramos, *Beyond the Alamo: Forging Mexican Ethnicity in San Antonio, 1821–1861* (University of North Carolina Press, 2008), 145–46.
19. Jesús F. de la Teja, "Juan N. Seguín. Federalist, Rebel, Exile," in *Tejano Leadership in Mexican and Revolutionary Texas*, ed. Jesús F. de la Teja and Raúl A. Ramos (Texas A&M University Press, 2010), 212–30. May 30, 1835. Ángel Navarro Informs on the Civic Militia Marching Toward Monclova, Bexar Papers, microfilm, reel 164, February 1835–May 1835, frame 0976.
20. Ramos, *Beyond the Alamo*, 147–48.
21. Josefina Zoraida Vázquez, "La Supuesta República del Rio Grande," *Historia Mexicana* 36, no. 1 (July–Sep. 1986): 52.
22. Juan José Gallegos, "Last Drop of My Blood. Col. Antonio Zapata: A Life and Times on Mexico's Río Grande Frontier, 1797–1840" (MA thesis, University of Houston, 2005), 102–3; Roberto Mario Salmón, "Zapata, Antonio," *Handbook of Texas Online*, Texas State Historical Association, accessed May 1, 2024, https://www.tshaonline.org/handbook/entries/zapata-antonio.
23. Gallegos, "Last Drop of My Blood. Col. Antonio Zapata"; Zoraida Vázquez, "La Supuesta República del Rio Grande"; Cesar Morado Macías, "Aspectos Militares: Tres Guerras Ensambladas (1835–1848)," in *La guerra México-Estados Unidos: su impacto en Nuevo León, 1835–1848* (Senado de la República, 2003), 74–79.
24. David Vigness, "Republic of the Rio Grande," *Handbook of Texas Online*, Texas State Historical Association, accessed May 1, 2024, https://www.tshaonline.org/handbook/entries/republic-of-the-rio-grande; Gallegos, "Last Drop of My Blood. Col. Antonio Zapata"; Zoraida Vázquez, "La Supuesta República del Rio Grande"; Morado Macías, "Aspectos Militares: Tres Guerras Ensambladas (1835–1848)."
25. Gallegos, "Last Drop of My Blood. Col. Antonio Zapata," 110–12.
26. October 20, 1839. Report of Two Thieves Who Identified Themselves as Federalists, Trinity University, microfilm, Mexican Collection, reel 936, AMB, vol. 11, 1839.
27. February 21, 1839. Investigation into Individuals from San Miguel Joining the Federalist Rebellion, Trinity University, microfilm, Mexican Collection, reel 936, AMB, vol. 11, 1839.
28. January 4, 1840. Zapata Requests a Loan of 500 Pesos, Trinity University, microfilm, Mexican Collection, reel 937, AMB, vol. 12, 1841.
29. September 4, 1839. Report of Lampazos on the Federalist Uprising, Trinity University, microfilm, Mexican Collection, reel 741, AML, vol. 14, 1838–1839.

30. September 4, 1839. Report of Lampazos on the Federalist Uprising, Trinity University, microfilm, Mexican Collection, reel 741, AML, vol. 14, 1838–1839.
31. September 30, 1839. List of Individuals from Lampazos Pardoned for Their Participation in the Federalist Rebellion, Trinity University, microfilm, Mexican Collection, reel 742, AML, vol. 14, 1838–1839.
32. September 7, 1839. Army Section Assigned to Lampazos, Trinity University, microfilm, Mexican Collection, reel 180, AML, vol. 8, 1841–1842.
33. September 4, 1839. Report of Lampazos on the Federalist Uprising, Trinity University, microfilm, Mexican Collection, reel 741, AML, vol. 14, 1838–1839.
34. Isidro Vizcaya Canales, *Tierra de Guerra Viva: Incursiones de Indios y otros Conflictos en el Noreste de México durante el Siglo XIX, 1821–1885* (Academia de Investigaciones, 2001), 87.
35. September 30, 1839. List of Individuals from Lampazos Pardoned for Their Participation in the Federalist Rebellion, Trinity University, microfilm, Mexican Collection, reel 742, AML, vol. 14, 1838–1839.
36. 1840. Request to Use the Vecinos as Spies, Trinity University, microfilm, Mexican Collection, reel 180, AML, vol. 7–8, 1838–1841.
37. Gilberto Miguel Hinojosa, *A Borderlands Town in Transition: Laredo, 1755–1870* (Texas A&M University Press, 1983), 53. January 6, 1838. Decision to Support the Federalist Rebellion, Laredo Papers, microfilm, reel IX. Most of the garrison of the regular army of Laredo was composed of inhabitants of that town.
38. January 20, 1839. The Federalist Army Requests the Weapons from the Laredo Arsenal, Laredo Papers, microfilm, reel IX. January 29, 1839. About the Federalist Army's Request, Laredo Papers, microfilm, reel IX.
39. Omar S. Valerio-Jiménez, *River of Hope: Forging Identity and Nation in the Rio Grande Borderlands* (Duke University Press, 2013), 46, 120.
40. John Denny Riley, "Santos Benavides: His Influence on the Lower Rio Grande, 1823–1891" (PhD diss., Texas Christian University, 1976), 44–58.
41. Edward H. Moseley, "The Public Career of Santiago Vidaurri, 1855–1858" (PhD diss., University of Alabama, 1963), 52–60; Jesús Ávila, En el Reino de Catujanes." In *Santiago Vidaurri: La Formación de un Liderazgo Regional Desde Monterrey (1809–1867)*. (Universidad Autónoma de Nuevo León, 2012).
42. October 14, 1840. Vidaurri as Captain of a Force Assigned to Fighting "Indians," Trinity University, microfilm, Mexican Collection, reel 937, AMB, vol. 12, 1841. Santiago Vidaurri was born on July 25, 1809, the birthday of the apostle St. James [Santiago in Spanish]. He was named Santiago in honor of this religious figure who, for a long time, was fundamental in Lampazos's war traditions.

43. Sam W. Haynes, "Mexican Invasions of 1842," *Handbook of Texas Online*, Texas State Historical Association, accessed May 1, 2024, https://www.tshaonline.org/handbook/entries/mexican-invasions-of-1842.
44. Joseph M. Nance, "Somervell Expedition," *Handbook of Texas Online*, Texas State Historical Association, accessed May 1, 2024, https://www.tshaonline.org/handbook/entries/somervell-expedition.
45. Joseph M. Nance, "Mier Expedition," *Handbook of Texas Online*, Texas State Historical Association, accessed May 1, 2024, https://www.tshaonline.org/handbook/entries/mier-expedition.
46. Brian DeLay, *War of a Thousand Deserts: Indian Raids and the U.S.-Mexican War* (New Haven, CT: Yale University Press, 2008), 64–70.
47. DeLay, *War of a Thousand Deserts*, 71–75; Weber, *The Mexican Frontier, 1821–1846*, 86.
48. Hinojosa, *A Borderlands Town in Transition: Laredo, 1755–1870*, 50.
49. Vizcaya Canales, *Tierra de Guerra Viva*, 53–54.
50. J. Jesús Ávila, "Aspectos Sociales: Entre la Jara del Salvaje y el Rifle del Extranjero," in *La Guerra México-Estados Unidos: Su Impacto En Nuevo León, 1835–1848* (Senado de la República, 2003), 209–10.
51. Weber, *The Mexican Frontier, 1821–1846*, 86.
52. DeLay, *War of a Thousand Deserts*, 76–79.
53. July 16, 1837. Indigenous Attack in Laredo, Laredo Papers, microfilm, reel X; Vizcaya Canales, *Tierra de Guerra Viva*, 58–59.
54. Comanches were educated from childhood in the culture of revenge, which had a peculiarity. Although they sought to avenge actions they had suffered, it was not always against the direct enemies who had caused them harm but against a third party. On many occasions, the raids carried out by Comanches in Mexico were motivated by losses suffered at the hands of their Indigenous and Anglo-American adversaries. Also, in each raid conducted against Mexican villages, they suffered some deaths. So their Comanche relatives tried to return the following year seeking revenge, which created a geometric spiral of violence in northern Mexico during the 1840s. DeLay, *War of a Thousand Deserts*, 123–38; Pekka Hämäläinen, *The Comanche Empire* (New Haven, CT: Yale University Press, 2008), 220–38.
55. December 15, 1838. Preparations Before the Raid Against 300 Comanches, Trinity University, microfilm, Mexican Collection, reel 935, AMB, vol. II, 1838. December 29, 1838. Native Attacks, Trinity University, microfilm, Mexican Collection, reel 180, AML, vol. 7, 1838. December 31, 1838. Report on the Indigenous' Actions in Lampazos and San Miguel, Trinity University, microfilm, Mexican Collection, reel 180, AML, vol. 7, 1838; Vizcaya Canales, *Tierra de Guerra Viva*, 70–71.

56. January 22, 1839. Reports on the Robberies and Murders in San Miguel, Trinity University, microfilm, Mexican Collection, reel 936, AMB, vol. II, 1839. January 22, 1839. Reports of Robberies at Hacienda del Carrizal, Lampazos, Trinity University, microfilm, Mexican Collection, reel 180, AML, 1839; Vizcaya Canales, *Tierra de Guerra Viva*, 72–73.
57. February 19, 1839. Threat of Attack in Lampazos, Trinity University, microfilm, Mexican Collection, reel 180, AML, 1839.
58. February 21, 1839. Detection of Indigenous Party with Horses and Mules, Trinity University, microfilm, Mexican Collection, reel 936, AMB, vol. II, 1839.
59. February 27, 1839. Murder of a Muleteer, Trinity University, microfilm, Mexican Collection, reel 936, AMB, vol. II, 1839.
60. March 23, 1839. Two Indigenous Parties Were Detected in Lampazos, Trinity University, microfilm, Mexican Collection, reel 936, AMB, vol. II, 1839. March 24, 1839. Detection of "Indians" in the Area, Trinity University, microfilm, Mexican Collection, reel 936, AMB, vol. II, 1839.
61. November 20, 1839. Lampazos Preparations against Indigenous attacks, Mexican Collection, reel 180, AML, 1839.
62. October 29, 1839. Reports of Robberies at Hacienda del Carrizal, Lampazos, Trinity University, microfilm, Mexican Collection, reel 936, AMB, vol. II, 1839.
63. DeLay, *War of a Thousand Deserts*, 80–85.
64. October 7, 1840. Report of Attack in Lampazos, in Semanario Político del Gobierno de Nuevo León, Thursday, October 15, 1840, vol. 2, no. 85, Periódico Oficial, AGENL. October 21, 1840. Reports about the Resistance against the Comanches in Lampazos, Trinity University, microfilm, Mexican Collection, reel 180, AML, vol. 7, 1840. Isidro Vizcaya Canales, *La Invasión de los Indios Bárbaros Al Noreste de México en Los Años de 1840 Y 1841* (ITESM, 1968), 85–89; Bárbara Leticia Martínez Cárdenas, "Los Vecinos Lampacences: de Súbditos a Ciudadanos (1821–1867)," in *Apuntes Para La Historia de Lampazos de Naranjo, Nuevo León* (Universidad Autónoma de Nuevo León, 2003), 38.
65. October 14, 1840. Report of Attack in San Miguel, Semanario Político del Gobierno de Nuevo León, Thursday, October 29, 1840, vol. 2, no. 87, Periódico Oficial, AGENL; Vizcaya Canales, *La Invasión de Los Indios Bárbaros*, 85–89; David B. Adams, "Embattled Borderland: Northern Nuevo León and the Indios Bárbaros, 1686–1870," *Southwestern Historical Quarterly* 95, no. 2 (Oct. 1991): 205–20.
66. DeLay, *War of a Thousand Deserts*, 114–15; Hämäläinen, *The Comanche Empire*, 232; Vizcaya Canales, *Tierra de Guerra Viva*, 115–27; Vito Alessio Robles, *Coahuila y Texas. Desde la Consumación de la Independencia hasta el Tratado de Paz de Guadalupe Hidalgo*, vol. II (Porrúa, 1979), 234–37. January 15, 1841. Report of Attack in Saltillo, Semanario

Político del Gobierno de Nuevo León, Thursday, January 21, 1841, vol. 3, no. 3, Periódico Oficial, AGENL.

67. January 15, 1841. Report of Attack in Saltillo, Semanario Político del Gobierno de Nuevo León, Thursday, January 21, vol. 3, no. 3, Periódico Oficial, AGENL.

68. DeLay, *War of a Thousand Deserts*, 117.

69. May 29, 1836. Organization of the Townships of Nuevo León against the Indigenous Attacks, Trinity University, microfilm, Mexican Collection, reel 934, AMB, vol. 10, 1836.

70. May 20, 1836. San Miguel Men Are Requested to Help in Lampazos, Trinity University, microfilm, Mexican Collection, reel 934, AMB, vol. 10, 1836.

71. May 21, 1836. Organization of the Party to March to Lampazos, Trinity University, microfilm, Mexican Collection, reel 934, AMB, vol. 10, 1836.

72. February 13, 1837. Defense Plan in the North of Tamaulipas, Laredo Papers, microfilm, reel X.

73. March 5, 1837. Laredo's Offer to Have 50 Armed, Mounted Men, Laredo Papers, microfilm, reel X. May 29, 1836. Forces from Laredo Recover a Horse from Lampazos, Trinity University, microfilm, Mexican Collection, reel 179, AML, vol. 6, 1836.

74. February 4, 1838. A Judge Asked How to Proceed Regarding the Civic Militia against the Natives, AMM, Misceláneo, vol. 14, file 13. February 13, 1838. Governor's Order to Keep the Civic Militia Working, Trinity University, microfilm, Mexican Collection, reel 180, AML, vol. 6, 1836. June 5, 1840. Collection of the Civic Militia's Exemption Fee, Trinity University, microfilm, Mexican Collection, reel 937, AMB, vol. 12, 1841.

75. February 10, 1840. Orders to Call the Previous Militias to Arms, AMM, Correspondencia, no. 55, file 10, fol. 21.

76. September 29, 1840. Decree on the Creation of a Militia Unit, in *Semanario Político del Gobierno de Nuevo León*, Thursday, October 1, 1840, vol. 2, no. 83, Periódico Oficial, AGENL; Luis Medina Peña, *Los Bárbaros del Norte. Guardia Nacional y Política en Nuevo León, siglo XIX* (Fondo de Cultura Económica, 2014), 74. Vizcaya Canales, *La Invasión de Los Indios Bárbaros*, 110–12.

77. December 16, 1841. Formation of the Defensores de la Frontera Company in Laredo, Laredo Papers, microfilm, reel IX.

78. October 11, 1840. Appointment of Santiago Vidaurri as Captain of the Defensores de la Frontera Company, Trinity University, microfilm, Mexican Collection, reel 180, AML, 1840. February 7, 1842. 40 Men of the Defensores Company under the Command of Basilio Benavides Had Action against "Indians," Laredo Papers, microfilm, reel XI. March 30, 1841. Basilio Benavides Is Captain of the Defensores de la Frontera Company, Laredo Papers, microfilm, reel IX.

79. Medina Peña, *Los Bárbaros del Norte*, 77.

80. *Semanario Político del Gobierno de Nuevo León*, Thursday, August 11, 1842, vol. 3, no. 84, Periódico Oficial, AGENL.

81. March 15, 1837. Pacification Proposal through Colonization, Trinity University, microfilm, Mexican Collection, reel 740, AML, vol. 13, 1837.

82. February 14, 1837. Proposal of Laredo's Town Council to have a Campaign against "Indians," Laredo Papers, microfilm, reel X. March 5, 1837. The Northern Army General Thanks Laredo's Town Council for Its Enthusiasm in Launching a Campaign, Laredo Papers, microfilm, reel X. December 2, 1839. Proposal for a Campaign in Lampazos With the Help of San Miguel, Trinity University, microfilm, Mexican Collection, reel 742, AML, vol. 14, 1839.

83. DeLay, *War of a Thousand Deserts*, 182–93; Vizcaya Canales, *La Invasión de Los Indios Bárbaros*, 257.

84. July 6, 1841. Operations Instructions by the Northern Army Commander, AMM, Correspondencia, no. 62, 1841, file 7, fol. 3. Medina Peña, *Los Bárbaros del Norte*, 76–77.

85. July 11, 1842. Instructions for the Auxiliary Militia, Trinity University, microfilm, Mexican Collection, reel 181, AML, vol. 8, 1842.

86. August 28, 1841. Roll of Lampazos's Compañía de Defensores, Trinity University, microfilm, Mexican Collection, reel 742, AML, vol. 15, 1841. February 7, 1842. 40 Men of the Defensores Company under the Command of Basilio Benavides Had Action against "Indians," Laredo Papers, microfilm, reel XI.

87. Vizcaya Canales, *La Invasión de Los Indios Bárbaros*, 171.

NOTES TO PAGES 167–171

CONCLUSION

1. Raúl A. Ramos, *Beyond the Alamo: Forging Mexican Ethnicity in San Antonio, 1821–1861* (University of North Carolina Press, 2008), 173–99.
2. Ramos, *Beyond the Alamo*, 173–99.
3. David J. Weber, ed., *Foreigners in Their Native Land: Historical Roots of the Mexican Americans* (University of New Mexico Press, 1973), 178.
4. José Antonio Serrano Ortega and Josefina Zoraida Vázquez, "El Nuevo Orden, 1821–1848," in *Nueva Historia General de México*, ed. Erik Velásquez (El Colegio de México, 2010), 425–37; Jan Bazant, "De Iturbide a Juárez," in *Historia de México* (Crítica, 2001), 43–81.
5. Jesús F. de la Teja, "Juan N. Seguín. Federalist, Rebel, Exile," in *Tejano Leadership in Mexican and Revolutionary Texas*, ed. Jesús F. de la Teja and Raúl A. Ramos (Texas A&M University Press, 2010), 212–30; Hermenegildo Dávila, *Biografía del Sr. General don Juan Zuazua* (AGENL, 1983); John Eisenhower, *Tan lejos de Dios: la guerra de los Estados Unidos contra México, 1846–1848* (Fondo de Cultura Económica, 2000); Christopher D. Dishman, *A Perfect Gibraltar: The Battle for Monterrey, Mexico, 1846* (University of Oklahoma Press, 2010).
6. Omar S. Valerio-Jiménez, *River of Hope: Forging Identity and Nation in the Rio Grande Borderlands* (Duke University Press, 2013), 231–59; Jerry Thompson, "Benavides, Santos," *Handbook of Texas Online*, Texas State Historical Association, accessed April 25, 2024, https://www.tshaonline.org/handbook/entries/benavides-santos; Jose Francisco Segovia, "Botas and Guaraches," *Handbook of Texas Online*, Texas State Historical Association, accessed April 25, 2024, https://www.tshaonline.org/handbook/entries/botas-and-guaraches.
7. Luis Medina Peña, *Los bárbaros del Norte. Guardia Nacional y política en Nuevo León, siglo XIX* (Fondo de Cultura Económica, 2007); Luis Alberto García, *Guerra y Frontera: El Ejército Del Norte Entre 1855 Y 1858* (Archivo General del Estado de Nuevo León, 2007); Brian Hamnett, "Santiago Vidaurri, Northern Mexico, and Regional Identities, 1855–1864," *Tzintzun Revista de Estudios Históricos* 30 (1999): 85–119.
8. J. Jesús Ávila, "Aspectos Sociales: Entre la Jara del Salvaje y el Rifle del Extranjero," in *La Guerra México-Estados Unidos: Su Impacto En Nuevo León, 1835–1848* (Senado de la República, 2003), 209–10.
9. Ávila, "Aspectos Sociales: Entre la Jara del Salvaje y el Rifle del Extranjero," 267.
10. Mario Cerutti, *Economía de guerra y poder regional en el siglo XIX: gastos militares, aduanas y comerciantes en años de Vidaurri (1855–1864)* (Archivo General del Estado de Nuevo León, 1983); Mario Cerutti, "Una economía binacional en tiempos de guerra. El

Bravo, Texas y el Norte de México (1850–1870)," in *Encuentro en la frontera: mexicanos y norteamericanos en un espacio común*, coord. Manuel Ceballos Ramírez (El Colegio de México; El Colegio de la Frontera Norte; Universidad Autónoma de Tamaulipas, 2001), 159–89; Ronnie C. Tyler, *Santiago Vidaurri and the Southern Confederacy* (Texas State Historical Association, 1973).

11. Luis Alberto García, "Dominance in an Imagined Border: Santos Benavides and Santiago Vidaurri's Policing of the Rio Grande," in *Policing the North American Borderlands*, ed. Holly Karibo and George T. Díaz (University of Texas Press, 2020); Juan de Dios Arias, *Reseña histórica de la formación y operaciones del cuerpo de ejército del norte durante la intervención francesa, sitio de Querétaro: Y noticias oficiales sobre la captura de Maximiliano, su proceso íntegro y su muerte* (México: N. Chávez, 1867), 15–16; Caja 91, D/111/598, Julián Quiroga, AHSEDENA.

Bibliography

ARCHIVES

Archivo General del Estado de Nuevo León (AGENL)
Archivo General de la Nación, Mexico (AGN)
Archivo Histórico de la Secretaria de la Defensa Nacional (AHSEDENA)
Archivo Municipal de Bustamante (AMB)
Archivo Municipal de Lampazos (AML)
Archivo Municipal de Monterrey (AMM)
Bexar Papers (Microfilm), Southern Methodist University
Laredo Papers (Microfilm), Southern Methodist University
Mexican Collection (Microfilm), Trinity University
Briscoe Center for American History, University of Texas

MANUSCRIPTS AND OLD TEXTS

"1835 Acta del pronunciamiento del estado libre de Coahuila y Texas" (http://www.memoriapoliticademexico.org/Textos/2ImpDictadura/1835PEC.html). Accessed on January 10, 2015.

Arias, Juan de Dios. *Reseña histórica de la formación y operaciones del cuerpo de ejército del norte durante la intervención francesa, sitio de Querétaro: Y noticias oficiales sobre la captura de Maximiliano, su proceso íntegro y su muerte.* N. Chávez, 1867.

Constitución Política del Estado Libre de Coahuila y Tejas, sancionada por su Congreso Constituyente en 11 de Marzo de 1827. 1827. Imprenta a cargo de Mariano Arevalo. Calle de Cadena num. 2.

Constitución Política del Estado Libre y Soberano de Nuevo León sancionada en 5 de Marzo de 1825. Imprenta de Don Mariano Ontiveros.

Constitución Política del Estado Libre de las Tamaulipas sancionada por su Congreso Constituyente en 6 de Mayo de 1825. Imprenta del Congreso del Estado a cargo del C. Contreras.

Colección de leyes, decretos y circulares: expedidos por el gobierno del estado, desde el 10 de agosto 1824 hasta el 30 de diciembre de 1830. Tipografia del gobierno, 1882.

Dublán, Manuel, and José María Lozano. *Legislación Mexicana ó Colección Completa de las disposiciones legislativas expedidas desde la Independencia de la República.* Volumen II. Calle de Cordobanes número 8. Imprenta del Comercio a cargo de Dublán y Lozano, 1876.

Humboldt, Alexander von. *Ensayo Político Sobre El Reino de La Nueva España.* Editorial Porrúa, 1966.

Instrucciones del Virrey Bernardo de Gálvez para la defensa de las Provincias Internas del Norte. 1786. Boletín del Archivo General de la Nación. 1937, First Series, vol. VIII, no. 4, October-December, 491–540.

Linn, John Joseph, *Reminiscences of Fifty Years in Texas.* D. & J. Sadlier & Company, 1935.

Santa Ana, Benito Fernández de, *Letters and Memorials of the Father Presidente Fray Benito Fernández de Santa Ana, 1736–1754: Documents on the Missions of Texas from the Archives of the College of Querétaro,* Documentary Series / Old Spanish Missions Historical Research Library at Our Lady of the Lake University, no. 6. Old Spanish Missions Historical Research Library at Our Lady of the Lake University, 1981.

Reglamento General de la Milicia Cívica (http://bibliohistorico.juridicas.unam.mx/libros/6/2881/32.pdf). Accessed on January 6, 2015.

Reglamento para la Milicia Cívica del Estado de Coahuila y Texas, Monclova 1834, Imprenta del gobierno dirigida por el ciudadano Sisto Gonzalez.

Las Siete Partidas del rey don Alfonso el Sabio, cotejadas con varios códices antiguos por la Real Academia de la Historia: Partida segunda y tercera. En la Imprenta Real, 1807.

BIBLIOGRAPHY

BOOKS AND ARTICLES

Adams, David B. "At the Lion's Mouth: San Miguel de Aguayo in the Defense of Nuevo León, 1686–1820." *Colonial Latin American Historical Review* 9, no. 3 (2000): 324–46.

———. "Embattled Borderland: Northern Nuevo León and the Indios Bárbaros, 1686–1870." *Southwestern Historical Quarterly* 95, no. 2 (Oct. 1991): 205–22.

Aguilar Camín, Héctor. *La frontera nómada: Sonora y la Revolución Mexicana.* Siglo XXI, 1977.

Alonso, Ana María. *Thread of Blood: Colonialism, Revolution, and Gender on Mexico´s Northern Frontier.* University of Arizona Press, 1995.

Andrews, Catherine, and Jesús J. Hernández. "La Lucha por la supervivencia: El impacto de la Insurgencia en el Nuevo Santander, 1810–1821." In *La Independencia En El Septentrión de La Nueva España: Provincias Internas E Intendencias Norteñas*, edited by Ana Carolina Ibarra. Universidad Nacional Autónoma de México, 2010.

Andújar Castillo, Francisco. *Ejércitos y militares en la Europa moderna.* Síntesis, 1999.

———. *El sonido del dinero: monarquía, ejército y venalidad en la España del siglo XVIII.* Marcial Pons Historia, 2004.

Archer, Christon I. *The Army in Bourbon Mexico, 1760–1810.* University of New Mexico Press, 1977.

———. "Military." In *Cities & Society in Colonial Latin America*, edited by Louisa Schell Hoberman and Susan Migden Socolow. University of New Mexico Press, 1986.

———. *World History of Warfare.* Lincoln: University of Nebraska Press, 2002.

Artusi, Simona. "El Esplendor Islámico en Europa: La España Musulmana y Mozárabe." In *La Edad Media.1. Bárbaros, cristianos y musulmanes*, coordinated by Umberto Eco. Fondo de Cultura Económica, 2015.

Ávila, Alfredo. *En nombre de la nación: La formación del gobierno representativo en México.* Taurus: Centro de Investigación y Docencia Económica, 2002.

Ávila, Alfredo, and Pedro Pérez Herrero. *Las experiencias de 1808 en Iberoamérica.* Universidad de Alcalá / Universidad Nacional Autónoma de México, 2008.

Ávila, Alfredo, and Luis Jáuregui. "La Disolución de la Monarquía Hispánica y el Proceso de Independencia." In *Nueva Historia General de México*, edited by Erik Velásquez. El Colegio de México, 2010.

Ávila, Carlos Lázaro. *Las Fronteras de América y los Flandes Indianos.* Consejo Superior de Investigaciones Científicas, Centro de Estudios Históricos, Departamento de Historia de América, 1997.

Ávila, J. Jesús. "Aspectos Sociales: Entre la Jara del Salvaje y el Rifle del Extranjero." In *La Guerra México-Estados Unidos: Su Impacto En Nuevo León, 1835–1848.* Senado de la República, 2003.

———. "En el Reino de Catujanes." In *Santiago Vidaurri: La Formación de un Liderazgo Regional Desde Monterrey (1809–1867).* Universidad Autónoma de Nuevo León, 2012.

———. "Lampazos: Entre la Insurrección y el Desafío Continuo." In *Apuntes para la historia de Lampazos de Naranjo, Nuevo León.* Vol. 1. UANL: Patronato de Lampazos. 2003.

Ayala Martínez, Carlos de. "Las órdenes militares castellano-leonesas y la acción de frontera en el siglo XIII." In Universidad Autónoma de Madrid y Casa de Velázquez, *Identidad y Representación de La Frontera En La España Medieval, Siglos XI-XIV: Seminario Celebrado En La Casa de Velázquez y La Universidad Autónoma de Madrid, 14–15 de Diciembre 1998.* Collection de La Casa de Velázquez vol. no. 75, Universidad Autónoma de Madrid, 2001.

Baschet, Jérôme. *La Civilización Feudal: Europa Del Año Mil a La Colonización de América.* Fondo de Cultura Económica, 2009.

Bazant, Jan. *A Concise History of Mexico from Hidalgo to Cárdenas, 1805–1940.* Cambridge University Press, 1977.

———. "From Independence to the Liberal Republic, 1821–1867." In *Mexico since Independence,* edited by Leslie Bethell. Cambridge University Press, 1991.

———. "De Iturbide a Juárez." In *Historia de México.* Crítica, 2001.

Benson, Nettie Lee. *The Provincial Deputation in Mexico: Harbinger of Provincial Autonomy, Independence, and Federalism.* University of Texas Press, 1992.

Black, Jeremy. *Warfare in the Eighteenth Century.* Collins/Smithsonian, 2006.

Blanco Valdés, Roberto Luis. *Rey, Cortes y Fuerza Armada en los Orígenes de la España liberal, 1808–1823.* Institució Valenciana d'Estudis i Investigació; Siglo Veintiuno Editores, 1988.

Blyth, Lance R. *Chiricahua and Janos Communities of Violence in the Southwestern Borderlands, 1680–1880.* University of Nebraska Press, 2012.

Bolton, Herbert Eugene. *Texas in the Middle Eighteenth Century: Studies in Spanish Colonial History and Administration.* University of California Press, 1915.

BIBLIOGRAPHY

Britten, Thomas A. *The Lipan Apaches: People of Wind and Lightning*. University of New Mexico Press, 2009.

Brooks, James. *Captives & Cousins: Slavery, Kinship, and Community in the Southwest Borderlands*. University of North Carolina Press, 2002.

Campbell, Camilla. "Navarro, Angel." *Handbook of Texas Online*. Texas State Historical Association. Accessed May 1, 2024. https://www.tshaonline.org/handbook/entries/navarro-angel

———. Navarro, José Angel [The Elder]." *Handbook of Texas Online*. Texas State Historical Association. Accessed May 1, 2024. https://www.tshaonline.org/handbook/entries/navarro-jose-angel-the-elder

Cañizares-Esguerra, Jorge. Puritan Conquistadors: Iberianizing the Atlantic, 1550–1700. Stanford University Press, 2006.

Carlisle, Jeffrey D. "Apache Indians." *Handbook of Texas Online*. Texas State Historical Association. Accessed April 29, 2024. https://www.tshaonline.org/handbook/entries/apache-indians

Cavazos Garza, Israel. *Diccionario Biográfico de Nuevo León*. Universidad Autónoma de Nuevo León, 1984.

Cerutti, Mario. "Una economía binacional en tiempos de guerra. El Bravo, Texas y el Norte de México (1850–1870)." In *Encuentro en la frontera: mexicanos y norteamericanos en un espacio común*, coordinated by Manuel Ceballos Ramírez. El Colegio de México; El Colegio de la Frontera Norte; Universidad Autónoma de Tamaulipas, 2001.

———. *Economía de guerra y poder regional en el siglo XIX: gastos militares, aduanas y comerciantes en años de Vidaurri (1855–1864)*. Archivo General del Estado de Nuevo León, 1983.

Céspedes del Castillo, Guillermo. *América Hispánica, 1492–1898*. Marcial Pons Historia, 2009.

Chavero, Alfredo, ed. *El Lienzo de Tlaxcala*. Editorial Cosmos, 1979.

Chipman, Donald E., "De Leon, Alonso." *Handbook of Texas Online*. Texas State Historical Association. Accessed May 2, 2024. https://www.tshaonline.org/handbook/entries/de-leon-alonso

———. "Ramón, Domingo." *Handbook of Texas Online*. Texas State Historical Association. Accessed April 27, 2024. https://www.tshaonline.org/handbook/entries/ramon-domingo

Chipman, Donald E., and Harriet Denise Joseph. *Spanish Texas 1519–1821*. University of Texas Press, 2010.

Chust, Manuel. "La Nación en Armas. La Milicia Cívica en México, 1821–1835." In *Revolución, Independencia y Las Nuevas Naciones de América*, edited by Jaime E. Rodríguez. Madrid: Fundación MAPFRE TAVERA, 2005.
Chust, Manuel, and José Antonio Serrano Ortega. "Milicia y Revolución Liberal en España y México." In *Las Armas de La Nación: Independencia y Ciudadanía En Hispanoamérica (1750–1850)*, edited by Manuel Chust Calero and Juan Marchena Fernández. Frankfurt am Main: Iberoamericana; Vervuert, 2007.
Crisp, James E. "José Antonio Navarro. The Problem of Tejano Powerlessness." In *Tejano Leadership in Mexican and Revolutionary Texas*, edited by Jesús F. de la Teja and Raúl A. Ramos. Texas A&M University Press, 2010.
Dávila, Hermenegildo. *Biografía del Sr. General don Juan Zuazua*. Monterrey: AGENL, 1983.
DeLay, Brian. *War of a Thousand Deserts: Indian Raids and the U.S.-Mexican War*. Yale University Press, 2008.
Devaney, Thomas. *Enemies in the Plaza: Urban Spectacle and the End of Spanish Frontier Culture, 1460–1492*. University of Pennsylvania Press, 2015.
Diccionario Porrúa de Historia Biografía Y Geografía de México. Editorial Porrúa, 1976.
Dishman, Christopher D. *A Perfect Gibraltar: The Battle for Monterrey, Mexico, 1846*. University of Oklahoma Press, 2010.
Domínguez, María Esther. *San Antonio, Tejas, En La Época Colonial (1718–1821)*. Ediciones de Cultura Hispánica: Instituto de Cooperación Iberoamericana, 1989.
Duverger, Christian. *Crónica de La Eternidad: ¿quién Escribió La Historia Verdadera de La Conquista de La Nueva España?* Taurus, 2012.
Eisenhower, John. *Tan lejos de Dios: la guerra de los Estados Unidos contra México, 1846–1848*. Fondo de Cultura Económica, 2000.
Elliott, John Huxtable. *Imperial Spain, 1469–1716*. Penguin, 1970.
English, Richard. *Modern War: A Very Short Introduction*. Oxford University Press, 2013.
Fernández-Armesto, Felipe. *The Canary Islands after the Conquest: The Making of a Colonial Society in the Early Sixteenth Century*. Oxford University Press, 1982.
Fisher, Lillian Estelle. *Viceregal Administration in the Spanish-American Colonies*. University of California Publications in History, vol. 15. Russell & Russell, 1967.
Folsom, Bradley. *Arredondo: Last Spanish Ruler of Texas and Northeastern New Spain*. University of Oklahoma Press, 2017.
Fowler, Will. *Santa Anna of Mexico*. University of Nebraska Press, 2007.

BIBLIOGRAPHY

Galaviz de Capdevielle, María Elena. "Descripción y pacificación de la Sierra Gorda." *Estudios de Historia Novohispana* 4, no. 4 (1971).

Gallegos, Juan José. "Last Drop of My Blood. Col. Antonio Zapata: A Life and Times on Mexico's Río Grande Frontier, 1797–1840." MA thesis, University of Houston, 2005.

García Fernández, Manuel. "Violencia y Sociedad Feudal. Reflexiones desde la Frontera del Islam Península (Siglos XIII–XV)." In *La Violencia En La Historia: Análisis Del Pasado y Perspectiva Sobre El Mundo Actual*. Universidad de Huelva, 2012.

García Fitz, Francisco. "Una Frontera Caliente: La Guerra en las Fronteras Castellano-Musulmanas (Siglos XI–XIII)." In *Identidad y Representación de La Frontera En La España Medieval, Siglos XI–XIV: Seminario Celebrado En La Casa de Velázquez y La Universidad Autónoma de Madrid, 14–15 de Diciembre 1998*. Collection de La Casa de Velázquez, vol. no. 75, Universidad Autónoma de Madrid, 2001.

———. "La Reconquista y la Formación de la España Medieval (de mediados del siglo XI a mediados del siglo XIII)." In *Historia Militar de España*, edited by Miguel A. Ladero and Martín Almagro Gorbea. Spain: Ediciones del Laberinto, 2010.

García, Luis Alberto. "Dominance in an Imagined Border: Santos Benavides and Santiago Vidaurri's Policing of the Rio Grande." In *Policing the North American Borderlands*, edited by Holly Karibo and George T. Díaz. University of Texas Press, 2020.

———. *Guerra y Frontera: El Ejército Del Norte Entre 1855 Y 1858*. Archivo General del Estado de Nuevo León, 2007.

Garza-Martínez, Valentina. "Poblamiento y Colonización en el Noreste Novohispano Siglos XVI–XVII." PhD dissertation, El Colegio de México, 2002.

Gerhard, Peter. *The North Frontier of New Spain*. University of Oklahoma Press, 1993.

Gibson, Charles. *Tlaxcala in the Sixteenth Century*. Yale University Press, 1952.

Los Gobernantes de Nuevo León: Historia (1579–1989). J. R. Fortson y Cia, 1990.

Gradie, Charlotte M. "Discovering the Chichimecas." *The Americas* 51, no. 1 (July 1994): 67–88.

González de la Vara, Martín. "La Lucha por la Independencia en Texas." In *La Independencia en el Septentrión de La Nueva España: Provincias Internas e Intendencias Norteñas*, edited by Ana Carolina Universidad Nacional Autónoma de México, 2010.

Guardino, Peter, ed. *La independencia de México y el proceso autonomista novohispano, 1808–1824.* Universidad Nacional Autónoma de México/Instituto Mora, 2001.

Guerra, François-Xavier. *Modernidad e independencias: Ensayos sobre las revoluciones hispánicas.* Fondo de Cultura Económica / Fundación MAPRE-Tavera, 1992.

Gutiérrez Cruz, Rafael. *Los Presidios Españoles Del Norte de Africa en tiempo de los Reyes Católicos.* Ciudad Autónoma de Melilla, Consejería de Cultura, Educación, Juventud y Deporte, Servicio de Publicaciones, 1997.

Hämäläinen, Pekka. *The Comanche Empire.* Yale University Press, 2008.

Hamnett, Brian. "Santiago Vidaurri, Northern Mexico, and Regional Identities, 1855–1864." *Tzintzun Revista de Estudios Históricos* 30 (1999): 85–119.

Haynes, Sam W. "Mexican Invasions of 1842." *Handbook of Texas Online.* Texas State Historical Association. Accessed May 1, 2024. https://www.tshaonline. org/handbook/entries/mexican-invasions-of-1842

Hernández Chávez, Alicia. *La tradición republicana del buen gobierno.* Fondo de Cultura Económica; El Colegio de México, 1993.

Hernández, Eligio Edelmiro. *Secuestro y venta de los bienes de Don Juan Ignacio Ramón, héroe de la Independencia.* Universidad Autónoma de Nuevo León, 2010.

Herzog, Tamar. *Defining Nations: Immigrants and Citizens in Early Modern Spain and Spanish America.* Yale University Press, 2003.

Hess, Andrew C. *The Forgotten Frontier: A History of the Sixteenth Century Ibero-African Frontier.* University of Chicago Press, 1978.

Himmerich y Valencia, Robert. *The Encomenderos of New Spain, 1521–1555.* University of Texas Press, 1991.

Hinojosa, Gilberto Miguel. *A Borderlands Town in Transition: Laredo, 1755–1870.* Texas A&M University Press, 1983.

Howard, Michael. *Clausewitz: A Very Short Introduction.* Oxford University Press, 2002.

———. *War in European History.* Oxford University Press, 2001.

Hoyo, Eugenio del. *Esclavitud y Encomiendas de Indios en el Nuevo Reino de León, Siglos XVI Y XVII.* AGENL, 1985.

———. *Historia del Nuevo Reino de León (1577–1723).* Fondo Editorial de Nuevo León, 2005.

———. *Indios, Frailes Y Encomenderos En El Nuevo Reino de León: Siglos XVII Y XVIII.* Archivo General del Estado de Nuevo León, 1985.

BIBLIOGRAPHY

Jaureguí, Luis. "El Primer Federalismo en Nuevo León: Prácticas, Dificultades y Fracasos, 1825–1835." In *Práctica y fracaso del primer federalismo mexicano (1824–1835)*, coordinated by Josefina Zoraida Vázquez and José Antonio Serrano Ortega. El Colegio de México, 2012.

———. "Las Tareas y Tribulaciones de Joaquín de Arredondo en las Provincias Internas de Oriente, 1811–1815." In *La Independencia en el Septentrión de la Nueva España: Provincias Internas e Intendencias Norteñas*, edited by Ana Carolina Ibarra. Universidad Nacional Autónoma de México, 2010.

Jenkins, John Holmes, ed. *The Papers of the Texas Revolution, 1835–1836*. Presidial Press, 1973.

Jones, Grant D. *The Conquest of the Last Maya Kingdom*. Stanford University Press, 1998.

———. *Maya Resistance to Spanish Rule: Time and History on a Colonial Frontier*. University of New Mexico Press, 1989.

Kahle, Günter. *El ejército y la formación del Estado en los comienzos de la independencia de México*. Fondo de Cultura Económica, 1997.

Katz, Friedrich. *The Secret War in Mexico: Europe, the United States, and the Mexican Revolution*. University of Chicago Press, 1981.

Kuethe, Allan J., and Kenneth J. Andrien. *The Spanish Atlantic World in the Eighteenth Century: War and the Bourbon Reforms, 1713–1796*. Cambridge University Press, 2014.

Kuethe, Allan J., Juan Marchena Fernández, and Lyle N. McAlister, eds. *Soldados Del Rey: El Ejército Borbónico en América Colonial en Vísperas de la Independencia*. Castelló de la Plana: Universitat Jaume I, 2005.

Ladero Quesada, Miguel Ángel. "Baja Edad Media 1250–1504." In *Historia Militar de España*, edited by Miguel A. Ladero and Martín Almagro Gorbea. Spain: Ediciones del Laberinto S. L., 2010.

———. *La España de los Reyes Católicos*. Madrid: Alianza Editorial, 2014.

———. *La formación medieval de España*. Madrid: Alianza Editorial, 2014.

Lafaye, Jacques. *Los conquistadores*. Mexico: Fondo de Cultura Económica, 1999.

León, Alonso de, Juan Bautista Chapa, and Fernando Sánchez de Zamora. *Historia de Nuevo León con noticias sobre Coahuila, Texas y Nuevo México*. Mexico: Fondo Editorial Nuevo León, 2005.

Lipscomb, Carol A. "Comanche Indians." *Handbook of Texas Online*. Texas State Historical Association. Accessed April 29, 2024. https://www.tshaonline.org/handbook/entries/comanche-indians

Lucena Giraldo, Manuel."El Reformismo de Frontera." In *El Reformismo Borbónico: Una Visión Interdisciplinar*, edited by Agustín Guimerá Ravina. Madrid: CSIC: Alianza Editorial, 1996.

Lynch, John. *Bourbon Spain, 1700–1808*. History of Spain. Oxford: B. Blackwell, 1989.

MacKay, Angus. *Spain in the Middle Ages: From Frontier to Empire, 1000–1500*. New Studies in Medieval History. London: Macmillan, 1977.

Marchena Fernández, Juan. *Ejército y Milicias en el Mundo Colonial Americano*. Madrid: Editorial MAPFRE, 1992.

Martínez Cárdenas, Bárbara Leticia. "Los Vecinos Lampacences: de Súbditos a Ciudadanos (1821–1867)." In *Apuntes para la Historia de Lampazos de Naranjo, Nuevo León*. México: Universidad Autónoma de Nuevo León, 2003.

Matthew, Laura E., and Michel R. Oudijk, eds. *Indian Conquistadors: Indigenous Allies in the Conquest of Mesoamerica*. Norman: University of Oklahoma Press, 2007.

McAlister, Lyle N. *The "Fuero Militar" in New Spain, 1764–1800*. Gainesville: University of Florida Press, 1957.

McEnroe, Sean F. *From Colony to Nationhood in Mexico: Laying the Foundations, 1560–1840*. Cambridge: Cambridge University Press, 2012.

Medina Peña, Luis. *Los bárbaros del Norte: Guardia Nacional y política en Nuevo León, siglo XIX*. Mexico: Fondo de Cultura Económica, 2007.

———. *Invención del Sistema político Mexicano: Forma de gobierno y gobernabilidad en México en el siglo XIX*. Mexico: Fondo de Cultura Económica, 2007.

Milton Nance, Joseph. "Mier Expedition." *Handbook of Texas Online*. Texas State Historical Association. Accessed May 1, 2024. https://www.tshaonline.org/handbook/entries/mier-expedition

———. "Somervell Expedition." *Handbook of Texas Online*. Texas State Historical Association. Accessed May 1, 2024. https://www.tshaonline.org/handbook/entries/somervell-expedition

Montejano, David. *Anglos and Mexicans in the Making of Texas, 1836–1986*. Austin: University of Texas Press, 1987.

Montemayor Hernández, Andrés. *La congrega: Nuevo Reino de León : siglos XVI–XVII*. Monterrey: AGENL, 1990.

Mora-Torres, Juan. *The Making of the Mexican Border: The State, Capitalism, and Society in Nuevo León, 1848–1910*. Austin: University of Texas Press, 2001.

Morado Macías, Cesar. "Aspectos Militares: Tres Guerras Ensambladas (1835–1848)." In *La Guerra México-Estados Unidos: Su Impacto En Nuevo León, 1835–1848*. México: Senado de la República, 2003.

Moreno Gutiérrez, Rodrigo. "Las Fuerzas Armadas en el Proceso de Consumación de Independencia: Nueva España, 1820–1821." PhD dissertation, Universidad Nacional Autónoma de México, 2014.

Moseley, Edward H. "The Public Career of Santiago Vidaurri, 1855–1858." PhD dissertation, University of Alabama, 1963.

Murphy, Retta. "The Journey of Pedro de Rivera, 1724–1728." *Southwestern Quarterly* 41, no. 2 (Oct. 1937).

Navarro García, Luis. *Don José de Gálvez y la Comandancia General de Las Provincias Internas del Norte de Nueva España*. Seville: Consejo Superior de Investigaciones Científicas, 1964.

Naylor, Thomas H., and Charles W. Polzer, eds. *Pedro de Rivera and the Military Regulations for Northern New Spain, 1724–1729: A Documentary History of His Frontier Inspection and the Reglamento de 1729*. Tucson: University of Arizona Press, 1988.

Nugent, Daniel. *Spent Cartridges of Revolution: An Anthropological History of Namiquipa, Chihuahua*. Chicago: University of Chicago Press, 1993.

O'Conor, Hugo. *The Defenses of Northern New Spain: Hugo O'Conor's Report to Teodoro de Croix, July 22, 1777*. Dallas: Southern Methodist University Press, 1994.

Ortiz Escamilla, Juan. *Guerra y Gobierno: Los pueblos y la independencia de México, 1808–1825*. Mexico: El Colegio de México; Instituto de Investigaciones Dr. José María Luis Mora, 2014.

Ortuño Sánchez-Pedreño, José María. *El adelantado de la Corona de Castilla*. Spain: EDITUM, 1997.

Osante, Patricia. *Orígenes Del Nuevo Santander (1748–1772)*. Mexico: Universidad Nacional Autónoma de México; Universidad Autónoma de Tamaulipas, 1997.

Palomo Acosta, Teresa. "Benavides, Basilio." *Handbook of Texas Online*. Texas State Historical Association. Accessed May 1, 2024. https://www.tshaonline.org/handbook/entries/benavides-basilio

Parker, Geoffrey. *The Army of Flanders and the Spanish Road, 1567–1659; the Logistics of Spanish Victory and Defeat in the Low Countries' Wars*. Cambridge: Cambridge University Press, 1972.

Peña Guajardo, Antonio. *La economía novohispana y la élite local del Nuevo Reino de León en la primera mitad del siglo XVIII*. Monterrey: Consejo para la Cultura y las Artes de Nuevo León, 2005.

Pérez, Joseph. *Carlos V, emperador de dos mundos*. Barcelona: Ediciones B, 1998.

———. *Historia de España*. Barcelona: Crítica, 2000.

Powell, Philip W. *Mexico's Miguel Caldera: The Taming of America's First Frontier, 1548–1597.* Tucson: University of Arizona Press, 1977.

———. *Soldiers, Indians, & Silver; the Northward Advance of New Spain, 1550–1600.* Berkeley: University of California Press, 1952.

Powers, James F. *A Society Organized for War: The Iberian Municipal Militias in the Central Middle Ages, 1000 –1284.* Berkeley: University of California Press, 1988.

Ramos, Raúl A. *Beyond the Alamo: Forging Mexican Ethnicity in San Antonio, 1821–1861.* Chapel Hill: University of North Carolina Press, 2008.

Rangel Silva, José Alfredo. *Capitanes a Guerra, Linajes de Frontera: Ascenso y Consolidación de Las Élites En El Oriente de San Luis, 1617–1823.* Mexico: El Colegio de México, 2008.

Reilly, Bernard F. *Cristianos y Musulmanes, 1031–1157: Historia de España, VI.* Crítica, 1992.

Remensnyder, Amy G. *La Conquistadora: The Virgin Mary at War and Peace in the Old and New Worlds.* Oxford: Oxford University Press, 2014.

Reséndez, Andrés. *Changing National Identities at the Frontier: Texas and New Mexico, 1800–1850.* Cambridge: Cambridge University Press, 2005.

———. *The Other Slavery: The Uncovered Story of Indian Enslavement in America.* Boston: Houghton Mifflin Harcourt, 2016.

Restall, Matthew, and Felipe Fernandez-Armesto. *The Conquistadors: A Very Short Introduction.* Oxford: Oxford University Press, 2012.

Richter, Daniel K. *Before the Revolution: America's Ancient Past.* Cambridge, MA: Belknap Press of Harvard University Press, 2011.

Riley, John Denny. "Santos Benavides: His Influence on the Lower Rio Grande, 1823–1891." PhD dissertation, Texas Christian University, 1976.

Robles, Vito Alessio. *Coahuila y Texas: Desde la Consumación de la Independencia hasta el Tratado de Paz de Guadalupe Hidalgo,* vol. I. Mexico: Porrúa, 1979.

———. *Coahuila y Texas: Desde la Consumación de la Independencia hasta el Tratado de Paz de Guadalupe Hidalgo,* vol. II. Mexico: Porrúa, 1979.

Rodríguez O., Jaime E. *The Independence of Spanish America.* Cambridge: Cambridge University Press, 1998.

———. *Nosotros somos ahora los verdaderos españoles: La transición de la Nueva España de un reino de la Monarquía a la República Federal Mexicana, 1808–1824.* 2 vols. Zamora: El Colegio de Michoacán: Instituto Mora, 2009.

Rothenberg, Gunther E. *The Napoleonic Wars.* Smithsonian History of Warfare. Washington, DC; New York: Smithsonian Books; Harper Collins, 2006.

Rucquoi, Adeline. *La Historia Medieval de la Península Ibérica*. Zamora: El Colegio de Michoacán, 2000.

Ruiz Guadalajara, Juan Carlos. "'... A Su Costa E Minsion... El Papel de los Particulares en la Conquista, Pacificación y Conservación de la Nueva España." In *Las Milicias Del Rey de España: Sociedad, Política e Identidad En Las Monarquías Ibéricas*. México: Fondo de Cultura Económica, 2009.

Salmón, Roberto Mario. "Canales Rosillo, Antonio." *Handbook of Texas Online*. Texas State Historical Association. Accessed May 2, 2024. https://www.tshaonline.org/handbook/entries/canales-rosillo-antonio

———. "Zapata, Antonio." *Handbook of Texas Online*. Texas State Historical Association. Accessed May 1, 2024. https://www.tshaonline.org/handbook/entries/zapata-antonio

Santoni, Pedro. "The Failure of Mobilization: The Civic Militia of Mexico in 1846." *Mexican Studies/Estudios Mexicanos* 12, no. 2 (Summer 1996): 169–94.

———. "A Fear of the People: The Civic Militia of Mexico in 1845." *Hispanic American Historical Review* 68, no. 2 (May 1988): 269–88.

Santoscoy, Maria Elena. "El Agua Organiza el Espacio." In Martha Rodríguez, María Eugenia Santoscoy, and Laura Elena Gutiérrez, *Coahuila: Historia Breve*. Fondo de Cultura Económica, 2011.

Seed, Patricia. *Ceremonies of Possession in Europe's Conquest of the New World, 1492–1640*. Cambridge University Press, 1995.

Segovia, Jose Francisco. "Botas and Guaraches." *Handbook of Texas Online*. Texas State Historical Association. Accessed April 25, 2024. https://www.tshaonline.org/handbook/entries/botas-and-guaraches

Serrano Ortega, José Antonio, "Epílogo. La República Federal desde los Estados, 1824–1835." In Josefina Zoraida Vázquez and José Antonio Serrano Ortega, *Práctica y fracaso del primer federalismo mexicano (1824–1835)*. El Colegio de México, 2012.

Serrano Ortega, José Antonio, and Josefina Zoraida Vázquez. "El Nuevo Orden, 1821–1848." In *Nueva Historia General de México*, edited by Erik Velásquez. El Colegio de México, 2010.

Sheridan Prieto, Cecilia. *Fronterización del espacio hacia el norte de la Nueva España*. Mexico: Centro de Investigaciones y Estudios Superiores de Antropología Social: Instituto Mora, 2015.

Siegel, Stanley E. "Navarro, José Antonio." *Handbook of Texas Online*. Texas State Historical Association. Accessed May 1, 2024. https://www.tshaonline.org/handbook/entries/navarro-jose-antonio

Teja, Jesús F. de la, ed. *A Revolution Remembered: The Memoirs and Selected Correspondence of Juan N. Seguín*. Texas State Historical Association, 2002.

Teja, Jesús F. de la. "Juan N. Seguín. Federalist, Rebel, Exile." In *Tejano Leadership in Mexican and Revolutionary Texas*, edited by Jesús F. de la Teja and Raúl A. Ramos. Texas A&M University Press, 2010.

———. "Seguin, Juan Jose Maria Erasmo de Jesus." *Handbook of Texas Online*. Texas State Historical Association. Accessed May 1, 2024. https://www.tshaonline.org/handbook/entries/seguin-juan-jose-maria-erasmo-de-jesus

———. "Seguin, Juan Nepomuceno." *Handbook of Texas Online*. Texas State Historical Association. Accessed May 1, 2024. https://www.tshaonline.org/handbook/entries/seguin-juan-nepomuceno

Tijerina, Andrés. "Under the Mexican Flag." In *Tejano Journey, 1770–1850*, edited by Gerald Eugene Poyo. University of Texas Press, 1996.

Treviño Villarreal, Héctor Jaime. "Lampazos: entre Catujanes y la Iguana (1698–1810)." In *Apuntes para la historia de Lampazos de Naranjo, Nuevo León*. vol. 1. Universidad Autónoma de Nuevo León, 2003.

Torres Sevilla, Margarita. "La España del Norte (Siglos VIII a XI)." In Miguel A. Ladero Quesada and Martín Almagro Gorbea, *Historia Militar de España*. Ediciones del Laberinto, 2010.

Tyler, Ronnie C. *Santiago Vidaurri and the Southern Confederacy*. Texas State Historical Association, 1973.

Valerio-Jiménez, Omar S. *River of Hope: Forging Identity and Nation in the Rio Grande Borderlands*. Duke University Press, 2013.

Van Young, Eric. *The Other Rebellion: Popular Violence, Ideology, and the Mexican Struggle for Independence, 1810–1821*. Stanford University Press, 2001.

Vigness, David M. "Republic of the Rio Grande." *Handbook of Texas Online*. Texas State Historical Association. Accessed May 1, 2024. https://www.tshaonline.org/handbook/entries/republic-of-the-rio-grande

Vizcaya Canales, Isidro. *En los albores de la independencia las Provincias Internas de Oriente durante la insurrección de don Miguel Hidalgo y Costilla, 1810–1811*. Fondo Editorial Nuevo León, 2005.

———. *La Invasión de los Indios Bárbaros al Noreste de México en los años de 1840 y 1841*. ITESM, 1968.

———. *Tierra de Guerra Viva: Incursiones de Indios y otros Conflictos en el Noreste de México durante el Siglo XIX, 1821–1885*. Academia de Investigaciones, 2001.

BIBLIOGRAPHY

Weber, David J. *Bárbaros: Spaniards and Their Savages in the Age of Enlightenment.* Yale University Press, 2005.

———. *Foreigners in Their Native Land; Historical Roots of the Mexican Americans.* University of New Mexico Press, 1973.

———. *The Mexican Frontier, 1821–1846: The American Southwest under Mexico.* University of New Mexico Press, 1982.

———. *The Spanish Frontier in North America.* New Haven, CT: Yale University Press, 1992.

Weckmann, Luis. *La Herencia Medieval Del Brasil.* Fondo de Cultura Económica, 1993.

———. *La Herencia Medieval de México.* El Colegio de México; Fondo de Cultura Económica, 1994.

Weddle, Robert S. "Ramón, Diego." *Handbook of Texas Online.* Texas State Historical Association. Accessed April 27, 2024. https://www.tshaonline.org/handbook/entries/ramon-diego

Zavala, Silvio A. *Las Instituciones Jurídicas en la Conquista de América.* Editorial Porrúa, 2006.

Zoraida Vázquez, Josefina. "Reflexiones Sobre el Ejército y la Fundación del Estado Mexicano." In *Fuerzas Militares En Iberoamérica: Siglos XVIII Y XIX*, edited by Juan Ortiz Escamilla. El Colegio de México; El Colegio de Michoacán; Universidad Veracruzana, 2005.

———. "La Supuesta República del Rio Grande." *Historia Mexicana* 36, no. 1 (July-Sep. 1986): 49–80.

Index

Abasolo, Domingo de, 54, 56
Adaes, 87
Adalides, 15, 16
Adams, Jeremy, x
Adelantado, 13, 20, 24, 44–46, 48, 50, 172
Aguascalientes, 31
Aguilar, Eduardo, x
Aguilar-Camín, Hector, viii
Alamán, Lucas, 126
Alaska, 82
Alazapas, 36, 55, 67
Alcantara (order), 10
Alfonso III, 9
Alfonso VI, 10
Almocadenes, 15, 16
Almogávares, 15–16
Almohads, 9, 10
Almonte, Juan Nepomuceno, 144
Almoravids, 9
Alonso, Ana María, viii
Ampudia, Pedro, 155, 169
Andalusia, 1, 10, 15, 25, 27, 28, 75
Andrien, Kenneth, ix, x
Apaches, 37, 41, 49, 56, 57, 58, 62, 63, 68, 70, 82–83, 84, 85, 90, 101, 108, 109, 110, 121, 130, 138, 150, 157, 163, 170
Alencastre Noroña, Fernando, 61
Algeria, 21, 76, 99
Alquilones, 79
Álvarez de Toledo, José, 104
Antilles, 23, 59

Apennine Peninsula, 21
Aquitania, Luis of, 7
Aragon, 8, 10, 14, 15, 71
Arellano, Ruben, xi
Argentina, ix, 177
Arista, Mariano, 151–53, 164–65
Arizona, ix, 81, 82, 83, 85, 87, 168
Arizona, ix, 81, 82, 83, 85, 87, 168
Army of the Three Guarantees, 133
Arredondo, Joaquín de, 104–9, 120, 132, 149
Arthur (heir to the English throne), 18
Artigas, José Gervasio, 177
Asturias, 7, 9
Austin, Moses, 142
Austin, Stephen F., 142–45
Ávila (city), 11, 75
Ávila, Jesús, x
Ávila, Melissa, x
Ayala, Mariano, 131
Aztec Empire, 1, 24, 25, 28, 33
Aztecs, 25, 35, 66
Azuara, Arturo, x

Babcock, Matthew, xi
Báez-Benavides, José María, 154
Baffin Bay, 44
Bakewell, Peter, x
Barbadillo y Victoria, Francisco, 61–62

INDEX

Barcelona, 7
Barradas's expedition, 116
Barrera-Enderle, Alberto, xi
Barrón, Luis, x
Behetrías, 8
Béjar. *See* San Antonio (Texas)
Benavides, Basilio, 131, 132, 154, 164, 170
Benavides, Juan V., 170
Benavides, Margarita de, 53
Benavides, Refugio, 131
Benavides, Santos, 50, 131, 154, 170, 172, 177
Benavides-Hinojosa, Artemio, x
Berlanga, José Luis, x
Bexar. *See* San Antonio (Texas)
Blanco, Victor, 162
Blyth, Lance R., viii
Boardman, Andrea, xi
Booth, Ryan, xi
Bourbon Administration, 3, 72, 80, 91, 99
Brussels, 18
Bucareli, Antonio María de, 87
Burgundy, 18, 68
Bustamante (San Miguel), 3, 100. *See also* San Miguel (Nuevo Leon)
Bustamante, Anastasio, 116, 137
Bustilla y Zevallos, Juan Antonio, 63
Palo Blanco, 162

Cabeza de Vaca, Alvar (Nuñez), 24
Cabeza de Vaca, Teresa, 24
Cabo Verde, 59
Cacciavillani, Pamela, x
Cadereyta, 44, 81
Cádiz Constitution, 5, 111–14, 117, 119, 120, 121, 125
Cadiz, 71
Calatrava (order), 10
Caldera, Miguel de, 43
California, ix, 83, 85, 87, 168

Calleja, Félix María, 99–106
Campillo y Cossio, José de, 72
Canada, 73, 82
Canales, Antonio, 150–53
Canary Islands, 6, 14, 20, 24, 35, 41, 43, 45, 57, 172
Cañizares-Esguerra, Jorge, 4
Canto, Alberto del, 43, 53, 59
Carbajal, Luis, 128
Cardenas, Jesús, 152
Caribbean islands, 23
Caribbean, 23, 35, 43, 59
Cartagena de Indias, 72
Carvajal y de la Cueva, Luis, 36, 42–44, 46, 172
Casa Mata Plan, 115
Casas, Juan Bautista, 104
Castañeda, Francisco de, 146
Castile, 1, 4, 6–15, 18, 19, 20, 21, 22, 24, 25, 32, 33, 51–53, 55, 64, 68, 75, 89
Catalonia, 71, 74
Catherine (daughter of the Catholic kings), 18
Catujanos, 94
Caudillo, 13, 50, 172, 177
Celaya, 31, 45
Cerralvo, 81
Charles I (of Spain), 18, 19, 25, 68
Charles III, 72–76, 78, 82, 85, 87
Chavez, John, x
Cheyennes, 157, 158
Chichimeca War, 4, 26–32, 36, 37, 41, 43, 59, 61
Chichimeca, 28–32, 55, 67, 90
Chihuahua, 158
Chile, ix
Cholultecas, 31
Cisneros, José, 130
City of Mexico. *See* Mexico City
Ciudad Victoria, 152
Civic Militia, 5, 111, 124–34, 136, 138, 142, 146, 148, 149, 163, 168, 175, 176
Clavijo (battle of), 9

239

INDEX

Coahuila, 31, 37, 41, 42, 44, 47, 48, 50, 59, 62, 81, 87, 90, 102, 104, 105, 106, 120, 125, 127, 130, 132, 144, 145, 146, 147, 148, 151, 152, 154, 158, 161, 162, 171
Colombia, 23
Colorado, 83, 84, 168
Columbus, 23
Comanche, 68, 70, 83–85, 90, 109, 110, 130, 134, 137, 140, 141, 148, 150, 156–63, 165, 167
Comuneros Rebellion, 18, 19, 25
Conrad, Paul, x
Cordoba, treaties of, 114
Cortés, Hernán, 1, 3, 21, 23–25, 29, 64, 66, 85, 172, 173
Countryman, Edward F., x
Covadonga (Battle of), 8
Croix, Carlos Francisco de, 88
Croix, Teodoro de, 49, 88, 101
Cruillas, Marquess of, 76
Cruz, Bartolomé de la, 123
Cruz, María Josefa, 159
Cuba, 23, 24, 71, 72, 77, 81, 86
Cuzco, 23

Damascus Caliphate, 7
DeLay, Brian, x
Díaz de Bustamante, Ramón, 100, 107
Díaz de Vivar, Rodrigo (Cid), 10, 11, 23, 172
Díaz del Castillo, Bernal, 19
Díaz, George, xi
Dodge, Col. Henry, 156
Durango, 158

Echeverría, Juan de, 44
Edwards, Hayden, 143
Elguezabal, Juan José, 162

Elmore, Ruth Ann, xi
Encomienda, 23, 25, 26, 28, 36, 43, 45, 51, 53, 59, 60, 63, 65, 175
England, 14, 18, 71, 82, 101, 106, 171
Enríquez de Almanza (Viceroy Martín), 29
Entradas, 29
Escandón, José de, 41, 44–46, 47, 62, 172
Espinosa, María del Carmen, 136
Espiritu Santo Bay, 85

Federalist Rebellion, 141, 148, 150, 152, 154, 164
Ferdinand VII, 103, 114, 115, 119, 126
Fernández, Patricia, x
Fernández de Córdoba, Gonzalo, 21
Fernández de Jáuregui, José, 46, 65
Fernández de Santa Anna, Benito, 63
Flanders, 43
Flores, Juan Ignacio, 61
Flores de Abrego, Pedro Joseph, 54, 55
Flores, Salvador, 148
Flores, Vicente, 104
Florida, 73
Frederick II, 74, 78
French Revolution, 5, 103, 111, 117, 118, 121, 125
Foley, Neil, x
French soldiers, 1, 3
Ferdinand of Aragon, 15, 18
France, 5, 14, 15, 18, 20, 21, 22, 70, 71, 72, 73, 74, 102, 110, 117, 118, 123

Galicia, 7, 9
Galindo, Alejandra, x
García-Ayulardo, Clara, x
García-Ibarra Gerardo, xi
García-Silva, Lily, xi

INDEX

Gibraltar, 14, 99
Goliad (Texas), 148
Gómez-Farías, Valentín, 142
González (Texas), 146
González-Quiroga, Miguel, x
Goríbar, José María, 161
Granada, 8, 10, 12, 14–17, 21, 23, 27
Great Basin, 83
Great Britain, 72, 73, 7, 110
Guadalete (Battle of), 8
Guadalquivir, 10
Guajardo del Hoyo, Sergio, xi
Guanajuato, 28, 45
Guatemala, 25, 44
Guerra Guerreada, 12, 16
Guerra, Donna, xi
Guerrero (Tamaulipas), 150, 151, 152, 155
Guerrero, Vicente, 116
Gulf of Cortés, 85
Gulf of Mexico, 37, 41, 85
Gutiérrez de Lara, Bernardo, 104
Guzman, Nuño de, 25

Habsburg Empire, 19
Hacienda de Patos, 161
Hasinais, 37
Havana, 72, 73, 76, 81, 82, 89
Henry IV, 14
Herrera, Jose Joaquín de, 169
Herrera, José Manuel, 104
Hidalgo (Mexico), 45
Hidalgo, Miguel, 49, 103
Homiciano, 16, 21
Hopkins, James, x
Huachichiles, 27
Huejotzingos, 31
Humboldt, Alexander von, 78, 98
Hundred Years' War, 14

Iberia, 1, 4, 13, 14
Idaho, 83
Iguala, Plan of, 114
Inca Empire, 28, 33
Isabella (Queen of Castile), 15, 18, 33
Italy, 6, 18, 21, 22, 24, 30
Iturbe, Manuel de, 103
Iturbide, Agustín, 114, 115, 122, 133, 137, 143
Iturri-Castillo, Manuel, 128

James, Saint, 9, 66, 67, 69, 95, 175, 176
Jerez de la Frontera (Mexico), 28, 31
Jerez de la Frontera (Spain), 24
Johnson, Ben, x
Juana (Queen), 18

Kansas, 83, 84
Karankawas, 37, 48
Katz, Friederich, viii
Kiowas, 156, 157, 158
Knock, Thomas J., x

Ladrón de Guevara, Antonio, 46, 62
Lake Texcoco, 24
Lakomäki, Sami, x
Lampazos, 3, 35, 37, 41, 48, 49, 54, 55, 56, 66, 81, 84, 89, 90, 91, 93, 94, 95, 96, 100, 101, 102, 103, 104, 106, 107, 108, 122, 123, 124, 127, 129, 130, 131, 135, 136, 137, 138, 141, 153, 154, 155, 156, 157, 158, 159, 161, 162, 163, 164, 165, 169, 170, 171

241

INDEX

Laredo, 3, 35, 41, 46, 47, 50, 84, 90,
    91, 93, 96, 97, 100, 104, 106, 107,
    122, 127, 131, 134, 135, 136, 137, 138,
    139, 141, 151, 152, 153, 154, 155,
    156, 157, 158, 162, 163, 164, 165,
    169, 170, 172
León (kingdom of), 7, 8, 9
León (México), 31
León, Alonso (the Younger), 44,
    48, 101
León, Alonso de, 44, 172
Lipans, 56, 62, 83, 84, 85, 90, 93, 134,
    137, 157, 158, 160, 165, 170
Llano, Manuel María de, 152, 155
Louisiana, 41, 82, 87, 102, 105, 132
Lugo, Alfonso de, 20
Lupkin, Joshua, xi

Madrid, 57, 72, 74, 98, 114
Maldonado, Juan de, 130
Mansolo, Anastasio, 130
Marinids, 10
Martínez-Cortés, Victoria Andrea,
    xi
Martínez-Serna, Gabriel, xi
Matamoros, 151, 171
Mazalquivir, 21
Mazapi, l36
Maximilian of Austria, 18
McCrossen, Alexis, x
McEnroe, Sean F., x
Medina, Battle of, 105
Medina del Campo, 19
Medina-Peña, Luis, viii, x, 3
Melilla, 21
Menchaca, José, 50
Menchaca, Luis Antonio, 49, 50
Menorca, 99
Mesoamerica, 26, 67
Mexico City, 26, 28, 29, 35, 44, 61, 85,
    97, 121, 132, 133, 134, 139, 141, 143,
    144, 147, 151, 164, 165, 168, 169, 172

Mexica Empire. *See* Aztec Empire
Mickey, Barbara, xi
Mickey, Bruce, xi
Mier (Tamaulipas), 151, 155
Mier y Terán, Manuel, 143, 144
Mier y Torres, Francisco de, 65
Mogadouro, 42
Monclova, 146, 148, 151, 154, 162
Monte Cassino, 21
Montecuesta, Narciso de, 46
Montegredo, Longinos, 150
Montemayor, Diego de, 43, 53
Morelos (Coahuila), 152
Movimiento de las Villas del Norte.
    See Federalist Rebellion
Morales, José María, 128
Mexico, viii, ix, 1, 3, 4, 5, 24, 26, 64,
    85, 96, 98, 103, 111, 113, 114, 116,
    123, 124, 125, 131, 137, 140, 141,
    143, 144, 146, 147, 148, 156, 157,
    158, 162, 165, 167, 168, 169, 170,
    171, 172, 173, 174, 177
Málaga, 17, 20
Moors, 3, 8, 10, 12, 14, 15, 16, 17, 20,
    21, 24, 27, 30, 33, 52, 69
Mexica, 3, 26, 27

Nacogdoches, 49, 87, 102
Napoleon, 103, 111, 114, 118
Naranjo, Francisco, 171
Nasrid dynasty, 10
Natchitoches, 37
National Guard, 5, 124, 126, 163,
    168, 169, 170
National Militia, 5, 111, 119, 120, 121,
    122, 123, 124, 132
Navarre, 10
Navarro, Angel, 131
Navarro, José Ángel, 132, 148, 149
Navarro, José Antonio, 132, 149, 167
Nayarit, 81, 99
Neches River, 49

Netherlands, 71
Nevada, 83
New Granada, 71, 72
New Kingdom of León, 35, 36, 37, 38, 41, 42, 43, 44, 46, 47, 48, 51, 53, 54, 59, 61, 62, 63, 64, 65, 66, 81, 83, 87, 89, 90, 91, 93, 95, 99, 101, 102, 103, 104, 105, 127
New Mexico, ix, 1, 64, 81, 82, 83, 84, 85, 87, 168
Nichols, James, x
Noche Triste, 25
Nolan, Philip, 101, 102
Nueces River, 37, 41, 48, 168
Nuestra Señora del Pilar de Bucareli, 87
Nueva Vizcaya, 59, 81
Nuevo Santander, 35, 40, 41, 45, 46, 47, 62, 68, 69, 87, 91, 96, 97, 99, 102, 103, 104, 105, 122, 127
Nugent, Daniel, viii
Nuevo León, 3, 28, 42, 122, 125, 127, 129, 139, 144, 151, 152, 154, 157, 158, 163, 164, 169, 171, 172
New Spain, 3, 4, 5, 25, 26, 33, 35, 36, 37, 41, 42, 43, 44, 45, 48, 49, 50, 55, 59, 64, 65, 66, 67, 68, 69, 70, 76, 77, 78, 80, 81, 82, 83, 85, 86, 88, 89, 99, 102, 103, 104, 105, 111, 112, 113, 114, 119, 120, 121, 134, 173, 175
Navas de Tolosa (Battle of), 10, 11
Naples, 18, 21, 72

O'Conor, Hugo, 86–88, 92
O'Donoju, Juan, 114
Obregón, Álvaro, 177
Oklahoma, 84
Oran, 21
Ordoño II, 9
Oregon, 83
Orlovsky, Daniel T., x

Osages, 156
Ostia, 21
Otomies, 29, 31
Otumba, 25

Panama, 23
Panuco, 25, 42
Paraguay, 24
Parras, 146, 162
Patiño, José, 71–72
Pelayo, 7
Peten, 44, 45
Peter I, Tsar, 86
Philip II, 33, 36, 46
Philip IV, 44
Philip the Beautiful, 18
Philip V, 71
Philippines, 30
Pierson, Sharron, xi
Pinkston, Mildred, xi
Pizarro, Francisco, 23, 64, 66
Portugal, 14, 42, 71, 86, 105
Presidial Soldiers. *See* Presidial troops
Presidial troops, 1, 30, 31, 41, 44, 46, 48, 49, 62, 66, 68, 81, 82, 83, 86, 93, 97, 98, 99, 100, 104, 105, 109, 134, 135, 136, 138, 153, 155
Presidio, 1, 3, 21, 22, 30, 31, 32, 37, 41, 44, 46, 47, 48, 49, 50, 58, 62, 66, 68, 80, 81, 82, 83, 85, 86, 87, 93, 97, 98, 99, 101, 105, 132, 134, 135, 153, 164
Provincial Militia, 109, 119, 120, 121, 123, 134
Prunecha, Juan Bautista, 41
Prussia, 70, 74, 118
Puebloans, 3
Puerto de Santa María, 99
Pyrenees, 7

INDEX

Querétaro, 45

Ramiro I, 9
Ramón, Antonia, 49
Ramón, Antonio, 48
Ramón, Diego (Father of Domingo Ramón), 48, 49
Ramón, Diego (Son of Domingo Ramón), 48
Ramón, Domingo, 48, 49, 50
Ramón, Joseph (brother of Domingo Ramón), 48
Ramón, Joseph (Father of Diego and Antonio Ramón), 48
Ramón, Juan Ignacio (Son of Antonio Ramón), 48, 101, 102, 104, 106
Ramos Arizpe, Miguel, 113, 120
Reconquest, 4, 6, 8–15, 17–21, 22, 28, 33, 35, 42, 50, 66, 67, 69, 94, 126, 166, 173, 174
Reconquista. *See* Reconquest
Repartimiento, 20, 23
Requerimiento, 20, 63, 64, 65, 69, 175
Resendez, Andrés, x
Revillagigedo, Count, 99
Rex, David, xi
Reyes, Isidro, 161
Richmond, 172
Richter, Daniel K., 4
Riego, Colonel Rafael de, 114, 119
Rio Bravo. *See* Rio Grande
Rio Grande, ix, 41, 44, 60, 156, 161, 163, 166, 168, 171, 172
Ripperda, Baron of, 93
Rivera, Pedro de, 80–82, 85, 86
Robertson, Sarah, xi
Rodrigo (King), 8
Rodríguez, Mónica, 53
Rolón, Javier, x
Rosas, José Manuel de, 177
Rubi, Marquis of, 83, 85–87, 90
Rubio, Jesús, x

Saint James (Order), 10
Salado (battle of the), 10
Salado River, 158
Salamanca, 11
Salinas, José, 128
Saltillo, 31, 36, 43, 53, 59, 104, 144, 145, 151, 152, 161, 162, 169
San Agustín de Ahumada, 87
San Antonio (New Kingdom of Leon), 36
San Antonio (Texas), 3, 35, 37, 37, 41, 42, 47, 48, 49, 50, 57, 58, 62, 63, 68, 81–85, 90, 92, 93, 97, 101, 102, 104, 105, 107, 109, 121, 122, 123, 127, 128, 130, 131, 132, 135, 137, 138, 141, 145–49, 150, 152, 155, 156, 167, 168, 169, 171
San Fernando, 41
San Francisco de los Tejas, 37, 44
San Jacinto, 147
San Juan Bautista, 48
San Luis Potosí, 27, 43, 99, 103, 169
San Miguel (Guanajuato), 28–29, 31
San Miguel (Nuevo Leon), 35–37, 41, 42, 48, 55, 67, 81, 84, 89, 90, 91, 95, 107, 108, 122, 123, 127, 129, 136, 137, 141, 152–59, 161, 162, 163, 165, 170
San Patricio (Texas), 148
Sánchez, Aaron, xi
Sánchez, Cándido, 109
Sanchez, Tomas, 41, 47, 50, 131
Santa Anna, Antonio López de, 63, 116, 126, 142, 147, 165, 169, 170
Santa María (New Kingdom of Leon), 55
Santa María, Manuel de, 103
Santiago de Compostela, 10
Santiago. *See* Saint James
Santos Olivares, Margarita de los, 53
Segovia, 11, 75
Seguín, Erasmo, 132, 149
Seguín, Juan Nepomucenno, 132, 148, 149, 150, 151, 167, 168, 169, 177

INDEX

Seman, Jennifer, xi
Seno Mexicano, 41, 46
Seven Years' War, 72
Seville, 10, 71
Sierra Gorda, 45, 46, 62, 169
Siete Leyes, Las, 142, 146
Siete Partidas, 13
Sioux, 157
Slave Hunting, 23, 175
Smith, Sherry L., x
Sobrevilla, Andres de, 106, 138
Sonora, 81, 87
Spain, 1, 3, 4, 5, 6, 7, 8, 9, 10, 14, 18, 19, 20, 21, 22, 23, 24, 25, 26, 30, 32, 33, 37, 42, 44, 48, 50, 57, 66, 68, 69, 71, 72, 73, 74, 75, 76, 100, 101, 110, 111, 112, 114, 118, 119, 120, 124, 128, 165, 173, 175, 176
Stoessle, Philipe, x

Tabasco, 165
Tamesi River, 36
Tampico, 42, 144, 150, 151, 171
Tancahuayas, 68
Tartars, 86
Tello, Osvaldo, x
Tenochtitlan, 24, 25, 35, 43
Tercios, 22
Texas, ix, xi, 3, 35, 37, 39, 41, 42, 44, 46, 48, 49, 57, 62, 63, 68, 81, 83, 84–87, 90, 91, 93, 98–106, 109, 122, 125, 127, 129, 130, 132, 141–52, 154–57, 162, 164, 167–72
Tlaxaguichi, 37
Tlaxcala, 1, 24, 80, 123
Tlaxcalan, 1, 3, 24, 25, 31, 36, 37, 55, 67, 89, 90, 91, 95, 96, 107, 108, 123
Tobosos, 36, 55
Toledo, 104
Torget, Andrew, x
Travieso, Francisco, 104

Treaty of Guadalupe-Hidalgo, 168, 171
Treviño, Jerónimo, 171

United States, 3, 4, 102, 104, 106, 110, 124, 126, 143, 144, 145, 156, 163, 167, 168, 169, 171, 174
Urrutia Ramon, Antonia, 49
Urrutia, José de, 49, 50
Urrutia, Toribio de, 49
Ursúa y Arizmendi, Martin de, 45
Uruguay ix, 177
U.S. See United States
Utah, 168, 83

Valencia, 23
Valero, Marquis of (Viceroy), 61
Vázquez-Borrego (family), 154
Vecindad, 20, 51–58, 112, 123, 124, 125
Vecino, 37, 41, 45, 46, 51–58, 60, 61–64, 67, 68, 69, 87, 89, 90, 91, 92, 93, 94, 95, 96, 97, 100, 102, 106, 108, 109, 122, 159, 163, 164, 171, 174
Vela, Manuela, 53
Velasco y Castilla, Luis de (Viceroy), 31
Venezuela, 23
Vera, Pedro de, 24
Veracruz (city), 24, 76, 88, 134
Veracruz (state), 41, 104
Vidal de Lorca, Melchor, 66
Vidaurri-Valdés, Santiago, 106, 155, 164, 169, 170, 171, 172, 177
Vidaurri-Villaseñor, Francisco, 152, 154
Viesca, Andrés, 146, 147
Villa, Francisco, 177
Villalba y Angulo, Juan de, 77

War of Jenkins' Ear, 72
War of the Quadruple Alliance, 71
Washington, 172
Weber, David J., ix, x, 144
Wellman, Kathleen A., x
Woll, Adrián, 155
Wright, Claire, x
Wyoming, 83

Yamparikas, 157
Yucatan, 44, 45, 80, 169

Zacatecas, 26, 27, 28, 29, 36, 43, 59, 116, 126, 142, 144, 146, 147, 161
Zacatecos (Indigenous), 27
Zamora, Leandro, 123
Zapata, Antonio, 150–54
Zaragoza (city), 10
Zaragoza-Seguín, Ignacio, 131, 171
Zavala, Agustin de, 43
Zavala, Martin de, 43, 44, 46
Zozaya, Juan Miguel de, 96
Zuazua, Carlos, 131
Zuazua, Francisco, 131
Zuazua, Juan de (father), 106, 130, 132
Zuazua, Juan, 106, 131, 169

www.ingramcontent.com/pod-product-compliance
Lightning Source LLC
Chambersburg PA
CBHW020945230426
43666CB00005B/170